"TO THE LAST MAN"

"TO THE LAST MAN"

*The Battle for Normandy's Cotentin
Peninsula and Brittany*

RANDOLPH BRADHAM

FRONTLINE
BOOKS

First published in Great Britain in 2008
Reprinted in this format in 2012 by
Frontline Books
an imprint of
Pen & Sword Books Ltd
47 Church Street
Barnsley
South Yorkshire
S70 2AS

ISBN 978 1 84832 665 1

A CIP catalogue record for this book is
available from the British Library

First published in 2008 by Praeger Security International,
an imprint of Greenwood Publishing Group, Inc
in the United States of America.

Printed and bound in England
by CPI Group (UK) Ltd, Croydon, CR0 4YY

For a complete list of Pen & Sword titles please contact
PEN & SWORD BOOKS LIMITED
47 Church Street, Barnsley, South Yorkshire, S70 2AS, England
E-mail: enquiries@pen-and-sword.co.uk
Website: www.pen-and-sword.co.uk

Contents

Profiles

Special

Preface

DURING THE LAST FIVE months of this campaign, I served with the 66th Infantry (Black Panther) Division as a twenty-year-old staff sergeant squad leader. The 66th Division's mission was to contain the Germans in St. Nazaire and Lorient.

Following retirement as a thoracic and cardiovascular surgeon in 1995, I began to make periodic visits to Normandy and Brittany to study the campaign westward from the Normandy beaches. While visiting the towns, villages, hills, and rivers referred to herein, I gained a profound respect for those who fought in the bitterly contested battles. Seeing the many white crosses and monuments to the Allied soldiers scattered throughout the region was a very humbling and sobering experience.

It makes one realize that freedom is not a gift but is only achieved by the fortitude and sacrifice of many people. Thousands of Allied soldiers entered many small villages such as La Haye-du-Puits, Carentan, Avranches, Bouvron, and many more only to die there in an effort to preserve freedom for their country and for the world. We should never forget their sacrifices nor should we ever take freedom for granted.

Acknowledgments

I THANK MY son, John, who took time from his busy law practice in New York to go with me on several visits to France to research this campaign. He was baggage boy, chauffeur, reservationist for travel and hotels, and a wonderful companion.

I thank Luc and Marc Braeuer, owners and curators of the Grand Boock-haus Museum at Batz-sur-Mer, France, and the Memorial de la Liberté Retrouvée Museum at Quinéville, France, for opening their files to me and sharing interesting photographs and documents, including their own publications on the campaign.

I thank John Bussjager, a friend and an excellent graphic artist, who took complicated and detailed military maps and reduced them to simple "reader friendly" versions to help readers follow the course of the campaign.

I thank Mary Ilario, in the Still Pictures section of the National Archives, for locating excellent combat photographs of the campaign.

I thank Adam Heath, editorial content manager at Praeger Security International, for his guidance and professional expertise in helping me organize my material into a detailed but readable book on the campaign. I especially appreciate his allowing me the freedom to express some of my own thoughts about this bitter struggle.

Last but not least, I thank our seven pups—Sammy, Nelly, Winnie, Mattie Lou, Loo-Loo, Boo-Boo, and Joey—for waking me every morning at 5:00, when there is nothing else to do but write a book.

Introduction

THIS IS A CAMPAIGN which began when the first paratrooper landed on Normandy, June 5, 1944, and ended when Gen. Herman Kramer, commander of the 66th Infantry Division, accepted the surrender of German general Werner Junck at Bouvron, France on May 11, 1945, several days following the capitulation of the main German army. This campaign of the Cotentin Peninsula and Brittany has received little attention yet it was one of the most costly campaigns fought in the European theater of operations (ETO). Success hung in the balance on many occasions. "Citizen soldiers," yet untried in battle, were pitted against battle seasoned Wehrmacht troops. Generals Bradley, Middleton, Collins, Ridgway, Taylor, and Gavin were opposing Germany's premier commanders, generals von Rundstedt, Rommel, von Schlieben, von Kluge, Ramcke, Haussar, and von Choltitz, and Colonel von der Heydt, all chosen by Hitler personally. All had pledged to Hitler that they would defend their positions "to the last man."

The Americans were faced with launching an offensive in bocage (hedgerow) country laced with marshes, streams, and rivers against an enemy that effectively utilized the terrain for their defensive positions. The only approaches to some of the objectives were over open causeways where the American infantry had to advance on the run without cover. Many soldiers were killed during these assaults and rolled off the causeway into the water or marsh.

In spite of a greatly flawed airborne assault with paratroopers widely scattered and the loss of many gliders and soldiers, the troopers immediately began to band into small groups and head for a known objective such as the bridges exiting from Utah Beach essential for the 4th Infantry Division to cross and begin the journey toward Cherbourg, a port considered necessary to support the Allied advance.

Battles at Ste. Mère Église, the Carentan causeway, Carentan, the La Fière causeway, Chef-du-Pont, Sauveur-le-Vicomte, Valognes, and Montebourg were won with a casualty rate approaching 50 percent. The commanders were on the frontline with their troops encouraging them toward their objectives. The battle for Carentan ended with grenades and bayonets. The American paratroopers captured Ste. Mère Église the night of June 5–6 but Colonel von der Heydte's young paratroopers took it back. The Americans counterattacked and secured it for good.

After gaining a significant base in the southeastern sector of the Cotentin Peninsula, the VII Corps advanced westward to cut off the Cotentin Peninsula at its base. Gen. Lawton Collins, commander of VII Corps, then turned his corps northward toward Cherbourg while Gen. Troy Middleton, commander of VIII Corps, took over the east-west defensive line across the base of the peninsula. His objective was to prevent reinforcements from entering the peninsula and entrapping those between his line and Cherbourg.

Three infantry divisions began moving toward Cherbourg along Route National 13 through Ste. Mère Église, Valognes, and Montebourg, the latter having been heavily fortified. Cherbourg was one of the five fortresses to be encountered during this campaign. All five fortresses, which included Cherbourg, St. Malo, Brest, Lorient, and St. Nazaire, had been built into impregnable bastions by the Todt Organization and all were bristling with guns. Surrounding each fortress were multiple defensive perimeters encompassed in tank obstacles, barbed wire, and minefields. Each line of defense was punctuated with cement pillboxes housing cannons and machine guns.

Cherbourg was approached with the 79th, 9th, and 4th Infantry divisions abreast. On the morning of the attack, the worst storm in forty years hit the English Channel, wrecking the landing beaches at Normandy and destroying one of the prefabricated harbors. This severely curtailed the inbound supplies.

Gen. Karl von Schlieben was commander of Fortress Cherbourg and was dedicated to holding it "to the last man." Overcoming the defenses surrounding Cherbourg was costly for the Americans. Cherbourg was bombed numerous times and bombarded incessantly before it was taken. Von Schlieben repeatedly appealed to General Rommel for help but none was forthcoming. Finally von Schlieben with many wounded and exhausted soldiers surrendered Fort du Roule on June 27 after completely destroying the port.

It became obvious to the high command as the battle progressed that the number of German troops on the Cotentin Peninsula and in the Breton ports had been grossly underestimated. Gen. Troy Middleton was one of the few commanders who had anticipated this fierce resistance as he had spent considerable time pouring over aerial photos that revealed many gun positions. The time had come to break out of Normandy and into Brittany which would favor a mobile tank war. Field Marshalls von Rundstedt and Rommel visited Hitler on June 29 to request that they withdraw to another defensive line as their forces were becoming depleted in Normandy. Hitler would have none of this attitude and ordered them to hold the Allies on the beaches. Rommel went so far as to tell Hitler that it was time to end the war. Hitler informed him to do as ordered and let him, Hitler, worry about the war. Von Rundstedt was soon thereafter relieved as commander in the west as he continued to disagree with Hitler. Rommel was severely injured by an Allied plane strafing his command car.

General Middleton's VIII Corps had been stopped until General Collins's VII Corps could completely neutralize Cherbourg. On June 26 General Bradley resumed Middleton's advance toward Coutances in the southwestern part of the peninsula. The VII Corps was to proceed along the Carentan-Périers road to Coutances. Again, the troops were in hedgerow country and the VII Corps was confronted with the Carentan marshes. The Germans reorganized with Field Marshall Guenther von Kluge replacing von Rundstedt. Generals Eberbach, Hausser, and von Choltitz were placed under von Kluge's command.

The attack began with both corps headed to Coutances. The going was difficult and slow with a high casualty rate as again the Germans had the advantage of well-concealed defensive positions and possessed the high ground around La Haye-du-Puits. The 79th Infantry Division. was depleted and demoralized. On July 7 the entire advance stalled. At one point Middleton's VIII Corps advanced only 12,000 yards in twelve days. Gen. Omar Bradley aborted the attack toward Coutances and selected the St. Lo–Périers road (east-west) as a substitute for the St. Lô–Coutances road as a departure site to break out of Normandy. He marked off a carpet three and one-half miles in length and one and one-half miles in depth. Operation Cobra was formulated, which would consist of saturation bombing of this carpet followed by a breakthrough with infantry and exploitation of the break in the Germans' line with armor.

By July 24 all preparations for Cobra were complete and the attack was aborted due to bad weather. Some of the planes had left England and could not be recalled, making their bombing runs as planned. Unfortunately, short bombing occurred, killing twenty-five soldiers and wounding 131 more of the 30th Infantry Division. The attack was resumed the next day and again short bombs resulted in numerous casualties in the 30th and 9th Infantry divisions. Gen. Leslie McNair, chief of procurement of U.S. forces and an observer, was killed. Infantry and armor poured through the break and advanced to capture Coutances and Avranches. The Americans had defeated the German 7th Army and captured 20,000 prisoners. The Germans began retreating and many reached St. Malo, Lorient, St. Nazaire, and Brest, where they would fight the Americans again.

The U.S. Third Army with Gen. George Patton as commander was committed on August 1, 1944. General Bradley was commander of the newly formed 12th Army Group and Lt. Gen. Courtney H. Hodges took Bradley's place as U.S. First Army Commander. General Patton did not want to go into Brittany but was prevailed upon to do so by generals Eisenhower and Bradley. A concession allowed Patton to send only one corps into Brittany, which was General Middleton's VIII Corps.

General Middleton ordered generals John Wood and Robert Grow, commanders of the 4th and 6th Armored divisions respectively, to advance south and secure Avranches, which they did, thus securing the gateway into Brittany. General Wood was then diverted to Rennes and General Grow toward Brest. The Free French of the Interior (FFI) had become very active since the Allied invasion of France and joined the Americans at Lorient and Brest, giving the Americans considerable support. The rapidity of the Armored divisions reaching their objectives was unprecedented. They overran their communications, equipment, and maps. With the help of the FFI and elements of the 8th Infantry Division, General Wood secured Rennes, Nantes, and Vannes. As the 4th Armored approached Lorient the advance element encountered withering artillery fire in a field near Pont Scorf. Twenty-one soldiers were killed and fifty more wounded in a two-hour period. The German artillery observers were searched out and killed. which was the only thing that stopped the attack.

As the 6th Armored Division approached Brest, a large German force was found to be headed for Brest behind them. This necessitated a turnaround to confront the Germans. After an intense battle the trailing German force was defeated. General Grow then sent a surrender request into Brest, which was refused.

General Middleton had the responsibility of clearing Brest with his VIII Corps. He had grave concerns about taking Brest with a single Armored division and ordered General Grow to maintain a holding pattern.

As the VIII Corps began to approach Brest, they received significant bombardments from St. Malo. Middleton ordered Maj. Gen. Robert C. Macon, commander of the 83rd Infantry Division, with attached units, to capture St. Malo. The Allies did not realize that St. Malo was commanded by three commanders, colonels Aulock, Bacherer, and an unknown colonel who would not give his name. All were fanatically dedicated to Hitler. Each of the three commanders controlled his own bastion and all would fight "to the last man." The complex of forts in St. Malo had been prepared to withstand any bombardment and the battle for this port was a repeat of the battle for Cherbourg. It took relentless air, sea, and land bombardments and a costly battle by the 83rd Infantry Division to capture St. Malo, one fortress at a time. Finally on August 17, 1944, a white flag appeared and Colonel Aulock surrendered the Citadel. Other smaller forts surrendered shortly thereafter. The 83rd Infantry Division performed superbly and captured 10,000 prisoners. The tenacity of the German troops during the battle for St. Malo was a testimony to Hitler's orders to fight "to the last man." The port facilities had been destroyed.

The battle for Brest was next and would be equally as intense and difficult as the battles for Cherbourg and St. Malo. Until this late date, there remains a controversy among scholars and the military whether the Allies should have taken Brest as it was a costly battle and did not produce a usable port.

The commander of Brest was chosen by Hitler for its defense. He was Gen. Hermann Bernhard Ramcke who had come up through the ranks and had distinguished himself in many other campaigns including North Africa. General Ramcke finally surrendered to General Middleton on September 19, 1944, after sustaining a ground attack by four U.S. infantry divisions and multiple bombardments by sea, air, and land. He and Middleton carried on a correspondence during this battle related to problems each addressed to the other. This correspondence continued after the war born out of respect for each other as professional soldiers.

Following the bitter and costly battles for Cherbourg, St. Malo, and Brest, a decision was made to contain Lorient and St. Nazaire as both were probably the most heavily fortified as they were Hitler's premier U-boat bases. The 83rd Infantry Division, and the 4th and 6th Armored divisions all had short stays containing the two fortresses and were aided greatly by the large numbers of FFI units which had concentrated their efforts there in support of the Allies.

The 94th Infantry Division relieved the 6th Armored Division in September 1944, and Maj. Gen. Harry Maloney, commander of the 94th Infantry Division, performed a superb job of training and supplying the FFI units and gaining the confidence of their commanders who came under Malony's overall command.

In late December 1944 the 94th Infantry Division was relieved by the 66th Infantry Division. One of the troop ships bringing the 66th Division across the English Channel on Christmas Eve was torpedoed, with the loss of 802 soldiers and many more being injured. Gen. Herman Kramer, commander of the 66th Infantry Division, with the help of approximately 35,000 FFI troops contained the Germans until their final capitulation on May 10 (Lorient) and May 11 (St. Nazaire), 1945. These two fortresses and the surrounding countryside had been under attack for five years since the British started bombing them in 1940. Their surrender brought peace to Brittany.

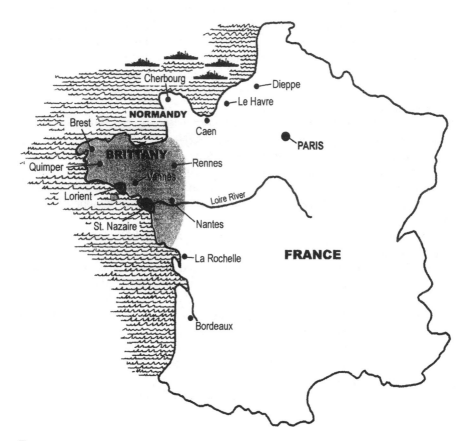

France

Prelude

CHERBOURG WAS ONE of the most heavily fortified bastions in the world. Its commander swore to Hitler that he would defend it "to the last man." If he succeeded, the invasion of Normandy would fail as the Allies were depending upon the capture of Cherbourg for a port with the capacity to land the supplies necessary to maintain the advance of the Allied forces. Therefore, it was essential for the Allies to capture Cherbourg.

In April 1942, not long after the United States. entered the war, generals George Marshall and Dwight Eisenhower presented a plan to President Roosevelt detailing a massive assault (Operation Sledgehammer) in the fall against the Germans in northwestern France. The British military leaders were appalled as they knew that the Americans, having been in the war for only several months, were not prepared for such an attack and that ultimately it would fail miserably with the loss of many men. The Germans were there waiting with twenty-five well-equipped divisions.

DIEPPE

The British conceived the idea of an assault on Dieppe with approximately six thousand men. Its origin and principal sponsors were never known but Winston Churchill heartily endorsed this raid. It was believed that Churchill knew the raid would fail but he felt it better to sacrifice this smaller group of men now to convince the Americans that their plan was too premature and save the thousands that would be lost with an invasion in 1942.

The raid took place on August 19, 1942, with 6,058 men and was complete chaos with the loss of 60 percent of the raiders. One hundred and six badly needed British planes were destroyed. The British navy lost 550 men, a warship, and thirty-three landing craft. On that same day Field Marshall Gerd Von Rundstedt notified Hitler that no armed Englishmen remained on the

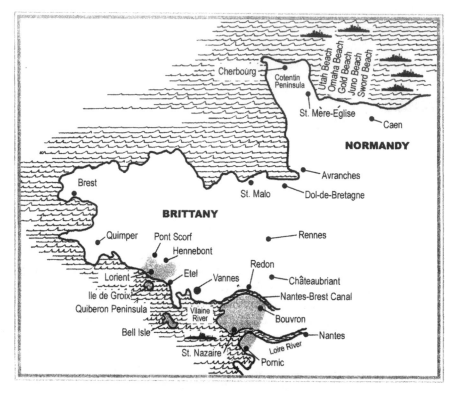

Normandy and Brittany

continent. Operation Sledgehammer failed. Churchill thought that the results justified the heavy losses. However, this alerted Hitler to the fact that a properly organized attacking force was plausible but could be defended against by building a super-strong Atlantic wall with which to stop the Allies at the beaches. Von Rundstedt was not enthusiastic about the Atlantic wall and thought it a waste of time and materials. He favored building up a strong reserve force that could quickly and effectively defend against an attacking force.

The Allies, having fought the Germans in North Africa, Sicily, and Italy, were organizing and building a massive assault team for a cross-Channel invasion of France. Meanwhile, the Germans were building 15,000 concrete and steel bunkers impenetrable to Allied bombs and artillery shells, intending to thwart any invasion attempt by the Allies. It was to be finished by May 1, 1943.

The French Resistance organization, Centurie, was instrumental in providing the Allies with an extremely accurate drawing of the Atlantic Wall extending from the northwest corner of the Cotentin Peninsula to Ouistreham, 100 miles to the east. Hundreds of members of the Centurie passed along any drawing or piece of information they had about the Atlantic Wall to a central collecting point at Caen. Cartographers organized this material into a detailed map, which was then sent to a nondescript building in Paris where it was further refined. From there, it was flown to London from a grassy field near Paris. The material was examined further and copies distributed to military officers. The maps were detailed and extremely accurate.

CONTROVERSY

As plans were being made for the invasion of the European continent, included was the immediate capture of a large port so as to maintain a rapid build-up of men, supplies, vehicles, and weapons necessary for the rapid growth of the Allied forces. Gen. Omar Nelson Bradley, commander of the U.S. First Army, had a plan for the capture of Cherbourg and was convinced that if this could not be done rapidly, the entire Overlord project would be in jeopardy. He was stunned when a delegation of staff officers from Washington visited Supreme Headquarters Allied Expeditionary Forces (SHAEF) in February 1944 and presented plans to General Eisenhower which had been formulated by General Marshall and Gen. H. "Hap" Arnold to carry out an airborne deployment between Evreux and Dreux, located forty miles from Paris and seventy miles from the invasion beaches.

The projected airborne assault would capture airfields and pave the way for two infantry divisions to be flown in as well as thousands of tons of supplies. This preposterous plan was quickly shot down by generals Eisenhower and Bradley. Gen. Bernard Montgomery considered the plan "nonsense." Gen. Matthew B. Ridgway, commander of the 82nd Airborne Division and the leader of the parachute elements of the 82nd considered the plan a "suicide mission." General Bradley wanted the 82nd and 101st Airborne Divisions dropped at the base of the Cotentin Peninsula to defend the 4th Infantry Division destined to land on Utah Beach and also to prevent the Germans from reinforcing defenses around Cherbourg.

Another furor erupted at the headquarters of the 21st Army Group which would be in command of the Overlord ground forces. British Air Marshal Sir Trafford Leigh-Mallory, air commander for Overlord, proposed that the airborne assault by the 82nd and 101st Airborne Divisions be canceled. He felt that the losses would far surpass the gain from this deployment. General Bradley countered with eliminating Utah Beach as he would not land troops there without protected exits behind it. Leigh-Mallory then made it clear to all that if Bradley persisted with this plan, he would have to take full responsibility. Bradley again countered with a statement that he was in the habit of accepting full responsibility for all of his operations. Leigh-Mallory appealed to Eisenhower, who sided with Bradley's plan. Bradley was well aware of the risk involved but also was aware that the failure to capture Cherbourg early would severely endanger Overlord.

On March 20, 1944, Hitler held a meeting of his top military officers and informed them that an Allied invasion of Europe was inevitable and must be stopped within hours or at most days. He expressed the opinion that capture of a large port was essential for the Allies to sustain a beachhead. Cherbourg and Brest were the two likely targets. As the meeting adjourned, plans were initiated to immediately to strengthen the Atlantic Wall on the Normandy coast. The Panzer Lehr Division and the 21st Panzer Division were transferred to Normandy in the vicinity of Caen.

Late in May preparation for the massive military attack on Nazi-occupied France began its final stages. Fifty-five thousand American troops were to be put on shore at Utah and Omaha beaches. Troops began moving into their last staging areas before crossing the Channel. The 82nd and 101st Airborne troopers were placed at airfields in southern England. Air Marshal Leigh-Mallory persisted in his contention that the airborne attack by the two American airborne divisions behind Utah Beach be canceled. General Bradley was furious and refused to cancel this phase of Overlord. Finally Leigh-Mallory again appealed to General Eisenhower and protested vehemently the slaughter of the two American airborne divisions. He predicted 75 percent casualties among the glider troops and 50 percent among the parachute troops. This was a bitter prediction, especially from someone with the experience and position of Leigh-Mallory. Eisenhower, already with more responsibility and anxiety than few men could bear, had to suffer the anguish that Leigh-Mallory could be right and if so, the Utah landing would be a disaster and the primary objective, Cherbourg, would be lost as well as hundreds of young troopers. To supply the troops on the beaches, a port such as Cherbourg was essential to prevent the possibility of another Dunkirk. After pondering long and hard, he remained the consummate professional soldier and realized the risk was high, but higher if he canceled the airborne attack. After a period of deliberation, Eisenhower called Leigh-Mallory and informed him that the attack would proceed as planned. This decision took unprecedented courage as Leigh-Mallory's opinion was not to be taken lightly. He was an extremely capable British officer. Eisenhower's decision to continue with the original plan exemplified the foresight and courage of our own general officers that took place repeatedly in the European war.

Meanwhile, in a meeting with reporters General Bradley was asked how soon he expected to take Cherbourg. Bradley informed them that he would gladly settle for D+15, even D+20. Another asked him why the map in front of them was marked D+8. Bradley replied that that was before Field Marshal Erwin Rommel started pouring troops into the Cotentin Peninsula. Bradley never sought publicity from the press and always reported to them in a factual and professional manner.

CHERBOURG, MAJOR OBJECTIVE

Cherbourg is a port on the north coast of the Cotentin Peninsula, which projects out into the Atlantic. The peninsula is about twenty-five miles from tip to

OMAR NELSON BRADLEY

Gen. Omar Bradley was born on February 12, 1893, to a poor family near Clark, Missouri. He was the only surviving child of John and Sarah Elizabeth Bradley. He attended Higbee Elementary School and Moberly High School, where he excelled in baseball. Upon graduation he went to work for the Wabash Railroad, hoping to save enough money to attend the University of Missouri. His Sunday school superintendent recognized Bradley's intelligence and leadership ability and recommended that he take the exam for West Point which he did and placed first in his district. Congressman William Rucker offered him an appointment to West Point and he entered the Military Academy in the fall of 1911. Bradley graduated in 1915 in the same class with Dwight Eisenhower and many others who would be generals in World War II. The class of 1915 is known as "the class the stars fell on."

From these humble beginnings Bradley ascended to the rank of general of the U.S. Army (five stars). At the end of World War II, he commanded the 12th Army Group, the largest ever commanded by an American general. It was composed of the First (Lt. Gen. Courtney H. Hodges, the Third (Gen. George Patton), the Ninth (Lt. Gen. William Simpson) and the Fifteenth (Lt. Gen. Leonard Gerow) armies. The 12th Army Group had under its command 1.3 million men organized into twelve corps made up of forty-eight divisions

After graduating from West Point, Bradley fist served with the 14th Infantry Regiment, which was sent to the Mexican border. The 14th became part of the 19th Infantry Division, which was slated to be deployed to Europe, but the flu epidemic and the armistice prevented them from joining the U.S. forces there.

Essentially, from 1920 until World War II began, Bradley served either as a student or instructor at West Point, the Infantry School at Fort Benning, the Command and General Staff School at Fort Leavenworth and the Army War College. He worked at the War Department in 1936 directly for Army Chief of Staff George Marshall, who would subsequently have a significant effect on Bradley's career. In 1941 Bradley was promoted to brigadier general and took command of the 82nd Infantry Division, later transferring to the 28th Infantry Division. His leadership and training programs had a profound effect on both divisions. While at Fort Benning, Bradley greatly influenced the development of airborne and tank warfare and organized the Officers Candidate School.

General Eisenhower sent General Bradley to North Africa in 1943 to serve under General Patton and to be Eisenhower's "eyes and ears" in that theatre. He became commander of II Corps when Patton began planning the invasion of Sicily. He led the II Corps through the final battles of North Africa and on into the battle for Sicily. He was chosen to command the 1st U.S. Army for the invasion of Normandy, which included the V, VII and XIX Corps. During the Normandy campaign a major reorganization took place on August 1, 1944, and Bradley became commander of the 12th Army Group. The 12th Army Group was engaged without respite for the remainder of the war, finally meeting up with the Russian's near the Elbe River.

The premier World War II news correspondent, Ernie Pyle, himself beloved by the troops in Europe, was the first to bring to the public's attention this polite and courteous man who subsequently became known as "the soldiers' general." Will Lang, chief correspondent for *Life* magazine during World War II and a Bradley admirer, once told Bill Mauldin (cartoonist for *Stars and Stripes*) that this quality of gentleness, set against a background of horrendous, grinding cruel warfare, was the thing he found most fascinating about General Bradley. While presiding over an army involved in this kind of fighting, Bradley was never known to issue an order to anybody of any rank without saying "please" first.

Postwar, General Bradley was placed in charge of the Veterans Administration for two years, greatly improving its health care and assuring veterans of educational benefits under the G.I. Bill of Rights. Bradley also served as chairman of the Joint Chiefs of Staff and as chairman of the NATO Committee. He died April 8, 1981.

the base near the large swamp Prairies Marecageuses de Georges. The base, on a line from the mouth of the Douve River on the eastern shore to Cateret on the west coast, is thirty miles. Two large rivers, the Douve and Merderet, drain the peninsula generally from north to south and run parallel to each other until the Douve turns east. The Merderet terminates into the Douve near the village of Beuzeville la Bastille. The presence of these two rivers was a geographic defense factor for the Germans that created offensive nightmares for the Americans.

As is well known, the invasion of France was delayed because of worsening weather conditions, too severe for a beach landing. Ships already underway were signaled to return. Finally, Capt. James Martin Stagg, chief meteorologist for the Royal Air Force, found a window in the weather and informed General Eisenhower. Eisenhower made the decision and gave the order to set D-day for Tuesday, June 6, at 6:30 A.M.

On the evening of June 5 General Eisenhower had dinner with Gen. Maxwell Taylor, the forty-two-year-old commander of the 101st Airborne Division. After dinner they visited several airfields where the paratroopers were putting on their gear in preparation to board the planes that would ferry them to their drop zones on the Cotentin Peninsula. Eisenhower continued to be disturbed profoundly by Air Marshall Leigh-Mallory's statement that the airborne troops would be slaughtered if the present plan for them was carried out. Never has any leader of our country borne more of a burden than Eisenhower did on this eve of the invasion. Leigh-Mallory's predictions of high casualties among the airborne troops continued to haunt him. The soldiers bolstered his morale by their positive comments and letting him know that he could count on them. This was a courageous young group of young American soldiers who firmly believed in their mission. Many would die carrying it out, but in so doing they would bring the world a little closer to freedom.

The mission for the 101st Airborne Division was to capture the five cause-ways leading into the Cotentin Peninsula from Utah Beach. The mission of the 82nd Airborne Division was to land astride the Merderet River near Ste. Mère Église, capture Ste. Mère Église, and cross over the Merderet River at La Fiere and Chef-du-Pont. They were to deny German reinforcements access to the roadways in that area and to protect the VII Corps' left flank as it entered the Cotentin Peninsula from the landing beaches.

No better warriors could be found to lead this massive airborne assault than generals Matthew Ridgway, who would lead the 82nd Airborne Division, and Maxwell Taylor, who would lead the 101st Airborne Division. Under their commands were generals James Gavin and Anthony McAuliffe, both of whom would lead distinguishing careers as airborne commanders. These four were pioneers in the development of airborne warfare in the United States. After the war they clearly recognized the perils inherent in "massive retaliation" as advocated by others and were dedicated to pursuing the concept of "flexible response" to counter low-level aggression.

MATTHEW BUNKER RIDGWAY

Matthew Ridgway was born in 1895, the son of a former West Point graduate who was a professional soldier. As a young man, Ridgway was good-looking, physically fit, and charismatic, and possessed other qualities consistent with becoming a born leader. He graduated from West Point in 1917.

His first assignment was to the Third Infantry Regiment stationed on the Mexican border, where he spent fifteen months. He was then stationed at West Point for six years as a language instructor and then to Fort Benning, Georgia, to take the Company Officers Course. Following the course at Fort Benning, he served under Lt. Col. George C. Marshall with the Fifteenth Infantry Regiment in Tientsin, China. Ridgeway rose quickly through the ranks.

By 1939 General Ridgway was assigned to the War Plans Division of the War Department in Washington as a lieutenant colonel. General Marshall had become Chief of Staff of the Army. Ridgway and Marshall became close friends and Marshall sent Ridgway to Latin America on diplomatic missions due to his foreign-language skills, his pleasing personality, and his intent on succeeding in any mission given him. Ridgway brought Maxwell Taylor, who was fluent in several foreign languages and a gifted diplomat, into the department.

Ridgway was promoted to full colonel four days after Pearl Harbor and assigned to the reactivated 82nd Infantry Division under General Bradley, division commander. The 82nd Infantry Division had earned a distinguished reputation in World War I, having participated in many of the crucial battles. Sergeant Alvin York was a member of that division.

General Marshall decided to move General Bradley to the 28th Infantry Division to bring them up to combat readiness. He promoted Colonel Ridgway to major general and made him commander of the 82nd Infantry Division on June

26, 1942. Soon thereafter, the 82nd Infantry Division was converted into the 82nd Airborne Division with General Ridgway as commander and Col. Maxwell Taylor as chief of staff.

General Ridgway commanded the 82nd Airborne Division in the Sicily, Normandy, Northern France, Rhineland, and Ardennes campaigns. He was awarded many decorations, including two Distinguished Service medals, two Silver Stars, two Bronze Stars with "V" for valor and a Purple Heart for having been wounded in action. He became commander of the XVIII Airborne Corps, which encompassed all American airborne troops in Europe.

At the end of World War II General Ridgway was commander of the Mediterranean theater of operations and then the U.S. Army representative to the United Nations Military Staff Commission and senior U.S. delegate to the Inter-American Defense Board. He became Commanding General of the Eighth U.S. Army, Korea, in 1950 and replaced Gen. Douglas MacArthur as Commander in Chief, Far East Command. As Supreme Commander for Allied Powers, Ridgway took command of an Army that had suffered greatly and overall had a very low morale. With his dominant, positive personality and his efficiency, he brought new life and success to this rehabilitated Army. His final assignment on active duty was Chief of Staff of the U.S. Army. After retirement he continued to work tirelessly to help the United States maintain a strong national defense. President Truman sent him on many diplomatic missions to other countries where problems of diplomacy surfaced.

Here was a general who had parachuted into Normandy with his troops and became another "rifle" fighting along with them. An exceptional soldier.

MAXWELL DAVENPORT TAYLOR

Maxwell Taylor was born in Keytesville, Missouri, in 1901. He attended West Point and finished fourth in his class of 1922. As an engineer officer, he served in Hawaii for three years with the 3rd Engineers. He married Lydia Gardner Happer in 1925. Taylor was a language instruction at West Point from 1928 to 1932. Attendance at the Fort Sill, Oklahoma, artillery school for a year was followed by a session of the Command and General Staff School at Fort Leavenworth, Kansas, in 1935. He attended the American War College 1939–40.

In 1941, as a colonel, Taylor was appointed chief of staff to Gen. Matthew Ridgway's 82nd Infantry Division, which would be converted to the 82nd Airborne Division in July 1942. The 82nd Airborne Division was split in two, creating the 101st Airborne Division (which General Taylor would later command on D-day). He remained with the 82nd Airborne Division and went with them to North Africa in 1943. He commanded artillery units in the Sicilian campaign and while there went on a daring mission to Rome to determine if an airborne attack had value. His report was unfavorable and the proposed landing near Rome was abandoned.

General Taylor was ordered to Great Britain to take over as commander of the 101st Airborne Division and parachuted into Normandy with the unit the night of June 5, 1944, capturing Carentan after a bitter struggle. When their mission was completed, the 101st was pulled back to England for regrouping and then dropped near Eindoven during Operation Market Garden. Stiff German resistance prevented the capture of the bridge over the Rhine, which was the major objective. Because General Taylor was in Washington at the time the 101st was entrapped at Bastogne, Gen. Anthony McAuliffe assumed command. Taylor subsequently returned and led his division through Alsace and the Rhineland and on through southern Germany to Berchtesgaden.

Following World War II, General Taylor became superintendent of West Point from 1945 to 1949. He then served as chief of staff of forces in Europe, followed by commander of U.S. forces in Berlin. In February 1953 Taylor was appointed commander of the Eighth Army in Korea. After the armistice, he was promoted to full general and made commander of all U.S. forces in the Far East. Taylor followed General Ridgway as Chief of Staff of the Army in June 1955. He retired in 1959. He became a military advisor to President Kennedy and continued to render service, becoming chairman of the Joint Chiefs of Staff during the Cuban missile crisis. After a second retirement, Taylor served as ambassador to South Vietnam and special counsel to Pres. Lyndon Johnson. He died on April 19, 1987.

2

The Assault and Bridgehead on the Cotentin Peninsula

ONSET

THE BATTLE TO capture Cherbourg began when the first pathfinders, who were volunteers, dropped into Normandy the night of June 5 to set up signal lights to guide the oncoming troop carriers filled with paratroopers of the 101st and 82nd Airborne divisions. Unfortunately, the airborne assault became disorganized and did not go well.

Many troopers were dropped well out of their zones. The 101st Airborne Division was scattered over twenty-eight miles, some troopers landing only a few miles south of Cherbourg. General Ridgway's 82nd Airborne encountered similar adversity. Dropped one hour after the 101st Airborne, they were scattered from Carentan at the base of the peninsula to Valognes. Some planes filled with troopers were shot down by German antiaircraft guns and others had to drop the troopers prematurely because of on-board fires or such damage that made the plane difficult to control. Many planes were too low and too fast when the troopers were forced to jump. The shock of the chute opening under these conditions injured the troopers, and rupture of chute panels accelerated the descent, which resulted in death or injury. Many troopers landed in flooded areas, swamps, rivers, and streams. Some managed desperately to cut themselves out of their chutes and unload some of the heavy equipment each carried, thus escaping drowning. Many others were not so fortunate.

The wide scattering of troopers made it difficult to assemble them into units in which they had trained. With their "crickets" as a means of identification during the dark hours, they teamed up with others and headed to an objective usually chosen by the ranking officer or noncommissioned officer (noncom) in the group. Members from different companies, battalions, and regiments were often banded together from a few to as many as 100 troopers

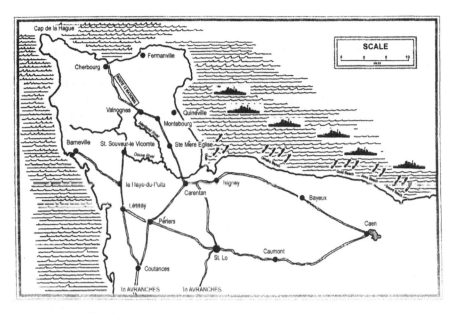

The Cotentin Peninsula

with two purposes in mind: to defeat the enemy and to provide protection for those soldiers who would soon be landing on the beaches. The officers provided superior leadership, each gathering as many men as he could find and leading them as a newly formed combat unit, no matter how large or small. Unlike many combat units, the officers in the airborne units jumped in with the men or were in the gliders with them and thus were subjected to the same discomfort and hazards as the frontline soldier. It was not unusual for a captain, major, or colonel and a few enlisted men to group together, sharing ammunition, food. and the dangers of the battle.

There were many acts of courage among the entire group fending their way through swamps and hedgerows and engaging the enemy no matter what the odds were. It was a desperate period for them and for the Allied countries and they rose to the occasion. Those who entered Ste. Mère Église were shocked to see their fellow troopers dangling by their parachutes from trees and buildings, dead before reaching the ground. Many personal stories are well presented in Phil Nordyke's book *All American All the Way,* which is an excellent combat history of the 82nd Airborne Division during World War II and exemplifies the courage that existed in our airborne landing in Normandy.

Another shocking sight that the troopers witnessed shortly after daylight on June 6 was the fate of so many incoming gliders filled with soldiers and equipment. Some of the gliders were on fire, others were badly damaged from antiaircraft fire and crashed, killing all on board. Others crashed into hedgerows, trees, and other gliders.

THE FIRST DAY

Gradually, as the troopers began moving toward their objectives, their situation became more orderly. The 101st Airborne Division captured the five causeways leading in from Utah Beach. The Stars and Stripes were raised over Ste. Mère Église by the 82nd Airborne at 6:45 A.M., June 6, 1944. A perimeter defense began to materialize. A group of citizen soldiers became veterans over night and quickly turned the negative of their dispersed landing into the positive of quickly regrouping and securing their objectives.

Fortunately, Air Marshall Leigh-Mallory's predictions were wrong. He subsequently apologized to generals Eisenhower and Bradley for having made such remarks that had added to their burdens associated with Overlord. Although many casualties were associated with this airborne assault, it is very probable that the casualty rate of the troops landing on the Normandy beaches would have been much higher had not these brave young soldiers been there in intense battle with the Germans when the invasion began.

On June 6 at 4:45 A.M., fifty-six-year-old Brig. Gen. Teddy Roosevelt and his 600 men of the 4th Infantry Division climbed down the rope net from the deck of the *Bayfield*. Roosevelt was a spare one-star general who had no assignment but had begged his way on to the first assault wave by appealing to Gen. Raymond O. ("Tubby") Barton to let hem go along with the troops. He was refused at first but finally sort of wore General Barton down by persuading him that he could bolster the spirits of the soldiers who were in combat for the first time. He told General Barton that if they saw a general on the beach they would not be afraid as they would think the beach was a safe place. He was well known for his courage and casualness under fire. This attitude was prevalent among men young and old when our country became involved in World War II.

As Roosevelt and his 4th Infantry troops clambered into the landing craft that would carry them into Utah Beach, the capture of Cherbourg had already begun. Their assignment was to begin to attack toward Cherbourg as soon as the beach was secured.

The Navy and Air Force laid down a concentrated carpet of bombs and artillery shells as the small boats approached the beach. This naturally gave the incoming soldiers a lot of encouragement, knowing that the Germans were taking a terrific pounding before they stepped on to the beach.

As the contingent of assault troops approached the beach, General Roosevelt realized that they were not headed for their designated landing target. When the ramp of his boat went down, Roosevelt and his men struck out for the beach in waist-high water. The Germans, after recovering from the terrific shelling that they had endured, opened up with machine guns, mortars, and the deadly accurate flat-trajectory 88mm cannon. The troops found cover behind a concrete barricade and Roosevelt had a moment to look at his maps. He determined that they were 2,000 yards south of the target beach.

Undaunted, Roosevelt climbed over the barricade and set out on a one-man reconnaissance patrol through the dunes ahead. He continued until he found the causeways that the 4th Infantry Division would use to push on into the Cotentin Peninsula and to begin their trek toward Cherbourg. He started the troops forward and the men of the 4th Infantry assault wave, without hesitation, followed and slogged through a flooded area toward a causeway three miles inland. The 82nd and 101st Airborne Divisions were battling furiously to prevent any attack on the incoming 4th Infantry and to secure the bridges necessary for the 4th Infantry soldiers to exit Utah Beach into the base of the Cotentin Peninsula. It was one group of GIs looking out for another.

Meanwhile, at 9 A.M. Gen. J. Lawton "Lightning Joe" Collins, commander of VII Corps, at his command post on the *Bayfield*, finally received a message from Col. Jim Van Fleet that he was with Lt. Col. Conrad C. Simmons and General Roosevelt and that they were steadily advancing. After hours of anxiety, Collins was finally able to relax a bit.

Early in the afternoon, the seaborne group of the 82nd Airborne Division began landing on Utah Beach, delivering field artillery units, antitank units, various headquarters units, an engineer battalion, an ordinance company, quartermaster company, a medical detachment, and other support units. By 6 P.M. the 4th Infantry Division with its vehicles and more than 1600 tons of supplies had landed at Utah with very few casualties. Omaha, the other American beach, was a catastrophe and came near to being eliminated as a landing beach. The weather cleared and the Allied air support came in on time. Unfortunately, the bombardment was too far inland and virtually ineffective. The Germans held their fire until the GIs were crossing the beach and then bombarded them with machine guns, mortars, and artillery, creating a bloodbath among the incoming troops.

The glider troops had prepared back in England to board the gliders and be ferried to the landing zones in Normandy. The gliders carried not only troops but also jeeps, cannon, ammunition, and other essential supplies. British and American gliders were used, both made of plywood and both operated by two pilots. All were overloaded, some so much so that contents had to be jettisoned in flight to maintain altitude. The tow planes were predominantly C-47s. The first flights left England between 4:00 and 5:00 A.M. on June 7, touching down at approximately 7:00 A.M.

In addition to the obstructions placed by the Germans and the multiple hedgerows, other unanticipated factors played havoc with the landings. Many of the gliders were released too low and at too great a speed. In practice the glider was released at an altitude of approximately 700 feet to allow the pilot to execute a 180-degree turn, which slowed the descent and gave him time to pick out a landing site. With a release too low and too fast, the pilot could not execute the 180-degree turn without potentially stalling and therefore not being able to slow the glider. In this situation, the pilot would have to pick out a landing site immediately and put the glider down. Understandably, this led to many crash landings. Had the tow pilots ascended to 700 feet prior to releasing the glider, the casualty rate would have been much less. Needless to say, many of these plywood gliders burst apart when they hit the ground.

While the first wave of gliders was landing, the second wave was departing from England, designated to land astride Highway N-13 southeast of Ste. Mère Église. The 325th Glider Infantry Regiment of the 82nd Airborne Division, having been subject to these faulted landings, regrouped with the survivors and arrived at Ste. Mère Église just in time to face a counterattack by the Germans on the town. Bitter fights continued all day at Chef-du-Pont, the La Fière and Chef-du-Pont causeways, across the Merderet River and at Hill

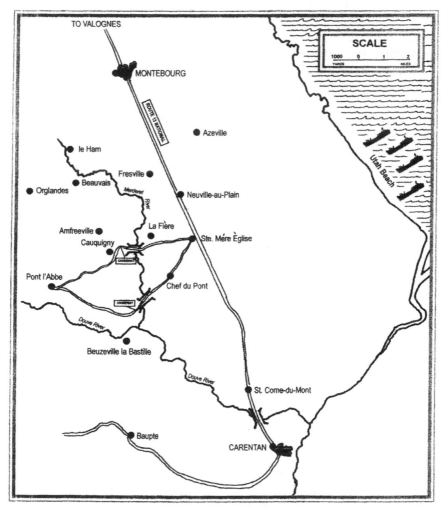

La Fiere and Chef-du-Pont Causeways

30, a high hill desired by the Germans and Americans because of its vantage point. As June 6 neared its end, the exhausted paratroopers of the 101st and 82nd Airborne divisions formed perimeter defensive positions around their designated site and dug in with the hope of getting a few hours sleep between guard duty and patrol duty. Time to eat a K-ration was a welcomed event for those who could do so. As evening approached, forward reconnaissance patrols of the 4th Infantry Division began to arrive, which was a great relief for the exhausted troopers. They had survived the first day and secured the majority of their objectives with weapons that they carried on their backs. Truly, they were a unit of warriors for whom we should always be proud.

At the end of this first day, the Atlantic Wall had been breached by a force of 57,000 American and 75,000 British and Canadian soldiers. Approximately 23,000 American airborne troops were battling the Germans on the southeast end of the Cotentin Peninsula.

COUNTERATTACK

At midnight on June 6, preparations began for the German attack that was sure to come before dawn. Although they were sleep-deprived, hungry, and exhausted, the troopers maintained a vigilant guard against a night attack. Perimeter defenses were established and soldiers began "digging in." On Hill 30 so many dead and wounded from both sides needed evacuation. Among the living and still functional was a group of approximately 400 troopers representing all of the regiments of the 82nd and 101st Airborne divisions, attributable to the widely scattered units during the drop from the transport planes. Although many troopers could find no one familiar to them, they banded together to set up roadblocks and to launch reconnaissance and combat patrols. Others were sent out to recover equipment bundles that had been dropped. This rapid regrouping into an effective combat force was a tribute to the outstanding leadership of the two airborne divisions.

The Germans attacked Hill 30 at dawn from multiple directions, but after a vicious battle at close range they were driven back. Some of the fighting was hand to hand with bayonets. Cauquigny remained in German hands. In another dawn attack the Germans began an assault on Ste. Mère Église, coming down from the north. They were well fortified with infantry and artillery and supported by a number of self-propelled guns. A group of less than thirty 82nd Airborne troopers defended this northern section along Route 13, being outnumbered twenty to one. The American artillery gave them superb support but the fighting remained intense. As usual during these early days following D-day, acts of courage were abundant and allowed the depleted platoon to hold on.

One officer on a one-man reconnaissance patrol found that the German infantry was using a sunken road between two hedgerows as cover and concealment to approach the Americans. He directed a mortar crew to traverse the road several times, dropping shells every few feet. He also set up a machine gun at one end of the sunken road which fired on those in the road and on those who broke out on both sides into fields to escape. The Germans rapidly retreated northward on both sides of Route 13. General Ridgway was very concerned about holding on to Ste. Mère Église so he sent a small patrol the four miles back to Utah Beach to seek tank support for the 4th Infantry Division. Five tanks were sent, arriving in early afternoon.

Since the Germans did not launch another attack on Ste. Mère Église, the Americans decided to go on the offensive at 5:15 P.M. Tanks and infantry from the 4th Infantry began arriving at 4 P.M., just in time to add welcomed strength to the attacking force. The battle became an intense one but the Americans overwhelmed the Germans, capturing several hundred prisoners and killing many more who were trapped in ditches and sunken roads where they had sought cover. The newly arrived tanks drove the Germans up Route 13 to Neuville-au-Plain. Sixty more Germans were captured. By nightfall, the Americans were moderately secure in Ste. Mère Église.

On that same day a bitter battle began at the La Fière causeway where the Americans repeatedly drove the Germans back. Initially the Germans attacked with tanks. When these were knocked out, the German infantry assaulted the American position, but many of them were killed. The American group guarding the west end of the causeway suffered greatly also and were reduced to a group of approximately fifteen men.

FIGHT TO HOLD THE BRIDGEHEAD

General Gavin ordered Lieutenant Colonel Maloney to take seventy-five troopers to capture the causeway across the Merderet River a few miles southwest of Chef-du-Pont. This group found the village deserted and quickly seized it. They then stormed the western end of the causeway but failed to secure it. The eastern end remained in American hands.

Colonel Maloney headed back to La Fière to support that battle with the majority of the force. The small group left at the eastern end of the Chef-du-Pont causeway suffered numerous shellings and lost half of their group of approximately thirty-four troopers. They were ordered to "hold at all cost" but actually they were not holding anything of strategic value as they had not secured the east end of the causeway.

The town of Carentan southwest of Utah Beach became an important target for the Allies as it would have to be neutralized so that the forces of Utah and Omaha could join, leaving no gap that Rommel could exploit with a counterattack. General Eisenhower conveyed to General Bradley that this gap must be closed as soon as possible, which General Bradley then passed on to General Collins, VII Corps commander, who would be in charge of this attack on Carentan.

On June 8 the 101st Airborne Division captured Saint-Côme-du-Mont a few miles northwest of Carentan and had set up a defense line facing south. The area around Carentan had been flooded so it was accessible only along causeways through the low areas.

Elements of the 505th Parachute Infantry Regiment (82nd) continued to attack to the north targeting Grainville and Fresville as the next targets. While this offense was in progress, the Germans again launched an attack on Hill 30, desperate to gain some high ground so as to control a wide area with their very effective artillery. Again, the Americans, quite physically depleted and low on ammunition, tenaciously held on and again denied the Germans the Hill. Let us never forget their courage and determination. After a brutal attack with tanks and infantry, Grainville fell to the Americans late in the afternoon of June 8.

Early morning on June 9 elements of the 505th Parachute Infantry Regiment (82nd) and the 325th Glider Infantry Regiment (82nd) combined forces and advanced northward toward Montebourg, which they knew would be heavily defended. Casualties were numerous and some of the troopers stated that this battle was worse than any that they had experienced while fighting in Italy. By the end of the day, June 9, they were midway between Fresville and Montebourg.

Two major players in the battles of the Cotentin Peninsula were generals Joseph Collins and Troy Middleton. Both were outstanding combat soldiers and had difficult baptisms of fire prior to landing at Normandy. Both men were dedicated to their profession and to defeating the Germans as quickly and as decisively as possible. They were given a formidable assignment to capture Cherbourg and rid the Cotentin Peninsula of all German forces knowing that if their efforts failed, Normandy could become another Dunkirk.

Unforeseen serious events took place, making their assignments even more difficult. The airborne assault was badly flawed with the paratroopers scattered from just south of Cherbourg to the base of the peninsula, creating a nightmare of reorganization. The Germans had flooded much of the terrain in the lower peninsula, making it difficult for the infantry to maneuver and limiting greatly any use of tanks. The worst storm in many years in the Channel, June 19 23, suspended debarkation of supplies, equipment, and soldiers and destroyed much of the docking facilities. In spite of all the adversity, the performance of generals Joe Collins (VII Corps) and Troy Middleton (VIII Corps) was superior. No one could have chosen more outstanding commanders. They are profiled in this story in some detail to highlight their superior capabilities and to honor their service to our country.

COLLINS ORDERED TO CROSS THE COTENTIN PENINSULA

On June 9 General Bradley directed General Collins to give top priority to sealing off the Cotentin Peninsula so as to prevent the Germans from reinforcing the defense of Cherbourg. This required Collins to change direction of the

JOSEPH LAWTON "LIGHTNING JOE" COLLINS

Joseph Lawton Collins grew up in Algiers, Mississippi, a small town on the west bank of the Mississippi River south of New Orleans. He was one of eleven children and when he was old enough worked in the family general store. At the age of sixteen, he attended Louisiana State University on a scholarship. He entered West Point in 1913, graduating in 1917. He was sent to Fort Hamilton, New York, and after a period of training was sent to France in 1919, just after the armistice was signed. He attained the permanent rank of major in the early 1930s and became a lieutenant colonel at age forty-four.

Collins married Gladys Easterbrook in 1921. Soon after his marriage, he was sent to West Point as an instructor and then to Fort Benning and Fort Leavenworth. Major Collins served in the Philippines from 1933 to 1936, where he helped build a defensive system against the Japanese and trained the Philippine soldiers to prepare for such an attack. He attended the Army Industrial College and the War College from 1937 to 1940.

Subsequently, Collins was assigned to the VII Corps as chief of staff and participated in the Tennessee maneuvers in 1941. After Pearl Harbor, he was sent to Hawaii as Chief of Staff of the Hawaiian Department responsible for ground defenses and training troops of the 24th and 25th Infantry divisions. He was promoted to major general and placed with the 25th Infantry Division as its commander. The division was sent to Guadalcanal in January 1943. The code name of his headquarters was "lightning" and the men of his division began to refer to him as "Lightning Joe," a sobriquet that remained with him throughout his service. The division fought a vicious battle with the Japanese, finally clearing the island in February 1943.

Following this tour of duty, General Marshall chose Collins to command the VII Corps, which was in England preparing for the invasion of France. The VII Corps landed on Utah Beach and proceeded immediately to begin a bloody battle up the east coast of the Cotentin Peninsula to capture Cherbourg. They then turned south and joined the VIII Corps to secure the peninsula. Following this battle, the VII Corps joined the U.S. eastern front and fought many battles against the Germans until the Germans capitulated. His VII Corps met up with the Russians on the Elbe River.

Postwar, General Collins was Chief of Staff of the Army and a member of the Joint Chiefs of Staff during the Korean War. General Eisenhower appointed him as a special representative of the United States in Vietnam. He retired from the Army on March 31, 1956. As a civilian, he joined Charles Pfizer and Company as a member of its board of directors, serving as vice chairman of its international division for twelve years.

main effort of his corps from north to the west coast. It was necessary to secure the north flank of his corps by capturing Quinéville ridge through the action of the 4th Infantry Division then underway. Collins's corps would eventually turn north again and proceed to Cherbourg.

To embark on this westward advance, General Collins would need a secure point of departure and the west bank of the Merderet River was selected. To traverse the Merderet River was going to be difficult as Germans on the west bank had established a formidable defensive position. Between the opposing forces was a flooded area, several miles long and five hundred yards across traversed by the La Fière causeway. The 325th Glider Infantry Regiment, commanded by Col. Harry L. Lewis was given the assignment to force this crossing. A ford was found a few hundred yards north of La Fière bridge, and during the dark hours the first battalion of the glider regiment slipped across the river. Resistance was minimal initially, but then the glider men encountered a brutal attack by small arms, mortars, and artillery. They were driven back across the river, leaving many of their dead and wounded on the west bank.

BATTLE FOR THE LA FIÈRE CAUSEWAY

General Gavin was informed that the Germans were strengthening their forces at the west end of the La Fière causeway, which spanned the Merderet River. He assumed that an assault was forthcoming and that it was critical to deny the Germans this pathway to Utah Beach. Also, securing this causeway was important for VII Corps' move west. General Ridgway agreed and ordered an attack across the causeway to establish a bridgehead at the west end. Tanks and artillery were acquired for the battle and the plan issued to the officers of the units that would be involved. The battle for the La Fière causeway would be costly for the Americans. The artillery bombardment was planned to begin at 10:30 A.M., June 9, and last for thirty minutes. A dozen Sherman tanks were lined up at the east end. The first shells of the bombardment would be smoke shells to help conceal the infantry that would begin charging across the causeway as soon as the bombardment ended. Its major purpose was to rescue Lt. Col. Charles Timmes and his group of troopers, who had been trapped there since D-day. After fifteen minutes of bombardment, the troops were given the "go" sign and began running across the causeway led by one of their captains. The Germans opened fire and men began to fall, some rolling off of the causeway into the marsh. Chaos ensued. Gavin signaled a unit of the 82nd Division troopers to charge across the causeway in an effort to get the glider men to follow.

Capt. John Sauls, who led the glider troops, and approximately thirty of his men reached the far side. This group was isolated as those following were cut off. Finally, more men, guns, and a few tanks pushed across the causeway. Within an hour a small area of the west bank of the Merderet had been established as a bridgehead.

Once General Gavin made the crossing, he was appalled to see the might of the guns opposing his small group. General Ridgway entered the battle and tried to move the troops forward over the causeway. Some troopers later stated that Ridgway probably saved their lives as many would have been

La Fiere Causeway

killed if they continued to lie down on the causeway. Outstanding leadership was given by other officers at this critical time. The Germans were either dead by their guns or had fled, abandoning much equipment. Later in the afternoon the 82nd Airborne Division soldiers reached two isolated pockets of fellow troopers who had been entrapped since bailing out. A bridgehead was established by one of the bloodiest battles of the campaign.

As more troopers moved to the west end of the causeway, some fanned out north and south to expand the bridgehead and to destroy German machine-gun positions along the shore. Dead and wounded covered the causeway. The troopers and glidermen, shoulder to shoulder, were resolute in getting the job done. Never had there been such a strong association between them. The same was true for the officers and enlisted men. Rank made no difference as all were soldiers fighting together against almost impossible odds to rescue Colonel Timmes and his band of troopers.

General Gavin exemplified so many of our military commanders in World War II. The U.S. Army was fortunate to have recently grown from a small, rather dormant army to one bristling with a cadre of extremely competent army, corps and division commanders. Gavin returned to his command post near Ste. Mère Église in order to report to General Ridgway. While he was there he received an urgent message that the Germans were attacking. He raced back to the bridgehead to find that the 325th Glider Infantry Regiment (82nd) was about to withdraw. Gavin informed the glider troops commander that they would not pull out and everyone would join in a counterattack. He placed two of his staff officers on the bridge and instructed them to let no one withdraw. General Gavin found every available man and directed them to firing positions. With a gallant effort, by nightfall, the potential rout of the American troops was converted to a successful counterattack, setting up a westbound advance by VII Corps to cross the Cotentin Peninsula, which would entrap the German garrison in Cherbourg.

Hundreds of acts of heroism abound in a battle of this intensity but unfortunately many are never cited due to the confusion and violence of battle. It was an indomitable spirit that carried this mixed force across the treacherous exposed causeway to establish a small bridgehead on the west bank of the Merderet River. This small American foothold became a gateway to the western sector of the Cotentin Peninsula. The battle was an example of the many seemingly small fights in World War II which had a great impact on the eventual victory over the Germans. Had not this brave group of men secured the causeway, the German troops could have retaken Utah Beach. While fanning out, one group moved on to Motey and, although subjected to heavy shelling, held their ground and were relieved the next morning by elements of the 90th Infantry Division. Colonel Timmes and his troopers were freed from their entrapment.

In 1983 Gen. James Gavin, who led the La Fière causeway attack stated to author William Breuer, "It is impossible to put into words the holocaust that took place there, but the attack was crucial to gain a bridgehead for the drive west to cut off the peninsula."

On June 10 the 90th Infantry Division began relieving the exhausted troopers and glider infantrymen who had been fighting continuously since arrival. The wounded and dead were retrieved and the airborne troops began to regroup. Le Motey and Grainges were secured and Montebourg station was

JAMES MAURICE GAVIN

James Gavin was born in Brooklyn, New York, on March 22, 1907. His parents placed him in an orphanage and he was adopted by Martin and Mary Gavin when he was two years old. Mr. Gavin was a coal miner and young Jim did not want to become one, so he ran away to New York on his seventeenth birthday. As soon as he arrived, he telegrammed his parents to let them know that he was all right. He lied about his age and joined the U.S. Army Two sergeants in his company recognized that he was very smart and that he read a lot. They encouraged him to go to an army school that coached young soldiers who had academic potential in studies that would prepare them to take the West Point entrance exam. With the help of the school and a lieutenant who tutored him, Gavin passed the entrance exam and entered West Point the summer of 1925. Graduating in 1929 as a second lieutenant, he was assigned to Camp Harry J. Jones near the Mexican border, where he stayed for three years. In 1936 he was posted to the Philippines and improved considerably the defenses and the training of the troops.

Eventually, Gavin was ordered to West Point and assigned to the Tactics Faculty where he began to shine. Germany had begun its Blitzkrieg and the Tactics Faculty was requested to study and analyze this German aggression. At this time Gavin began talking about airborne forces. He studied the German airborne assault on the Fort Eben-Emael in Belgium in May, 1940, and was so enthusiastic about the value of airborne units that he joined the paratroopers in April 1941 at Fort Benning. He became known to his troopers as "Jumpin' Jim."

In 1942 Gavin attended the Command and General Staff College at Fort Leavenworth, Kansas. He subsequently became commanding officer of the 505th Parachute Infantry Regiment (82nd) and began a very intensive physical training program with realistic sessions to bring the regiment up to combat readiness. His dictum was that the "officers were first out of the plane and last in the chow line."

The 505th was sent to North Africa, arriving in Casablanca on May 10, 1943, and on July 9, 1943, was the first U.S. parachute regiment to conduct a regimental-sized parachute assault when they parachuted into Sicily. The unit repeated this feat when the 505th was dropped into Salerno on September 13, 1943. Next was the airborne assault in Normandy (already covered in these pages). When General Ridgway was made commander of the XVIII Airborne Corps, he recommended that Gavin be made commander of the 82nd Airborne Division. With this appointment Brigadier General Gavin was promoted to major general and thus became the youngest two-star general since the War Between the States to command a U.S. Army division. On September 17 the 82nd Airborne Division made its fourth combat jump into the Netherlands as part of Operation Market Garden. In December the 82nd entered the Battle of the Bulge and were instrumental in helping to halt the German penetration. Gavin continued to lead the unit into the battle for Germany after crossing the Elbe River and advancing thirty-six miles in one day, following an opinion voiced by Gen. Bernard Montgomery that German opposition was too great to cross the Elbe.

Upon retiring in 1958 Lieutenant General Gavin twice served as the U.S. ambassador to France (1961–1963). General Gavin died February 23, 1990. It was very meaningful to the GI soldiers that General Gavin always carried an M-1 Garand Rifle as they did. Above all, he was a soldier.

taken later in the day. On June 11 Le Ham was captured at a price of many casualties. The Germans made several counterattacks on Grainges, causing the American troops to withdraw through a swamp. The Germans killed all of the wounded Americans in Grainges, as well as the battalion surgeon, his medics, and two priests.

The battle for the La Fière causeway was very costly with nearly 50 percent of the 325th Glider Infantry becoming casualties. It was one of those battles in this campaign that was equally as devastating to the troops as was Omaha Beach, yet little has surfaced about it or about its importance in taking the Cotentin Peninsula.

The next battle for Cherbourg would be no different. Col. Friedrich August Freiherr von der Heydte was commander of the German 6th Parachute Regiment, one of Germany's finest. This regiment was composed of seventeen- and eighteen-year-olds who were well trained and dedicated to Hitler. They were placed in a defensive position to block the 101st Airborne Division's advance to Carentan. This same regiment had attacked the 101st Airborne Division after the Americans had taken Ste. Mère Église the night of June 5–6. Von der Heydte's young troopers took it back. Now they were pulled back to the north to block Route National 13 and east of Carentan to protect it from an attack by the 101st Airborne Division from the north and any attack from the British sector east of Carentan. Although the young German paratroopers were short on ammunition and had no tank support and very little artillery, von der Heydte believed that they would hold their position. In their favor were the marshes just north of Carentan.

FRIEDRICH AUGUST FREIHERR VON DER HEYDTE

Colonel von der Heydte was not the usual tough paratrooper commander. He was an aristocrat, born of the nobility and an intellectual. He was a former professor of law at a German university. These were potential strikes against his military advancement but at the age of thirty-four, he was a lieutenant colonel for one reason: he had produced on the battlefield.

Von der Heydte had confidence in himself and was ready to argue with the Oberkommando der Wehrmacht (OKW) in Berlin for the supplies and equipment needed for his unit of young paratroopers. Although the OKW treated him with disdain, he would stand his ground during any controversy with them.

He had little respect for them as he felt none of them had been within 500 miles of a frontline. His young troopers had the greatest respect for their colonel and looked upon him as a father figure. In the battle for Carentan, von der Heydte knew that although his regiment had suffered many casualties and was short of weapons and equipment, they would stand their ground.

Von der Heydte was born into the nobility in Munich, Bavaria, on March 30, 1907. He was Roman Catholic and attended a Catholic school, making excellent grades. His father, a baron, distinguished himself in World War I. Friedrich entered the military but was released to attend Innsbruck University to study law. He attained his law degree in 1927. During his university years, he became very liberal and found himself at odds with the popular opinions in Germany, becoming involved in brawls with pro-Nazis students. He studied for two years at The Hague and again joined the military and attended a General Staff Officers' course in 1938–1939.

He commanded a paratroop battalion in Crete in 1941 and was awarded the Knight's Cross of the Iron Cross. He fought in Russia, North Africa, and Normandy, and was taken prisoner in the Ardennes counterattack (Battle of the Bulge). While in North Africa he was a member of "Ramcke's Brigade" at El Alamein. After the war, von der Heydte served in the reserves, reaching the rank of brigadier general. He died in 1994.

BATTLE FOR THE CARENTAN CAUSEWAY AND CARENTAN

Route National 13 ran south from St.-Côme-du-Mont to Carentan and was a hard-surfaced causeway across the marshes. The 101st Airborne Division would have to cross this exposed highway with no place to seek cover. They would attack from the north and east and try to capture a hill southwest of Carentan which would put them in a position to block any attempted exit south on Route National 13.

Von der Heydte's men were well hidden, which gave the Americans the impression that there were few German forces in Carentan. General Taylor ordered the 502nd Parachute Regiment (101st) to attack Carentan over the causeway. The 3rd Battalion under Lt. Col. Robert G. Cole would lead. A small patrol led by Lt. Ralph B. Gehauf set out to reconnoiter the causeway especially to determine if bridge 2 had been repaired by the engineers. The bridge had not been repaired and the patrol crossed the creek and proceeded down the elevated causeway to bridge 3 and then on to bridge 4 over a canal. At this point von der Heydte's troopers began firing on the Americans. A trooper was sent back to try to locate the advancing battalion and request urgent help to neutralize the machine guns confronting them. The attack on the night of June 9 was canceled.

On that same evening the 327th Glider Regiment began an amphibious attack across the Douve River just east of Carentan. The first elements reached the far shore at 1:45 A.M., June 10. By 6 A.M. the crossing was completed, three miles northeast of the Carentan causeway.

Meanwhile, Lieutenant Colonel Cole was ordered to attack once again over the causeway from the north. Suddenly, after reaching a point 600 yards from the outskirts of Carentan, the Americans were engulfed with machine-gun fire and had no place on the causeway to take cover. Mortar shells began to explode and there were immediately numerous casualties. The trap had been sprung. The German paratroopers had waited until the Americans were 100 yards from their guns before they began to fire. There was no place to maneuver. They were virtually pinned down and taking numerous casualties. Lieutenant Colonel Cole tried to get the troops moving forward but there were so many wounded troopers that this was difficult.

As night approached, a lone German fighter-bomber flew directly over I Company of the 3rd Battalion and dropped its bombs concomitantly with a hail of machine-gun fire. Company I faced annihilation. During the night of June 10–11, G and H Companies had completed the trip across the causeway and were on firm ground on the outskirts of Carentan. I Company was ineffective with only a few men and two officers functional. Although in a very untenable position, this brave battalion of the 502nd Parachute Regiment (101st) was out of the horrors of the causeway leading into Carentan. The battle for the causeway was another battle equal to Omaha Beach where young GIs committed numerous acts of heroism, most of which were never recorded. This was true in so many intense battles where there were not many left who could so honor the heroes with reports on the battle. During this battle, Lieutenant Colonel von der Heydte received a message from Hitler, "You are to defend Carentan to the last man and the last bullet." Veterans of the Carentan causeway attack and Bastogne maintained that the attack over the Carentan causeway was the bloodiest, most difficult of the war for the Screaming Eagles.

At 5:30 A.M. the next morning, Lieutenant Colonel Cole was advancing with H Company when they were suddenly assaulted with concentrated small arms and mortar fire. The Americans called in artillery and pounded the area from which the firing was coming from, but the young German paratroopers persisted. H Company was pinned down and Lieutenant Colonel Cole had to make the decision to either crawl back and lose the costly ground that they had gained or charge the group of farmhouses, knowingly at great risk. He decided on the latter but unfortunately, the troopers were scattered and all did not get the order. When he yelled out the order to charge with bayonets, fewer than half followed due to the flawed communication. Maj. John Stopka was with him and continued to yell to his men to keep going. The charging element of the second battalion reached the farmhouses and found them vacated except for the dead and wounded of which there were many. The attack continued at very close quarters. In some instances the bayonets were necessarily utilized in this desperate effort to overcome these die-hard German troopers. Evacuation of the wounded became a major problem. The Germans requested a truce to recover their large numbers of dead and wounded were scattered over a wide area. General Taylor issued a surrender ultimatum to them through an emissary. Von der Heydte refused to see the emissary. The Germans then ended the truce and began shelling the Americans again.

The Germans, having regrouped, counterattacked the Americans viciously. An intense firefight began at close quarters, so close that grenades as well as automatic rifles were being used by both sides. Small groups of the Americans were isolated in pockets, many wounded but refusing evacuation. Cole was contemplating withdrawal as the Germans were now on the next hedgerow and continuing to advance. He faced annihilation of his remaining troopers. Finally after much effort, the artillery fire center was contacted and artillery called for on the hedgerows right in front of the battalion command post. Within fifteen minutes artillery shells began coming in and hitting the target with great concentration and accuracy. When it lifted, Cole sent a patrol forward to find many dead Germans. Those who were able had fled. The Carentan causeway was secure but this bloody battle took its toll. Approximately 80 percent of the 650 American troopers had become casualties. Those remaining were relieved by another battalion. The high cost of freedom!

The Carentan causeway was secured but the town of Carentan was still occupied by von der Heydte's paratroopers. General Collins had to focus his attention on the progress of the 4th Infantry Division northward so he designated General Taylor to conduct the attack on Carentan. The attack by the 501st and 506th Parachute regiments (101st) and the 327th Glider Infantry Regiment (101st) would be under the battlefield command of Brig. Gen. Anthony J. McAuliffe, who would later say "Nuts" to the Germans when they requested his surrender at Bastogne. The attack began at 2:00 A.M. the night of June 11–12. The city was secured closing the gap between the V and VII Corps. On the morning of June 12, the 3rd Battalion of the 327th Glider Infantry Regiment (101st), which had been fighting its way into Carentan from the east, entered the city and linked up with the 506th Parachute Infantry (101st) coming into town from the southwest. Carentan was finally secured but the cost was high.

General Bradley related that on June 12 he was informed that a German counterattack was being planned for the next day and was to be spearheaded by a Panzer-grenadier unit from the 17th SS. He knew that General Taylor had formed a good defensive position in Carentan but had only few heavy weapons with which to repel a tank attack. He telephoned Lt. Gen. Leonard T. Gerow and instructed him to get Gen. Maurice Rose on the road immediately with a combat command from the 2nd Armored Division. General Gerow did not like the idea of moving Rose as this would expose General Huebner's flank. On the morning of June 13, the Germans struck as anticipated. They were held off by the American paratroopers with their small-arms fire. As the Germans got within 500 yards of the city, Rose's forces entered the city and drove the Germans back. General Montgomery moved part of the British 7th Armored Division to General Gerow's exposed flank, thus blocking the Germans from attacking the weakness that existed.

Hitler felt betrayed by his commanders and was enraged to hear of the loss of Carentan. On June 12 he sent this order to all German commanders in that area:

Explicit orders demand that everyone at strongpoints, points of resistance and other defensive positions surrounded by enemy units must defend the position to the last man and to the last bullet, in order to allow time for preparation for the counterattack and the recovery of the Normandy coast. No orders to retreat will be issued by any commander.

ACROSS THE DOUVE RIVER

During this same period, the 508th Parachute Regiment (82nd) was organized into a combat force to cross the Douve River and establish a beachhead on the southern bank at Beuzeville-la-Bastille. Some of the troops would cross the river in assault boats while others would cross a bridge. The attack began at midnight, June 12–13, and the town was quickly taken, followed by Crettsville. Three more villages, Coigny, Taillerfer, and Baupte, followed as the Germans were taken by surprise and gave up quickly. The French tanks used by the Germans were destroyed with bazookas and grenades.

The advance toward St.-Sauveur-le-Vicomte had stalled so elements of the 507th Parachute Regiment (82nd) were passed through the 90th Infantry Division to restore the initiative. The object of this plan was to cut off the Cotentin Peninsula.

The 401st Glider Infantry Regiment (82nd) secured Bonneville and Etienville the same day. Thousands of Germans were seen moving south through St.-Sauveur-le-Vicomte to escape capture. A massive barrage decimated this large force and many German vehicles fell to the Americans. A bridgehead was established toward La Haye-du-Puits. On June 19 Vindefontaine was captured. Although, the American encountered intense artillery and mortar fire, they continued to move south and secured the Bois de Limors Forest and Pretot.

3

Westward to Barneville, Northward to Cherbourg

THE VII CORPS had been making slow progress northward, impeded by many small streams and hedgerows that gave excellent defensive positions to the Germans who utilized them effectively in slowing the oncoming Allies. Gen. "Tubby" Barton and his 4th Infantry Division soldiers would have to slug it out with the Germans for every yard of advance. Basically, the capture of Cherbourg, the much-needed port, was going to be a costly campaign.

Four American infantry regiments—three were the 9th Infantry and the other the 505th Parachute Infantry Regiment (82nd)—began moving northward toward Cherbourg on June 8. At first progress was satisfactory, but resistance began to increase. The journey along Route National 13 would carry them through Ste. Mère Église and Montebourg, the latter having been heavily fortified to stop the Allied advance.

Colonel Jim Van Fleet's 8th Infantry Regiment (90th) reached the Montebourg-le Ham road which ran east-west. General Collins ordered them to dig in there as a defensive position to protect the flank of the American divisions that were attacking toward the west to cut off the Cotentin Peninsula, south of Van Fleet's position.

THE 90TH INFANTRY DIVISION FAILS

The newly arrived 90th Infantry Division in General Collins's VII Corps was assigned with the 4th Infantry to proceed toward Cherbourg while the 9th Infantry and the 82nd Airborne were directed toward cutting off the neck of the Cotentin Peninsula by advancing westward. On June 12 the 90th Infantry passed through the 82nd Airborne. Because of a poor showing by the green 90th Infantry, Collins made a change. Their new objective was a section of the Douve River just north of St.-Sauveur-le-Vicomte. The 90th Infantry Division was untested and failed from the beginning. The division's progress was

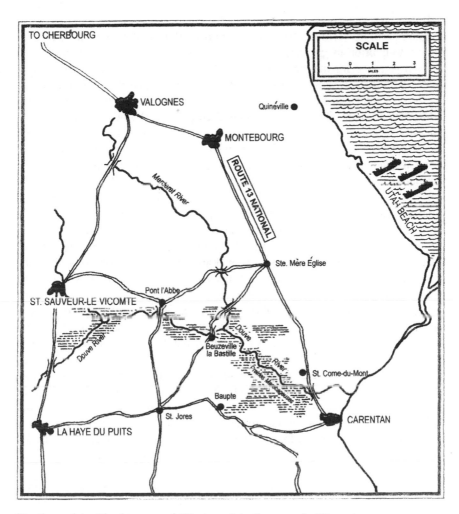

Northward to Cherbourg and Westward to Sauveur-le Vicomte

slow and casualties were high. Collins went forward into their zone on June 13 and could find no regimental command post (CP) and no officers until he finally ran into Lt. Col. William L. Nave, a battalion commander, who was killed two days later.

On the way back to the division CP, General Collins encountered a group of obviously malingering soldiers. Collins tried to appeal to their pride and ordered them back to the front. He finally found Gen. Jay W. McKelvie and confronted him with the division's poor incentive and performance. Collins recognized immediately that the division had poor leadership, with its senior officers having very little incentive to do what was required of them.

McKelvie, who had been made commander when the former commander was assigned a corps, seemed at a loss to improve things. Although he had performed well prior to entering combat, this former artillery commander was not well prepared for this new role. McKelvie had inherited some inept subordinates with this division. Collins requested relief of McKelvie without prejudice to his career and he was subsequently assigned an artillery position equal to his rank General Bradley found that during the first few days in combat, generally speaking, a new unit would suffer mental shock from the agony of the wounded and the finality of death, which creates fear and confusion. The troops needed to be led into an attack and sometimes even coaxed by their commanders. Within a few days, the shock usually abated and they would overcome their panic. With good command they would respond normally. Usually General Bradley would initially place a new unit in a quiet area before exposing them to the violence usually associated with an attack.

General Landrum, General Collins's deputy, replaced General McKelvie. After three weeks, the 90th failed again. Landrum had cleaned house but not well enough. Landrum was replaced by Brig. Gen. Raymond S. McLain. Bradley was convinced that the right commander could save this division. McLain studied the division for forty-eight hours and gave General Bradley a list of subordinates he did not want. Bradley had them reassigned. When McLain left the division in October to command a corps, it was one of the finest in the ETO.

General Collins decided to revamp his plan to secure the Cotentin Peninsula with the attack toward the west. The initial objective was to seize the line of the Douve River south of Terre-de-Beauval. He would pass the 9th Infantry Division and the 82nd Airborne through the 90th Infantry, and they would attack abreast with the 9th Infantry on the right. This was scheduled for June 14 but because of so much shuffling of troops, the attack actually began on June 18. The 90th Infantry would turn northeast after having been passed through and the 101st Airborne and would continue to protect the south flank of the VII Corps west of Baupte.

General Collins recommended that the 9th Infantry and the 82nd Airborne Division lead the attack to the west of the Cotentin Peninsula. At 3:00 P.M. on June 15, a platoon from the 505th Parachute Infantry Regiment (82nd), which would spearhead the attack, moved out. The terrain on the route westward would greatly favor the defenders. The advance would consist of two columns on parallel roads with the small seaport village of Barneville being the objective. Soon after passing through the 90th Infantry, the 82nd Airborne ran into intense resistance from small groups of Germans well concealed by the hedgerows.

The first and second battalions of the 505th Parachute Infantry Regiment (82nd) continued to press forward, periodically halting to wipe out opposing gun positions. Several hundred prisoners were taken. These two battalions reached the Douve River and dug in. The 60th Infantry Regiment (9th) was not faring as well on their route two miles to the north. German resistance brought them to a standstill. The 9th Infantry commander, Gen. Matt Eddy, committed the 47th Infantry Regiment (9th) and the two regiments then made good progress to reach Orglandes by nightfall.

On this night, June 15, Hitler unleashed his V1 bombs on London. Prior launching of these robots had failed but on this night the weapons hit the target. London was terrified.

BATTLE FOR ST.-SAUVEUR-LE-VICOMTE

On the morning of June 16, the battle for St.-Sauveur-le-Vicomte began. First was the pounding by the artillery and then the Allied fighter-bombers came in. The 82nd Airborne entered hard on the heels of the fleeing Germans to find the town completely destroyed and a few pitiful remnants of the population faced with the reconstruction of their homes and city buildings. The troopers fired into buildings as they passed to neutralize any remaining snipers or machine-gun units. The Germans began firing back into the town with 88mm cannon as the 82nd Airborne moved on through to the high ground to the right.

General Ridgway spotted the enemy pulling out of St.-Sauveur-le-Vicomte and immediately requested of General Collins permission to cross the Douve River and establish a bridgehead on the west bank. The request was granted and Collins asked General Ridgway to push his advance across the Prairies Marecageuses south of St.-Sauveur-le-Vicomte and reconnoiter the area south toward La Haye-du-Puits. Slightly north of the 82nd Airborne, the 60th and 47th Infantry regiments (9th) were experiencing counterattacks but in spite of this resistance pushed on to the Douve River near St. Colombe.

SEALING OFF THE COTENTIN PENINSULA

General Collins believed that they had the Germans on the run so he decided to immediately make a run for the coast to Barneville. He directed General Eddy, commander of the 9th Infantry, to send Colonel Smythe's 47th Infantry Regiment through the 82nd Airborne and on to the coast. A few miles north, the 60th Infantry Regiment (9th), commanded by Col. Frederick de Rohan, would attack toward Barneville.

Field marshalls Rommel and von Rundstedt were called to have a conference with Hitler. Hitler was very upset because they had allowed the Allies to secure Normandy. Both informed him that they and their men had done all that they could but were overwhelmed by the Allied superiority in tanks, planes, and weapons. Rommel added that Cherbourg would fall in a week and suggested pulling the German forces back from the range of the Allied naval guns. Rommel further advised Hitler that it was time to end the war. With this

Hitler became very angry and told Rommel not to worry about the war but to take care of his own front. Hitler warned them to hold Cherbourg at all costs and "to the last man." Rommel knew then that "school was out" and that his own future was in jeopardy. Rommel was actually subordinate to von Rundstedt, although Hitler dealt directly with Rommel. Von Rundstedt had little interest in the Atlantic Wall and did little to strengthen it. Rommel, whom Hitler had called in in 1943, had masterminded the fortification of the Atlantic Wall.

KARL RUDOLF GERD VON RUNDSTEDT

Field Marshall von Rundstedt was born into an aristocratic Prussian family on December 12, 1875, at Aschersleben in Saxony-Anhalt. He joined the German army in 1892 and entered Germany's elite military academy in 1922 where 75 percent of the academy's students were weeded out. In World War I, he was promoted to major and was chief of staff of his division. He stayed in the army and was made commander of the 3rd Infantry Division. He retired in 1938 following his objection to some controversy. In September 1939 von Rundstedt was recalled to lead the Army Group South during the invasion of Poland. He then participated in the battle for France as commander of seven Panzer divisions, three motorized infantry divisions and 35 regular infantry divisions.

Von Rundstedt called a halt to the German forces which were forcing the French and British troops westward. This allowed the British to evacuate their forces from Dunkirk. He forbade an attack on Dunkirk, which became a controversial subject, but von Rundstedt and others argued that Hitler had decided that Britain would more readily accept a peace treaty if he spared the evacuating expeditionary force. Von Rundstedt was promoted to field marshall June 19, 1940, and participated in the planning of Operation Sealion, which was subsequently called off.

In June 1941 von Rundstedt entered Operation Barbarossa with fifty-two infantry divisions and five Panzer divisions under his command. Kiev was captured and the Russians lost approximately 300,000 men. He moved his Army Group South to Kharkov and Rostov, strongly opposing a continuation of the advance into Russia. He advised Hitler to halt but this was rejected. At Rostov the Russians counterattacked and drove the Germans back. Von Rundstedt demanded to be allowed to withdraw and Hitler became furious and replaced him.

Hitler recalled von Rundstedt in March 1942 and placed him in the west to oppose any invasion of the continent by the Allies. Von Rundstedt defeated the English when they raided Dieppe, but he did little to secure the shoreline and as of autumn 1943 no worthy fortifications had been built. Field Marshall Rommel was placed under von Rundstedt and began to build the Atlantic Wall as it existed on D-day.

Von Rundstedt insisted that the armored reserves be held in the operational rear in order to be rushed to any sector under attack by the Allies. Rommel insisted that the armored forces be deployed near the shoreline just out of range of all Allied naval artillery. Von Rundstedt did not think an invasion would occur as far west as Normandy and that armor should not be committed there, so only one armored division was committed to Normandy. After the invasion began Von Rundstedt began to urge Hitler to negotiate a peace with the Allies. Hitler responded by replacing him with Gen. Guenther von Kluge. Because Von Rundstedt was of German aristocracy it was always thought that he looked down on Hitler. Hitler could not punish von Rundstedt as he would other high-ranking officers because of his heroic reputation with the German people, especially with the aristocracy.

Von Rundstedt surfaced again when von Kluge committed suicide in mid-August. He opposed Operation Market Garden launched by the Allies and won that battle. He commanded the German forces in an effort to retake Antwerp (the Battle of the Bulge) although he opposed this attack from its inception and did not pursue it as he knew the Germans were up against hopeless odds. He was relieved again after telling Wilhelm Keitel that Hitler should make peace rather than continue to fight a hopeless war.

Von Rundstedt was captured by the U.S. 36th Infantry Division on May 1, 1945. He was kept in prison in Britain and charged as a war criminal because of damning evidence that while in the Soviet territories he was involved in mass murders. Whether due to his poor health (two heart attacks) or because of some political considerations by the British, he was released in 1948 and lived in Hanover until he died February 24, 1953. During his career he had received every notable decoration presented to German soldiers. His last award was the Swords to the Iron Cross in 1945.

The 9th Infantry passed through the 82nd Airborne's lines and immediately ran into antitank, machine-gun, and rifle fire. Colonel Smythe outflanked the Germans with two battalions (47th Infantry) and progress resumed. Colonel de Rohan's 60th Infantry Regiment (9th) fought through initial resistance but by nightfall had reached Saint-Jacques-de-Néhou.

General Collins arrived in Saint-Jacques-de-Néhou, having followed the 9th Infantry advance all day, and was informed that the Germans were on the run. Collins immediately contacted the division commander, General Eddy, and asked him to meet with him. Collins told Eddy to push on to the coast that night. When Collins arrived back at his command post, he received a call from Eddy, who informed him that Colonel Smythe's 47th Infantry Regiment (9th) was two miles from the coast on the Barneville–La Haye-du-Puits road. Early the next morning the 60th Infantry Regiment (9th) reached the little port of Barneville. At 5:00 A.M., June 17, the 3rd Battalion of the 60th Infantry Regiment (9th) reached the hill overlooking Barneville and sent a company into the town. It was deserted except for a few German MPs. Cherbourg was thus sealed off on D-day plus 12.

Immediately following General Eddy's arrival on the west coast, Adolf Hitler sent a message to Gen. Karl Von Schlieben: "You are hereby appointed commander of Fortress Cherbourg. You will defend the city *to the last man and the last bullet.*" On June 18 General Bradley informed Gen. Troy Middleton, commander of VIII Corps, of the route north the VII would take on their way to Cherbourg. Bradley directed Middleton to place the VIII in a line of defense across the Cotentin Peninsula so as to protect the rear of the advancing VII Corps. From July 15 to July 19 General Middleton with the VIII Corps relieved the VII Corps of operations south of the line of Ste. Mère Église–Orglandes–St. Colombe–Barneville. The 82nd and 101st Airborne divisions and the 90th Infantry Division passed to the VIII Corps leaving the 4th, 79th, and 9th Infantry divisions with the VII Corps for the drive toward Cherbourg. Approximately 2,000 Germans had escaped the trap by heading south under the command of Col. Bernard Bachever. The Germans crossed the Ollande River and moved onto the high ground north of La Haye-du-Puits.

GENERAL COLLINS TURNS NORTH

Now the Americans would begin a two-pronged campaign, which, after many small and large battles, would free the Cotentin Peninsula of Germans. This was the beginning of the end for the Wehrmacht. Hitler would lose thousands of veteran soldiers as well as hundreds of field artillery pieces, self-propelled guns, tanks, and much equipment that would take months and years to replace. His edict of "to the last man" would prove crippling to the German forces. Perhaps the same would have happened had he allowed his generals to pull back to a natural defense line such as the Seine River. However, it is doubtful that the losses on the Cotentin Peninsula would have occurred so quickly and dramatically. With the Allies' superiority in planes and tanks, nothing other than innovative new weapons such as jet planes and accurate missiles could have brought about a different outcome.

General Collins turned north with three divisions. On the afternoon of June 19 the 4th Infantry Division started out without artillery. The 79th Infantry Division, commanded by Maj. Gen. Ira T. "Billy" Wyche, was positioned in the center and General Eddy's 9th Infantry Division was on the left. The target cities on Route National 13 of Montebourg and Valognes would be heavily defended. The two outside divisions would make the initial thrust with the less-experienced 79th Infantry in the center holding the corps together. The 39th Infantry Regiment (9th) jumped off at 5 A.M. and at 7:00 was in Briequebec without opposition. Meanwhile, Middleton's VIII Corps formed a defensive line across the peninsula and began to drive the German units southward.

THE CHANNEL STORM

The worst storm in forty years along the Channel was raging the morning of the attack. Until it began on the evening of June 18, the Allies had made momentous progress in landing men and equipment on the Normandy beaches and within the fabricated harbors of Gooseberries and Mulberries. Between 600,000 and 700,000 men had been landed with their vehicles, weapons, and supplies. The intensity of the storm was such that all beach unloading operations were brought to a halt on June 19.

This was a critical blow for the newly established beachhead as supplies of food, water, fuel, ammunition, and soldier replacements were critical to the success of the advance to Cherbourg. On the second day of the storm the beach was strewn with wrecked craft, and on the third day the artificial harbor on Omaha Beach buckled. Fortunately, the artificial harbor on the British sector survived. General Bradley went down to the beaches to assess the damage and found a very discouraging and critical condition. The beach personnel had climbed into their makeshift shelters. Operation Overlord was threatened. Hundreds of crafts were destroyed. The shutdown on the beaches severely curtailed the inbound tonnage needed for the ongoing battle for Cherbourg. It also gave the Germans a chance to bring up more reinforcements without being subjected to the deadly attacks by the Allied air forces. Everyone realized that it was now essential for Gen. "Lightning Joe" Collins to live up to his sobriquet and take Cherbourg quickly to alleviate the shortages with which the troops would be confronted.

The English Channel storm June 19–21 so devastated the landing beaches that the incoming supply of men and equipment had fallen far behind. This put more pressure on the Americans to capture Cherbourg as quickly as possible while General Middleton's VIII Corps cut off the Cotentin Peninsula and prevent the reinforcement of Cherbourg. The Douve River bridgehead was strengthened and the attack on La Haye-du-Puits would begin as soon as the rain stopped. It would be necessary to capture hills 131 and 95 prior to the assault on La Haye-du-Puits. Capture and control of the highway between St.-Sauveur-le-Vicomte and La Haye-du-Puits would prevent any more Germans from reinforcing Cherbourg and would entrap those north of the highway.

At this time Hitler appointed Gen. Karl von Schlieben commander of Fortress Cherbourg and instructed him to defend it to "the last man and the last bullet." Major Kuppers, the artillery commander at Montebourg, was ordered to defend this fortified city and to contain the advancing Americans. Lt. Erik Staake, an artillery officer, who had been wounded that morning, reported to Major Kuppers that they were able to stop the Americans but the town was now flanked on both sides by tanks and the infantry was fighting inside the town. Staake believed that if they stayed they would be captured. After considerable thought, even though he knew that Staake was militarily correct, because of his orders "to hold at all cost," Kuppers decided to do so.

One of Field Marshal Rommel's orders to von Schlieben, instructing him to withdraw the German forces into Cherbourg from its defensive ring outside of the city, was intercepted by British intelligence and passed on to General Bradley on the evening of June 10. This intelligence report was passed on to

KARL-WILHELM VON SCHLIEBEN

General von Schlieben was a large man. When he was captured by the Americans at Cherbourg on June 26, 1944, he weighed 200 pounds and was six feet and four and a half inches tall. He was born in Eisenach, Germany, in 1894. He joined the German army in August 1914 and a year later was promoted to the rank of lieutenant. His principal promotions were to major in 1935, to major general in 1943, and to lieutenant general on May 1, 1944.

During World War I, von Schlieben was wounded twice, once in 1914 and again in 1916. His father, Maj. Wilhelm von Schlieben was killed in action November 11, 1914, while commanding an infantry regiment. Following World War I, von Schlieben continued to rise in rank and commanded multiple cavalry, panzer and infantry units. In May 1943 he became commander of the 18th Panzer Division and in December 1943 von Schlieben became commander of the 704th Infantry Division. On June 23, 1944, Hitler chose him to be the commander of Cherbourg. He pledged to Hitler that he would defend "to the last man." When he surrendered, he was at his underground command post. He had requested air support numerous times during the battle but received none. Hitler was furious when von Schlieben surrendered. In spite of criticism in German military circles, there was little else von Schlieben could do as the Americans had blasted holes in Fort du Roule and were literally firing cannon shells into the interior of the fort.

General von Schlieben received many awards and decorations for valor during both world wars. He was decorated for valor on the Russian front as well as during his combat against the Allies in 1944. Some of his most prestigious decorations were the Knight's Cross of the Iron Cross, German Cross in Gold, Prussian Iron Cross, Medal for Winter Campaign in Russia, and Cross of Honor for Combatants.

General von Schlieben was interned at Island Farm with other German officers and was repatriated in 1947. He was not charged with any war crimes. He died June 18, 1964, in Giessen, Germany.

General Collins, who then urged his division commanders to pursue the fleeing Germans. The Germans had previously constructed a line of fortifications, all of which were on high ground, covering with fields of fire all approaches to Cherbourg.

The German defenses were well integrated with the terrain, which was ideal for positions with which to ward off the oncoming Americans. Streams, steep hills, deep valleys of the rivers, all contributing to the defensive fire. The French spy network, Centurie, had furnished the Americans with very accurate maps and drawings of the German positions. It was estimated that the total German forces would be 25,000 to 40,000 including coastal defense, antiaircraft, naval personnel, and organized labor battalions.

The Battle for Cherbourg

MONTEBOURG AND VALOGNES FALL

THE VII CORPS' attack began at 3:00 A.M. on June 19. Montebourg had been strengthened and at first the 4th Infantry Division made little progress but the 8th Infantry Regiment (4th) with a double-pronged attack secured Montebourg and by midnight June 1 the 8th and 12th Infantry regiments (4th) closed in on Valognes and secured it the next morning. The three divisions of the VII Corps were at the doors of the outer perimeter defense positions of Cherbourg. On the night of June 19 patrols reconnoitered the German defenses and confirmed that the enemy was withdrawing. The next morning the American troops began to move forward. General Collins planned an attack with three divisions abreast, the 4th, 79th and 9th Infantry divisions. This double-pronged attack had the 4th and 9th Infantry divisions attacking the defenses from east and west, with the 79th Infantry Division and the 4th Cavalry Squadron as the link between the two prongs.

Approach

The 4th Infantry Division on the right flank moved slowly, and General Collins admonished General Barton and told him to move forward. On the left flank, the 9th Infantry was making good progress up the west coast until they reached Flottemanville-Hague four miles west of Cherbourg. Here they sustained intense mortar, artillery, and machine-gun fire. They also ran into mine-fields and casualties increased. The German rifle squad had an advantage over the American rifle squad. Each German infantry squad had a rapid-fire machine gun upon which their tactics were based. The American rifle squad had one Browning automatic rifle per squad, which gave much less firepower than the German machine gun. The American infantry company had only two machine guns whereas the German company had thirteen.

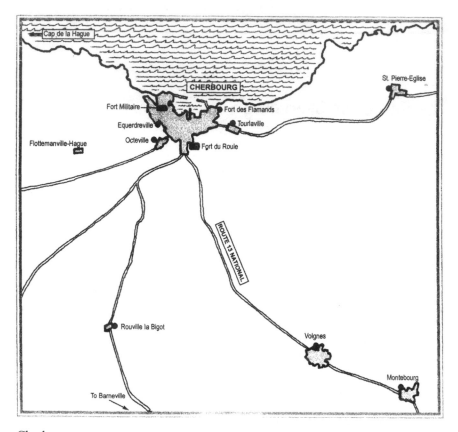

Cherbourg

In Cherbourg General von Schlieben was receiving repetitious orders from Hitler to hold Cherbourg at all costs. Von Schlieben knew that Cherbourg would fall as he did not have the men or munitions to last much longer, but he wanted to delay long enough to destroy the port. The violent storm that was pounding the Normandy coastline had not ceased. Urgent supplies for General Collins's VII Corps could not be unloaded. The attack on Cherbourg was in jeopardy. This worked very much in von Schlieben's favor, giving him and his forces somewhat of a respite.

General Bradley conferred with his staff, who informed him that supply of ammunition would be critical until they could recover and begin unloading activities. In view of this, Bradley called a halt to Middleton's VIII Corps advance across the peninsula so that Collins's VII Corps could utilize the limited supplies, especially ammunition. It would be two weeks before Middleton received enough supplies to resume his advance. The problems with ammunition supplies persisted all the way to the Ruhr, until the port of Antwerp was opened. During this crucial battle for Cherbourg, Maj. Gen. Elwood A. "Pete" Quesada relieved the situation a bit by flying in 500 tons a day.

General Collins was on the go in his armored scout car, urging each commander to speed up the advance. By June 21 he had organized a formidable attacking force around Cherbourg. The Germans were manning the outer belt of fortifications and von Schlieben issued orders to shoot any soldier who vacated his post. He was adamant to hold "to the last man." The three American divisions were making slow but steady progress against this perimeter defense.

Attack on the Perimeter Defense

As the 79th Infantry Division advanced, they ran into a grassy knoll which turned out to be an underground concrete fort with a gun emplacement for multiple 88mm and 40 mm cannon. It was obvious that having to fight through such defenses would take time and casualties would be high. The Germans were having a tough time also and began surrendering in small groups. Leaflets were dropped from planes in an attempt to convince the German soldiers to surrender. They were promised food, which was scarce in Cherbourg.

General Collins continued to encourage his VII Corps troops forward and was frequently on the battlefield to keep the pressure on the Germans and never give them a chance to regroup. By the evening of June 21 the Germans were confined to a small area of the fortress. General Collins appealed to von Schlieben to surrender and avoid further bloodshed. He threatened to destroy the garrison if they did not surrender by the following morning. Von Schlieben did not reply.

It was a difficult fight in very difficult terrain. In the seventeenth century the French had built forts around Cherbourg for its defense against the British. Napoleon Bonaparte improved them, and when building the Atlantic Wall the Todt Organization incorporated the old with the new. This improved the forts by virtue of constructing impenetrable cement walls for them.

With his three division commanders Collins prepared an attack for the next day which would begin with concentrated air bombardment. General Wyche's 79th Infantry Division would attack from the south, General Eddy's 9th Infantry from the west, and General Barton's 4th Infantry Division from the east. As of June 22, approximately 6,000 people remained in Cherbourg, contained there by the Germans. Most were living in cellars. The Americans began to bombard the city with artillery shells while the Germans worked around the clock to destroy the port facilities in an effort to deny the Americans a usable port. Early on the morning of June 22, General von Schlieben was handed a message from Adolf Hitler:

> I expect of you that you will conduct this action as Gneisenau once conducted the defense of Kolberg. As long as you still have ammunitions and rations, every enemy attack must be shattered by your inflexible will, the strength of your

wisdom, your skill and the bravery of your troops. Even if the worst should happen, it is your duty still to defend the last pillbox and to leave the enemy not a harbor but a field of devastation.

Prior to the assault on Cherbourg General Collins had requested of General Bradley to arrange an aerial assault destined to lower the morale of the German garrison and hopefully to effect a surrender. A plan was developed between generals Bradley, Collins, and Quesada of the IX Tactical Air Command. Bombing would start at H-hour minus eighty minutes and concentrate in front of the 79th and 9th Infantry divisions. Instructions were given to the ground troops to properly mark their fronts to guide the aerial assault. Multiple flights of British and American bombers and fighter bombers would make up the bombardment of the numerous fortresses and outlying strongpoints.

On the night before the attack, a multilingual broadcast was made to the German garrison telling them of their hopeless situation and warning that unless they surrendered, they could expect annihilation. No message was received so the attack began at 2:00 P.M. on June 22. For an hour approximately 400 fighter bombers concentrated on the targets and although no great damage was done, later interrogation of prisoners documented its effect on their morale. The aerial bombardment was followed by an artillery shelling.

On the morning of June 22, the American soldiers were busy preparing for the assault. Mortar squads placed their guns at strategic locations and hauled in shells and stacked them beside the mortars like firewood. Many rounds were smoke and white phosphorous, which would be used to mark targets for the soon-to-arrive dive-bombers. The mortarmen made sure the powder increments were dry so as to cause no malfunction. The bipods and the base plates were planted firmly into the ground. The thirty-mile infantry frontline was pulled back 100 yards to avoid casualties from the planned aerial bombardment.

The storm, which had brought havoc to the beaches, suddenly subsided. The first wave of bombers roared in shortly after noon. The German positions were bombed and strafed for more than an hour. The Germans shot down twenty-four Allied planes, which accounted for at least 150 airmen wounded, killed, or captured. Aerial dogfights broke out when a flight of Luftwaffe planes appeared and knocked down several American bombers. American P-47s and P-51s appeared and attacked the Luftwaffe planes. The aerial battle lasted for a quarter of an hour, during which time the American troops on the ground witnessed the intense confrontation. Finally outgunned, the German planes broke off the attack and headed for their home base.

Each of the three divisions advanced slowly but met stiff resistance. It was "do or die" time for the Germans who were firmly entrenched in their underground bunkers bristling with machine guns and 88mm cannon. In one single action a 4th Infantry Division battalion was caught in the open and thirty-one soldiers were killed and ninety-two wounded. The ground troops did not make much progress on July 22 but by July 24 closed in on the city from all directions. During this first day of the final attack on Cherbourg, both sides suffered many casualties. It became obvious to the German command that unless they could receive reinforcements quickly, they could not hold off the Americans.

Late on the evening of July 22, General von Schlieben, now very depressed, sent the following message to Field Marshall Rommel:

> The troops of 709 Division who have taken part in the fighting are numerically and physically exhausted. Fortress garrison itself not fit to withstand a severe strain. Men are over age, untrained and pillbox-minded. Reinforcements regarded as absolute necessary for a task which the Fuhrer has declared to be decisive.

On the morning of June 23 General Collins pondered the situation and realized that as on the preceding day, they had thrown everything they had at the Germans, but still this outer defense had not been breached. It was evident that the American advance had been halted by the Germans' fierce determination to allow no breakthrough. One major reason was that the bombs and artillery shells did little damage to the extremely thick walled German bunkers. Generals Eisenhower and Bradley paid a surprise visit to this front and upon arriving in the 79th Division area began moving around and visiting with the troops, a group that had been pulled back into a reserve position.

General Collins began the attack that day again with all three divisions, which were now fighting inside the defensive perimeter. During the day Eddy's 9th Infantry cleared out two strongpoints and by evening was on a ridge leading into Cherbourg. The 79th Infantry sustained heavy losses and did not reach La Mare aux Canards strongpoint on the Valognes-Cherbourg highway. The 4th Infantry Division, on the east, did not reach Tourlaville, their objective. The battle at the end of the second day remained at a standstill. Fortunately for the Americans the Luftwaffe had been absent.

General Collins, who was becoming increasingly concerned about the lack of progress of his VII Corps, appealed to Adm. Morton Deyo, skipper of Task Force 129. He requested that on the following day Deyo have his ships assault German gun positions from offshore. Admiral Deyo was enthusiastic but could not be ready and in position until June 25 as his task force was distributed to various British ports during the storm. As day faded on June 24 the sound of detonations could be heard from miles away as the Germans continued the destruction of the port.

From Fort du Roule, General von Schlieben's forces looked down on the Americans. The fort was on a hill that rose steeply behind Cherbourg, and from this vantage point its guns commanded the sea approaches and the streets of Cherbourg. General Bradley requested Adm. Alan R. Kirk to attack the fort's guns from the sea. Cherbourg was bristling with guns that outranged and outgunned those of some of Kirk's biggest ships. Kirk knew that this would be costly and asked Bradley if this attack was worth the risk he would be taking. Bradley assured him that it was essential to conquer Cherbourg as quickly as possible so as to get Collins's VII Corps turned around to help Middleton clear the Cotentin. Kirk promptly moved his ships in but they were outdueled and had to withdraw with slight losses. This gesture, however, allowed the infantry to scale the cliffs of Fort du Roule and attack it with satchel charges.

On June 24 the attack on Cherbourg resumed. The 9th Infantry fought its way to Octeville, a suburb of Cherbourg. The 79th Infantry finally cleared La Mare aux Canards. The 4th Division advanced to near Fort du Roule, which overlooked Cherbourg, but attempts to break through to the fort failed. The 8th Infantry Regiment (4th) was repulsed by German forces in concrete bunkers and thirty-seven men from that regiment were killed and approximately 106 wounded. The 12th Infantry Regiment (4th) captured Tourlaville after a vicious fight and hundreds of prisoners were taken in the process.

Von Schlieben reported the depressing news to Rommel. On the morning of June 25, under a white flag the Germans sent a German officer and a captured American pilot to ask that shelling around the hospital cease. The Americans sent back another request for surrender. There was no reply. General Bradley visited General Collins that day to discuss means of capturing Cherbourg. Both Bradley and Eisenhower urged Collins to resume the attack as supplies were so crucial and an adequate port was essential.

On the morning of June 25, a flight of P-47 Thunderbolts dropped their bombs on Fort du Roule, high atop a massive rock edifice that dominated the surrounding area. The only approach route was from the south along a narrow ridge that contained concentrated minefields. The bombs, unfortunately, missed the target, falling to the side.

FORTRESS CHERBOURG FALLS

As the planes departed the artillery and mortars began bombarding Fort du Roule. Again, because of the thickness of the concrete roof, the bombs did little damage. Two battalions of the 314th Infantry Regiment (79th) moved in. The leading battalion ran into heavy mortar and machine-gun fire, very costly to the Americans. Finally, the American firepower overcame their adversary's defense. The Germans tried to withdraw from their foxholes and many were killed. One by one the concrete bunkers were attacked.

Making slow progress, the troops finally reached Fort du Roule but had to assault the fort room by room. Hundreds of prisoners were taken. Hundreds more lay dead within and along the approach to the fort. Unfortunately, the American casualties were high as the battle had been vicious at close quarters.

The 313th Infantry Regiment (79th) was ordered to proceed on into Cherbourg. The 47th Infantry Regiment (9th) also began the attack on Cherbourg but promptly ran into severe resistance at the old fortress, Equerdreville. The approach was mined and the fortress had a moat. The tanks moved in and a squadron of planes attacked, followed by a barrage of artillery and mortar fire. The infantry began to move in. Shortly after the attack began, white flags began to appear and Equerdreville was in American hands.

The battle in the city limits of Cherbourg had begun. Admiral Morton Deyo and his task force of ships left Portland for Cherbourg to attack from the sea. As the ships approached land near Equerdreville, the Germans began to fire on them. Deyo's ships returned fire. The HMS *Glasgow* was hit. The firing continued and white flags began to appear. The ships then focused on shore batteries along the Cherbourg coast. The German gunners remained undaunted and continued to fire on the naval force. Once again they had been ordered to defend "to the last man."

The 4th Infantry Division, fighting its way into the city from the east, encountered heavy artillery fire from Fort des Flamands. Responding to a request for help two of Deyo's ships silenced the battery there. A formidable battery that the Germans called Hamburg, located six miles east of Cherbourg, took on the two battleships and five destroyers under Adm. C. F. Bryant's command. Two destroyers were hit by duds. The destroyer USS *O'Brien* was hit and thirteen sailors killed. The land-sea battle continued throughout the day. During the day of June 25, there was a continuous repetition of explosions as the Germans completely wrecked the port of Cherbourg. Buildings that were centuries old were not spared because as piles of rubble, they made it more difficult to resurrect the harbor. The harbor was filled with mines. All piers and docking sites were destroyed. By evening Cherbourg was a smoking inferno.

The maze of tunnels and underground rooms in the bunkers and forts were packed with exhausted and wounded German soldiers who had lost the will and ability to fight any longer. The Americans seized these forts one room at a time with subterranean hallways and emplacements that seemed endless. Still General von Schlieben encouraged the men to resist the Americans although he himself knew that it was sheer folly. He sent the following message to Field Marshal Rommel:

> Concentrated bombing and air attacks have split the front. Numerous batteries have been put out of action or have worn out. Combat efficiency has fallen off considerably. The troops squeezed into small areas will hardly be able to withstand an attack on the 25th.

During the fight, the American forces reorganized and prepared for the final attack on Cherbourg. Col. Warren A. Robinson, commander of the 314th Infantry Regiment (79th), discovered that morning that even though they had captured Fort du Roule the day before, there were still Germans in the fort in areas very near him. From the roof, Robinson and his men began dropping grenades and other explosives down on the guns projecting from apertures on the ground level. First Lieutenant Carlos C. Ogden, although he had sustained a head wound and faced enemy fire, alone disabled an 88mm cannon. At the same time, Cpl. John D. Kelly crawled up the hill under machine-gun fire and after two futile attempts finally succeeded in blowing open the rear door of the pill-box with a pole charge and forced the German crew to surrender. Both Ogden and Kelly received the Medal of Honor.

Again, von Schlieben appealed to General Rommel:

> Enemy superiority in material and enemy domination of the air overwhelming. Most of our own batteries out of ammunition or smashed. Troops badly exhausted, confined to narrow space, their backs against the sea. Loss of town unavoidable in nearest future as enemy has penetrated outskirts. Have 2,000 wounded without possibility of moving them. Is there any point, in view of the overall situation, in having our remaining forces entirely wiped out, as seems inevitable in the absence of effective counter-weapons? Request urgent instructions.

Rommel sent back the following message:

> In accordance with the Fuhrer's orders, you are to continue fighting to the last round.

How to root out the remaining die-hards occupying the lower levels of Fort du Roule with their 88mm cannon became a problem. Blasting through the walls with bazookas was attempted but fruitless. Some German groups continued to fight until they ran out of ammunition and, feeling that they had fought to the last cartridge, finally surrendered. Many of the German wounded were in critical condition and badly needed medical attention for survival.

The old forts in Cherbourg begun in the seventeenth century continued to protect the resistant German forces. After the battle had raged for more than twenty-four hours, a soldier emerged with a large white flag and requested to speak to the ranking American officer. An officer was detailed to go back into the fort with the German and escort von Schlieben out to surrender. More than 800 soldiers of varying units came out of the tunnel behind von Schlieben. German Adm. Walther Hennecke accompanied von Schlieben and both were escorted to General Collins. Von Schlieben made it clear that he was only surrendering the forces in the Fort Du Roule. Collins sent the two high-ranking officers to General Bradley's headquarters.

At 7:30 A.M. on June 27 the 47th Infantry Regiment (9th) was ready to attack Port Militaire, a virtual indestructible fort with plenty of guns, ammunition, and food with which to withstand a long siege. Maj. Gen. Robert Sattler and 400 men were contemplating whether to surrender or not. Like so many other German commanders, he was fanatic in adhering to Hitler's orders but in these final hours before annihilation he relented. He emerged and surrendered to General Eddy who had come to view the assault. Other than some isolated pockets of die-hards, the battle for Cherbourg was finally over.

General Collins and his staff made a French tricolor flag from colored parachutes and presented it to Paul Reynaud, the honorable mayor of Cherbourg, on the steps of the city hall. The city council members and the VII Corps division commanders, generals Ridgway, Taylor, Barton, Eddy, and Wyche, were there. General Collins gave a short speech in French relating that the Americans were proud to return to their sister republic its first city to be liberated by the Allies. Reynaud eloquently expressed the gratitude of his townspeople for being free from Nazi control and pledged eternal friendship of France to America. Glasses of champagne followed.

Following the official surrender, there were still well contested fights to finally subdue the Germans at Maupertus Airfield and Batterie Hamburg, as well as several forts on the outer breakwater: Fort Osteck (held out overnight until June 28), Fort du Hamet (fell on June 28), Fort West, and Fort du Centre (both surrendered on June 29). On June 29 soldiers of the 9th Infantry Division attacked the Cap de la Hague where 6,000 German troops remained. This fell after a bitter fight on July 1. Some 39,000 German personnel had been captured in and around Cherbourg.

_____

5

Clearing the Cotentin Peninsula

OFFENSIVE BEGINS

THE INVASION OF the Normandy beaches is well known. It was a major turning point for the Allies in World War II and because of its massiveness and drama, it has been publicized extensively. After landing, the Allies were contained there for almost two months. The longer they stayed in a defensive position, the longer the Germans had to build up their forces and supplies.

It was time now to organize and break out into open country. This was to be a very difficult task as the terrain surrounding the Normandy beaches was hedgerow country alternating with large areas of marsh and crossed by many rivers, tributaries, and lowlands. Most of the roads were narrow and sunken between two hedgerows. The paved roads were well defended by the Germans, who had had plenty of time to lay extensive minefields and place their guns and strongpoints in vital places. Many low-lying areas had been flooded.

The terrain markedly favored defense rather than offense. Each field was surrounded by hedgerows. When the farmers first cleared the fields, they stacked dirt and stones into walls that generally measured six feet at both base and height. When the natural vegetation took over, they matured into formidable brush- and tree-covered walls. The thick vegetation on the hedgerow concealed the German positions. Machine-gun embrasures that had been cut through the hedgerow were only a narrow slit, well concealed with brush. The strength of the hedgerow gave excellent cover to the German soldier during the Allied aerial bombardments and the artillery barrages. Hunkered down at the base of a hedgerow, a soldier was pretty well protected with the exception of an overhead burst or a direct hit on his position.

The Allied soldiers could expect one or more machine guns on each of the hedgerows confronting them as they tried to push forward. Narrow passageways existed at corners of the field and were often connected to a sunken road just wide enough for small carts or for cows to move from one field to another. This terrain covered much of the Cotentin Peninsula, making for slow progress from the beaches to open country. Avranches near the base of the peninsula would be the point of breakout into Brittany and into firm and open country where tanks could support the advance.

Lt. Gen. Omar N. Bradley was comfortable that having captured Cherbourg, an Allied offensive should begin. It was time to leave the static battle of the Normandy beaches and break out into a mobile war. Once beyond Caen and the Cotentin Peninsula, the Allies would be in tank country to the east and west of the peninsula.

France was to be liberated in stages. Gen. Sir Bernard Montgomery would hold Caen, and the Allied Army, using Caen as a pivot, would head eastward toward the Seine River. The U.S. First Army would advance westward and then south to Avranches, which was a gateway to Brittany. General Bradley evidently thought that Brittany would be taken with relative ease and that the Allies would not spend much time there. In his book, *A Soldier's Story*, he stated,

> We were to sweep south out of the Cotentin past Avranches and there cut off the Brittany Peninsula at its neck. After pausing only long enough to secure Brittany and its choice selection of deep water ports, the American Forces were to turn east and, with the right flank on the dry, sandy banks of the Loire, close to the Seine-Orleans gap south of Paris.

It is obvious that General Bradley had grossly underestimated the strength of these German ports, which were fortified fortresses. Their commanders had also been instructed by Hitler to hold them "to the last man." St. Nazaire and Lorient were to hold out until the end of the war, contained the last five months of the war by the U.S. 66th Infantry Division and units of the Free French of the Interior (FFI).

THE PLAN

Bradley's goal was to break out of the hedgerow country, avoid any semblance of a war in the trenches, and gain open country where tanks could move freely and establish a moving war. How was this to be done? The requisites were to find a weak spot in the enemy defense and concentrate the Allied forces against such a position, and then with heavy bombardment, break the frontline defenses and send in the mechanized units before the enemy reorganizes their defenses. The point selected would have to meet three criteria: It must be beyond the Carentan marshes, it must avoid the strongpoints, and it must have parallel roads available so that quick and efficient exit is possible. Although none of the routes considered was perfect, the west coast road from La Haye-du-Puits to Coutances was the most promising. An advance by this route would force the Germans to withdraw across the neck of the Cotentin Peninsula to avoid encirclement from St. Lô.

General Montgomery still had not taken Caen, a vital road junction that effectively would be the breakout point to the east toward the Seine River and Paris. Caen was the British objective for D-day but had been heavily defended especially with Panzer divisions. Montgomery was criticized repeatedly, especially by the press. He seemed undisturbed, however, as he believed that holding the Panzer divisions on his front allowed the Americans more freedom of movement and protected them from attack on the left. Montgomery, rather than capture a geographic location, believed it best to retain the initiative and avoid setbacks and reverses. To him, retaining the initiative did not necessarily mean areas had to be taken on a schedule or that an advance was necessarily ongoing. Montgomery's concept seemed to be that not allowing any deterioration in the battle or one's position was also a demonstration of initiative, maybe a more patient concept awaiting a better opportunity to advance, such as weather, reinforcements, and so on. However, Lt. Gen. Sir Miles Dempsey was urged to keep the Germans on the defensive with multiple limited attacks. He was always wary of a counterattack against the British army. At this stage of the game, the Germans were well able to launch a significant attack against the Americans or British.

Montgomery believed that if he kept a battle going on his front it would attract the stronger German units as the Germans were believed that the major landing of Allied troops had not taken place and that this would come in the Pas de Calais area, strengthening the British 2nd Army front. Eisenhower was in agreement with this, yet he could not give this information to the press for security reasons. This made it difficult for him to defend Montgomery.

Montgomery's role in the overall plan was to attract as much of the German force as he could to the British sector and to give every indication that the British would make the main thrust to break through the German defenses. This feint worked well and tied up some of the premier German units. The British endured the criticism of those who felt that they should be progressing forward as the Americans were doing. This was probably the basis for the strained relationship that existed later between the British and American commands.

ERWIN JOHANNES EUGEN ROMMEL

General Rommel, probably the most widely known commander of World War II, has become a legendary figure in world history. Loved by the German people, he was a favorite of Adolf Hitler and admired by Winston Churchill. His two outstanding qualities were that he was a superb military commander and followed the rules of war and chivalry. On one occasion in North Africa, Rommel rode up to a New Zealand field hospital in the desert and offered to send them medical supplies. He acquired the nickname "The Desert Fox" in North Africa and has been portrayed as such in numerous movies. He remained loyal to Hitler even though he knew that Germany would lose the war and that Hitler should be replaced to prevent further bloodshed. He incurred Hitler's wrath on several occasions when he expressed his honest opinion based on his experiences in Africa against the Allies' overwhelming air and ground support.

Erwin Rommel was born in Herrlingen, Germany, on November 15, 1891, the son of a Protestant headmaster of a secondary school. It was his father who influenced Rommel to join the 124th Wurthenberg Infantry Regiment as an officer cadet in 1910. Shortly thereafter he finished the Officer Cadet School in Danzig as a lieutenant. In World War I he fought in France, Italy, and Romania. It was in these early years that his qualities as a soldier and leader surfaced. He was wounded three times and awarded the Iron Cross and Prussia's highest medal, the Pour le Merite, an honor usually reserved for generals.

During the interwar years, Rommel worked closely with the Hitler Jugend, helping to set up rifle schools with qualified instructors. He rose to the rank of colonel and was appointed commandant of the War Academy and published several books on infantry and tank combat.

During World War II Rommel first served in Poland in 1939 and saw much of Hitler. He organized Hitler's victory parade in Berlin when that campaign was over. For the invasion of France in 1940, Rommel was made commander of the 7th Panzer Division, one of the first to reach the English Channel and the division that captured Cherbourg. He was then sent to Libya as commander of two Panzer divisions and formed the Deutsches Afrika Korps. It was in North Africa that his fame really began. His victory at Tobruk and defeat at El Alamein are well known. Although Rommel defeated the U.S. II Corps at Kasserine Pass, he was defeated by Montgomery's 8th Army at the Battle of Merdenine and left North Africa shortly thereafter for health reasons.

Hitler next assigned Rommel to the west coast of France to prepare the defenses for the anticipated Allied invasion. He worked tirelessly to fortify the coast, which produced the seemingly impregnable Atlantic Wall. Hitler and his staff believed that the invasion would come at Calais, but Rommel insisted it would come at Normandy. As a result, most of the Panzer divisions were deployed near Calais while only one was deployed at Normandy, which made a tremendous difference on D-day. Rommel wanted the tank forces dispersed in small units as close to the front as possible, but Hitler disagreed, another German error. Subsequently, Rommel was badly wounded when strafed by an Allied plane.

Rommel was thought to be involved in the plot to assassinate Hitler and was given the alternative to commit suicide or have his family murdered. He died after taking a cyanide capsule on October 14, 1944, and was given a state funeral. When the fall of Tobruk was debated in the British Parliament, Winston Churchill had said, "We have a very daring and skilled opponent against us, and may I say across the havoc of war, a great general." When Churchill heard of Rommel's death, he said,

He also deserves our respect because, although a loyal German soldier, he came to hate Hitler and all his works, and took part in the conspiracy to rescue Germany by displacing the maniac and tyrant. For this, he paid the forfeit of his life. In the somber wars of modern democracy, there is little place for chivalry.

By the end of June, Rommel had concentrated seven Panzer divisions on the British sector, leaving only one opposing the American line. Rommel feared that Montgomery would break out and begin a great pincer route calculated to join on the Seine River another Allied pincer move from Pas de Calais. The Germans believed that was the reason General Patton was in England with an army.

Montgomery found that he was confronted by six Panzer divisions. He requested of Gen. Dwight D. Eisenhower that the Third Army be assigned to him as a reserve in case the Germans launched a counterattack against the British sector. Bradley considered this unwise because he believed that he would have a hard time getting them back since England was encountering a manpower shortage. Bradley realized that Great Britain had been fighting much longer than the United States and profoundly appreciated the suffering and deprivation that they had endured. However, he was opposed to putting American troops under British command and met with Montgomery to discuss the matter. Montgomery was very reasonable about it and a compromise was reached. Lt. Gen. Leonard T. Gerow's V Corps extended its left boundary further to the left (east) to include some of the British sector thus, to some extent, lightening the load for the British. Gerow was agreeable to this arrangement This example of General Bradley's wisdom and courage to remain resolute to a plan that he had studied in detail was, in a sense, similar to his refusal to be swayed by Sir Leigh Mallory's criticism of his deployment of the 101st and 82nd Airborne divisions at Normandy.

The Overlord plan was to attack the Cotentin Peninsula immediately after D-day as breakout from the beaches could not be accomplished until Carentan, Cherbourg, and the entire peninsula were neutralized. Tying up the Panzer divisions allowed the American First Army to attack the Cotentin Peninsula with much less opposition had the Panzer divisions confronted it in force. This was to General Montgomery's credit.

HITLER AND HIS GENERALS DISAGREE

Field Marshall Gerd Von Rundstedt and Field Marshall Erwin Rommel visited Adolf Hitler on June 29 at Berchtesgaden to discuss strategy. This was shortly after the assassination attempt on Hitler's life with a bomb in a briefcase. Hitler was persistent about keeping the Allies on the beaches as he knew that the Allies outnumbered the Germans in tanks and in the air and he did not want them to gain a mobile war. The plan was for the German defensive line to be strengthened. Also, Hitler would urge Reich Marshall Herman Goering and Gross Admiral Karl Donitz to step up the air and submarine assaults in order to diminish supplies and reinforcements reaching the beaches as much as possible. The German antiaircraft defenses would be increased to protect the movement of men and supplies to the Normandy front. Having accomplished this, Hitler would then launch a large counterattack to try to eliminate the Allied beachhead.

Actually, the Allied buildup was progressing well, while the German supply line was in trouble mainly because the Allied air forces dominated the skies. Rundstedt and Rommel requested permission for a limited withdrawal but Hitler refused, claiming that if the Germans lost this battle at the beachhead, they would lose France. The two German generals returned to the front on June 30 and were dismayed to find that the German counterattack on Caen had failed. The Luftwaffe had made a token appearance but contributed little to the offensive. Hitler would not allow any defensive positions to be constructed as this would entice the weary soldiers to settle down to them. He also knew that once the Germans began to withdraw, the mobile Allies would overrun them. He was probably correct as this was exactly what happened when the Allies finally began to push the Germans out of the Cotentin Peninsula.

Hitler remained adamant about holding the position and building up the force. He planned a counterattack on Caen as soon as the forces there had acquired enough strength to do so. Rundstedt continued to disagree with Hitler and was relieved on July 2. Rundstedt, because of his elevated position in the German social society, probably always looked down on Hitler to some extent and resented his interference with the military. Hitler remained hopeful that Goering and Donitz would accomplish enough destruction of Allied supplies to level the playing field at Normandy. It is interesting that Hitler did not replace Goering as the Luftwaffe had failed miserably.

As of June 28 the German forces were divided into two sections, one on the east and the other on the west. The Seventh Army opposed the Allies on the western sector and Panzer Group West took the eastern half of the front. Panzer Group West had many more tanks than the German 7th Army.

FRANCE JOINS THE BATTLE

Now that the invasion of France was over, the Allies could begin to communicate and operate with the Free French of the Interior (FFI) more openly. This would have been a security breach before the invasion as details of the invasion was guarded very closely. Through the leadership of the French Resistance, many FFI units had been organized in France to harass and sabotage the Germans as much as possible. Their activity in Brittany was gaining momentum. The staff of SHAEF in June 1944 finally recognized Gen. Charles DeGaulle as the French leader and Pierre Koenig of the Free French headquarters in London as the commander of the FFI. The mission of the FFI demanded that they do everything possible to harass and impede the Germans. They were to destroy communications, harass the movement of troops, destroy railroad tracks, and steal and divert loads of ammunition and weapons to their own units. They were also to gather as much information as possible about bridges, crossroads, gun positions, and other vital installations. The FFI ranks were growing and the Resistance gave them as much training as time and facilities allowed, which was minimal. The British were parachuting weapons, ammunition, and medical supplies to them at selected drop zones. All of this movement had a disquieting effect on the German troops. The Resistance and FFI would prove invaluable to the Allies as the war progressed. Jedburgh teams consisting of a British or U.S. officer, a French officer, and a radioman were dropped into France to help the Resistance and FFI organize and to enhance the communication with the U.S. and British command.

THE JEDBURGHS

The story of the battle for Brittany would not be complete without honoring the Jedburgh teams of special forces formed jointly by the United States, Great Britain, and France. This three-powered organization consisted of of small teams of brave young men who parachuted into France before, during, and following the invasion in order to perform covert missions in France in preparation for the arrival of the Allied troops. Their dominant purpose was to work with the Resistance to encourage more young Frenchmen to join the FFI and to help train and supply them while maintaining a liaison with the Allied Command. Each team was made up of three men who volunteered for these dangerous missions behind enemy lines and who possessed certain essential qualities. Usually each team was composed of an American, a Frenchman, and a British soldier, one of whom spoke French and one of whom was a radio operator. Two members could be from the same country but all teams included at least one Frenchman. If one member was lost, there was no replacement. A team was not relieved until its mission was completed. They were to encourage the French Resistance to inflict as much damage against the Germans as possible and to capture and contain the bridges on roads and railroads likely to be used by the Allies. Another important mission was to radio Great Britain for necessary armaments and supplies and to submit to the Allies information on location and size of German units and ammunition depots.

The Jedburghs were forerunners of the special forces existing in Allied countries today. This type of warfare was heretofore unprecedented in its organization, scope, and methods of sabotage. Modern technology such as the airplane and shortwave communications equipment provided the means of delivering the Jedburgh teams to their destination and providing them with the training and equipment necessary for their covert missions. The "Jeds," as they were called, got their name from Jedburgh, Scotland, where they trained.

The Jedburgh program was developed over a three-year period prior to D-day. It was formed as a joint venture by the Office of Strategic Services (OSS) of the United States, the British Special Operations Executive (SOE), and the French Special Air Service (SAS). Very little has been published about the Jedburghs as their activities remained classified until the 1980s as a security measure to keep possible enemy countries from learning about the covert methods of operation by Allied countries. Many of their records were destroyed when there was any possibility of capture. They could not keep a daily official report as was done by many combat military units. Ten or more teams operated in Brittany. Lt. Col. (Ret.) Will Irwin published a book, *The Jedburghs*, in 2000 which gives details of many of their missions.

The first Jedburgh team that parachuted into Brittany was code-named Frederick. This team landed in an area near Guingamp, near the north coast in the department of Cotes Du Nord. Five more teams parachuted into the area around Breast and were instrumental in helping the French Resistance organize and train an FFI force of 5,000 men to aid the Americans in the battle for Brest. Some of them were actually in the city of Brest as snipers.

The joint effort of the Jedburghs and the Resistance was especially productive around the two large submarine bases at St. Nazaire and Lorient. These FFI units took their place on the line when the American troops arrived and aided the Americans greatly in the containment of these two fortresses. This same process of recruitment was repeated in many areas of Brittany.

In the final analysis, it seems that the most important function that the Jedburgh teams performed was the liaison that they established between the Allies and the Resistance, which supported the missions of sabotage. The FFI units, when properly trained and equipped, replaced Allied units that were needed on the eastern front. General Eisenhower credited them with shortening the war by several months. Some of the Jedburghs went on to the east to perform the same covert operations against the Japanese.

GETTING OFF THE BEACHES

Much of the Cotentin Peninsula was crisscrossed with hedgerows favoring defense. The terrain of marshes and creeks prevented the tanks from accompanying the infantry. Crossing these areas on causeways and poor roads greatly jeopardized the tanks as they became easy targets for the enemy German artillery. In many areas the infantry was completely exposed on causeways with no place to seek cover.

The American infantry and tank units had learned how to cooperate during "on-the-job training" in combat as this was not stressed for many units during training stateside. The tanks would pull up to a hedgerow and use it for cover while firing at positions on the next lateral hedgerow. Mortar fire was placed on the two perpendicular hedgerows of the next field. This slow but effective attack was followed throughout hedgerow country. Phones were placed on the outside of tanks so the infantry could communicate with the tank readily and without the tank commander being exposed through the turret. The artillery helped a great deal also by blasting the next hedgerow. The infantry would take cover along the perpendicular two hedgerows and proceed to the next.

The obstacle of the terrain made for slow progress and resulted in a large number of casualties, especially among the infantry as the Germans continued to pour artillery and mortar shells on the advancing Americans as well as lay extensive minefields. This was exhausting work for the infantry since they had to lug machine guns, mortars, rifle grenades, and fragmentation and white phosphorous grenades, as well as ammunition for each weapon. At the end of the day the infantryman was exhausted but had to face the nighttime duty of patrolling and standing his watch at his position. When advancing, the most he could expect was a cold K-ration for supper. Unfortunately the weather was rainy many of the days in June and July, eliminating air force support. Also, the roads became difficult and the soldiers spent a miserable existence being wet continuously. Young soldiers persistent against the difficult terrain and a formidable German defense. They would not be beaten!

At the beginning of July General Bradley, commander of the U.S. First Army, had under his command four corps headquarters, thirteen divisions of which nine were infantry, two armored and two airborne. Two of the infantry and one of the armored divisions were yet untested in combat. Because the storm in the Channel had wrecked so many facilities in the supply line, clearing of the Cotentin Peninsula would have to be delayed until Cherbourg was taken. The VIII Corps commanded by General Middleton with the assignment to clear the Cotentin of enemy was stopped until the VII Corps, commanded by General Collins, could complete the neutralization of Cherbourg. On June 26 General Bradley resumed the advance toward Coutances with Middleton's VIII Corps.

According to the plan, the VIII Corps would depart from La Haye-du-Puits and advance down the west coastal road to Coutances. The VII Corps was to proceed along the Carentan-Périers road with the same objective. The XIX Corps, commanded by Gen. Charles H. Corlett, would take an easterly course from Carentan to St. Lô. Each corps would advance independently as one was more ready than the other, and the delay for each was to be as short as possible.

The Germans had much in their favor. They were well camouflaged and dug into the hedgerows, had good fields of fire, and mortars zeroed in to cover the fields in front of them. Their artillery support was with 75mm and 88mm cannon in abundance. The Americans on the offensive had to break cover and move out along the hedgerows, which were in the same direction as their attack. Eisenhower was trying to get 90mm cannon and improved armor piercing ammunition from the United States as both were badly needed. The only good antitank weapon that the American infantry had was a hand-held bazooka with its complement of shells and ammunition.

The start of the First Army attack was delayed and gave General Bradley cause to fear a counterattack at the end of June. Reports showed evidence of a buildup of tanks by the Germans near Normandy. The delay gave the Germans time to bring in several more divisions from the Pas de Calais area. An earlier start by the Americans might have caused the Germans to abort the influx. It is interesting that the Germans, even at this late date, feared an attack at Pas de Calais.

GERMANS REORGANIZE

At the beginning of July some major changes in the command group of the Western front were made. Field Marshall Guenther von Kluge replaced von Rundstedt as commander in chief in the west. Gen. Heinrich Eberbach relieved Gen. Leo Freiherr Geyr von Schweppenburg as command of Panzer Group West. Col. Gen. Paul Hausser replaced Col. Gen. Friedrich Dollman, who died of a heart attack as commander of Army Group B.

HANS GUENTHER VON KLUGE

Hans Guenther von Kluge was born in Poznan, Germany, to a Prussian family on October 30, 1882. He joined the German army and served in World War I, participating in the Battle of Verdun. By 1933 von Kluge had become a major general and served in Westphalia.

In 1938 he objected to Hitler's aggressive foreign policy and was dismissed from the army. He was recalled and appointed commander of the German 4th Army that invaded Poland. Following the invasion of Poland, von Kluge led the 4th Army in the invasion of France in 1940 and was promoted to field marshall on July 19, 1940. Duty next sent him to Russia in Operation Barbarossa, still with his 4th Army, which took Smolensk in July 1941. He was then sent to Ukraine. He was ordered to attack Moscow but the operation was aborted because of a counterattack by the Russians. On October 27, 1943, von Kluge was badly injured in a car accident on the Minsk-Smolensk road. He returned to duty in July 1944 as commander of the German forces in the west as von Rundstedt's replacement. This occurred during the battle for the Cotentin Peninsula when the Allies were trying to breakout into Brittany.

Hitler had become very suspicious that von Kluge was in some way involved in the assassination attempts on his life and recalled him to Berlin after Stauffenberg's attempt to kill Hitler. Fearing that Hitler would punish him as a conspirator, von Kluge committed suicide by taking cyanide on the trip to Berlin. Historical notes place his death August 19, 1944, in Metz. Von Kluge left a suicide letter to Adolf Hitler:

> When you receive these lines I shall be no more. I cannot bear the report that I have sealed the fate of the West through faulty measures, and I have no means of defending myself. I draw a conclusion from that and am dispatching myself where already thousands of my comrades are. I have never feared death. Life has no more meaning for me, and I also figure on the list of war criminals who are to be delivered up. Our applications were not dictated by pessimism but by sober knowledge of the facts. I do not know if Field Marshall Model, who has been proved in every sphere, will still master the situation. From my heart, I hope so. Should it not be so, however, and your cherished new weapons not succeed, then, my Fuhrer, make up your mind to end the war. The German people have borne such untold

> suffering that it is time to put an end to this frightfulness. There must be ways to attain this end, and above all to prevent the Reich from falling under the Bolshevist heel.
>
> Hitler reportedly handed the letter to Alfred Jodl and commented that 'There are strong reasons to suspect that had not Kluge committed suicide he would have been arrested anyway."

Eberbach planned to use the hedgerows to his advantage. He designed his defenses in depth with strong formations behind the lightly staffed frontline. Panzer divisions were the last line of defense and placed there to counter any holes made in the German defense line. Hausser organized a shallow defense for his 7th Army with outposts in front to warn the larger body of troops behind them. Most of his troops were placed in a reserve position to act as a counterattacking unit if needed to overcome any breakthrough. These troops were equipped with tanks and assault guns to counterattack the flanks of any adversary.

German General der Artillerie Erich Marks, commander of the 7th Army's LXXXIV Corps had been killed and was to be replaced by Lt. Gen. Dietrich von Choltitz, who later would be the commander of Paris when it fell. General der Artillerie Wilhelm Fahrmbacher would command the corps temporarily. Von Choltitz assumed command on June 18 and Fahrmbacher returned to Brittany and would become commander of Hitler's U-boat fortress, Lorient, which he would hold until the end of the war, finally capitulating on May 10, 1945

The Germans were in an excellent defensive position but this was the last good one they would have between Normandy and the German border so it was essential that Eberbach and Hausser hold the British and Americans respectively on the beaches, build up reserves to reinforce this defense line, and hope Hitler's rockets or some other event would help them drive the Allies into the sea. Rundstedt and Rommel had formerly decided that if the Allies broke through, a major German retreat would have to take place quickly. They knew, however, that the mobility of the American forces far exceeded that of the German forces, indicating that the retreat might well turn into a rout. They would be opposed by General Middleton, commander of VIII Corps, who was given the assignment to clear the Cotentin Peninsula and Brittany.

TROY HOUSTON MIDDLETON

Troy Houston Middleton made outstanding contributions as the youngest colonel in the American Expeditionary Force in World War I. He spent more time in combat than any other general officer in World War II as commander of the 45th Infantry Division in Italy and of the VIII Corps in the ETO. He was involved in the major tactical decisions during the Battle of the Bulge. General Middleton rarely raised his voice but was firm, aggressive, and exemplified qualities of leadership that endeared his staff and his soldiers to him. As a strategist he was a genius with plans for battle, well researched and supported by detailed preparation. He was relentless in pursuing the enemy once he had them on the run, never allowing them the opportunity to set up another defensive line. Truly a soldier, gentleman, and student of war.

Troy Middleton was born near Georgetown in Copiah County, Mississippi, on October 12, 1889. After his initial education in Copiah County, Middleton attended Mississippi A&M College and upon graduation joined the U.S. Army in 1910 as a private. Twenty seven months later he was promoted to corporal. He was sent to Officer Candidate School and completed the course satisfactorily for a second lieutenant commission on March 3, 1913. In January 1915 he married Jerushia Collins. He served with the 7th Infantry in Mexico to help settle some internal problems there and to keep Pancho Villa from entering the United States.

In 1918 Captain Middleton was sent to Europe with the 4th Infantry Division and was promoted to major and given command of the 39th Infantry Regiment. He became a lieutenant colonel on September 11, 1918. He was awarded the Distinguished Service Medal for action at Bois de Foret and promoted to full colonel shortly thereafter, being the youngest regimental commander in the U.S. forces in Europe.

Post–World War I, Middleton became commander of cadets at Louisiana State University, taught at Command and General Staff School, and attended the Army War College. Four years after his retirement, he offered his services to the Army again the day after Pearl Harbor. He was quickly assigned to the 45th (Thunderbird) Infantry Division as a full colonel. The 45th Infantry Division invaded Sicily and fought the Germans continuously until relieved to participate in the invasion of Italy. It was in Sicily that General Patton and Middleton "crossed sabers" for the first time. It had to do with Bill Mauldin, an enlisted man whose cartoons of Willie and Joe appeared in the *Stars and Stripes* newspaper. The soldiers enjoyed these cartoons a great deal and looked forward to each publication of the *Stars and Stripes*. General Patton, a strict disciplinarian for proper appearance, was offended by these cartoons and mentioned this to Colonel Middleton several times. Colonel Middleton continued to defend Mauldin, so finally General Patton ordered him to get rid of Mauldin and the cartoons. Middleton, subordinate to Patton, looked him in the eye and said, "Put your order in writing, George." The subject was dropped, never to resurface.

During the Italian campaign, Gen. Mark Clark, commander of the 5th Army, told Colonel Middleton that he might have to pull out because of the severe German resistance. Colonel Middleton told General Clark, "Mark, leave enough ammunition and supplies. The 45th is staying." General Eisenhower gave Colonel Middleton a superior fitness report following the Italian campaign.

General Eisenhower requested of General Marshall that General Middleton be sent to him for the invasion of France. General Marshall informed General Eisenhower that General Middleton was hospitalized with severe arthritis in his knees, whereupon Eisenhower replied, "I don' give a damn about his knees. I want his head and his heart. I will take him into battle on a litter if we have to." General Middleton assumed command of the VIII Corps and crossed the Channel a few days after D-day, landing near Carentan. His record on the Cotentin is well addressed in these pages. After the battle for Brest, General Patton awarded General Middleton an Oak Leaf Cluster for his Distinguished Service Medal.

After the Cotentin and Brittany campaigns, the VIII Corps went to Bastogne where much of its forces were overrun. General Middleton quickly organized a defense that kept the Germans from taking Bastogne, a vital strategic crossroad that both sides needed badly. Following Bastogne, General Middleton with his VIII Corps helped greatly in bringing about the final capitulation of the German forces. He subsequently received many honors and praise from generals Patton, Bradley, and Eisenhower.

Postwar Middleton resumed his duties as comptroller of Louisiana State University where he subsequently became president in 1950. He died in 1976.

AMERICAN OFFENSIVE BEGINS

Preparations were made for the beginning of the attack to the south with the objective of freeing the Cotentin Peninsula of German forces, cutting off the peninsula, and entering Brittany through Avranches. The U.S. First Army would lead the attack. The VIII Corps with General Middleton in command would lead off and advance twenty miles along the west coast road to Coutances where it would occupy the high ground, thus becoming the western shoulder of the intended army line extending from Coutances to Caumont. Corps VII, V, and XIX would attack in their individual zones to gain their places in this line.

General Middleton placed the 79th Infantry Division (Maj. Gen. Ira T. Wyche commanding) on the west coast, the 82nd Airborne Division (Maj. Gen. Matthew B. Ridgway commanding) in the center and the 90th Infantry Division (Maj. Gen. Eugene Landrum commanding) on the eastern end of his sector of the line. Eventually, the 8th Infantry Division would replace the 82nd Airborne when they returned to England for restructuring with replacements and training for the next airborne attack.

Just prior to the attack, the Americans found evidence of increased German resistance. Rain that began to fall on July 2 by July 3 had turned into a hard rain, which was demoralizing to the ground forces. This did not delay the attack. The cannon began an intensive bombardment on July 3 and the attack was on.

General von Choltitz was on the scene, having recently arrived from the eastern front, and immediately determined that the German forces in his sector were weak and that he must use the terrain as an adversary to attack. He decided that the high ground around La Haye-du-Puits was his best bet to utilize as a defense line as it provided the best situation for observation and artillery fire. From the vantage point of the high ground, he would hopefully be able to control the surrounding country. His reserves would be on Montgarden ridge and on Mont Castre. This line would be his major defense line. However, Hausser moved von Choltitz and his corps to the eastern section of the corps sector. Meanwhile the American VIII Corps was advancing.

DIETRICH VON CHOLTITZ

Dietrich von Choltitz was born November 9, 1894, in Schloss Wiese, Silesia. He was a descendant in generations of Prussian militarism, leaving little room for an independent spirit. He was raised to do as he was told, a mindset that followed him into both world wars.

In World War I von Choltitz was promoted to lieutenant while serving on the western front. In 1929 he became a captain in the cavalry and in 1938 was promoted from major to lieutenant colonel. He earned the Iron Cross in 1940 when his battalion was engaged in the occupation of Rotterdam. He became commander of his regiment in September 1940, and promoted to full colonel His regiment was engaged in the siege of Sevastopol in June 1942. While fighting in Sevastopol, von Choltitz's 4800-man regiment was decimated, with only 347 soldiers surviving. He served in Italy in 1944 and soon thereafter was transferred to the western front where he fought the Americans in Brittany. By this time von Choltitz had been advanced to the rank of lieutenant general. While opposing the Americans, he was consistently in disagreement with General Hausser, his immediate superior. He had always followed Hitler's orders obediently and gained the reputation of leaving any city in scorched ruins.

In 1944 Hitler sent for von Choltitz, who realized that Hitler's health and mentality had deteriorated. Hitler no longer seemed as confident as he had when von Choltitz visited in the summer of 1943. Hitler decided that because von Choltitz's family heritage was one of generations of Prussian militarism, he would do as he was told. He informed von Choltitz that he had chosen him to be the fortress commander of Paris, instructing him to stamp out without pity all civilian acts of aggression. This clarified to von Choltitz that he had just been assigned another scorched earth mission. It struck him that this was not some unknown city in Russia but Paris, the most beautiful city in the world. He arrived in Paris in August 1944 as the city's governor, with detailed instructions from Hitler as to how to destroy Paris.

Von Choltitz, regardless of his Prussian heritage, was a logical man and destroying Paris was not logical. Therefore, von Choltitz requested of the French Resistance not to start an uprising and he surrendered the city intact and all German forces to the Allies. Hitler was furious.

General von Choltitz was a prisoner of war until 1946. He died in 1961 after a long illness and was buried in Baden-Baden. His funeral was attended by a number of high-ranking French army officers.

On July 3, even before the bombardment signaling the beginning of the VIII Corps attack, elements of the 82nd Airborne Division were already at work. The 505th Para Regiment (82nd) outflanked a German position on a hill at the edge of La Haye-du-Puits. For cover, they passed through the edge of a swamp and surprised the troops manning the position. The main body of the 505th Parachute Regiment (82nd) caught up and secured this assignment. The 508th Parachute Regiment (82nd) and a battalion of the 507th Parachute Regiment (82nd) moved in and secured their positions on the hills surrounding La Haye-du-Puits, leaving a few small pockets behind to be mopped up. The 325th Glider Infantry Regiment (82nd), although held up by mines initially, moved rapidly for a mile and was finally stopped by German artillery firing from Mont Castre. General Ridgway, commander of the 82nd Airborne, ordered a night attack on July 4 and the next morning Hill 95 was secured. By July 7 all enemy troops were cleared in the sector assigned the 82nd Airborne Division The 325th Glider Infantry had once again sustained heavy casualties.

The VIII Corps had begun their advance down the west coast road on July 3 but six days later had only advanced a few miles. The VII Corps was moving slowly through the marshes. The 82nd Airborne Division had taken its objective but was blessed with a wonderful incentive to do so. Upon completion of that mission, they were promised a return to England—a reward richly deserved. However, this was very unusual and General Bradley made the following comment about this in *A Soldier's Story*. It is repeated here as it was so true and very unusual for someone to express it so honestly.

> Incentive is not ordinarily part of an infantryman's life. For him there are no 25 to 50 missions to be completed for a ticket home. Instead the rifleman trudges into battle knowing that statistics are stacked against his survival. He fights without promise of either reward or relief. Behind every river, there's another hill–and behind that hill, another river. After weeks or months in the line, only a wound can offer him the comfort of safety, shelter, and a bed. Those who are left to fight, fight on, evading death but knowing that with each day of evasion they have exhausted one more chance for survival. Sooner or later, unless victory comes, the chase must end on the litter or in the grave.

Of course, the 82nd Airborne Division was sent to England where losses would be replaced and to prepare for another airborne operation. They had performed magnificently since being dropped into Normandy on the night of June 5–6. It has remained a premier unit.

By the end of the day on July 3, the 82nd Airborne Division had captured Hill 131 and the 325th Glider Infantry Regiment (82nd) was "dug in" at the base of Hill 95. The first attempt to capture La Poterie on July 4 was a disaster with very high casualties. It was during this attack that the soldiers experienced wounds from wooden bullets. The wooden bullet would fragment into many fine splinters on impact, eventually creating an infected wound that would not heal and usually required excision of the involved area before healing could begin. This kind of wound usually precluded a return to combat because of the time element in healing.

FIGHTING ON THE HIGH GROUND

The 79th and 90th Infantry divisions were having a much more difficult time on each flank of the 82nd Airborne. They ran into bitter resistance and had many casualties in the sector surrounding La Haye-du-Puits. The two major elevations in this area, Montgarden and Mont Castre, were held by the Germans and were superb vantage points. There was a mile-wide corridor between Mont Castre on the west and Prairies Marecageuses de Georges on the east. The 90th Infantry Division had to pass through it. Mont Castre had an elevation of 300 feet. From there the Germans commanded the corridor and could prevent passage through it. The ridge had to be captured so General Landrum assigned his three regiments, 357th, 358th, and 359th (90th Division) individual tasks. The attack to begin on July 3 lost any air support due to rain and the 90th Division gained only one mile and had 600 casualties.

An artillery duel began on the morning of July 4 and again the 90th Infantry Division attacked. The 359th Infantry Regiment (90th) advanced toward Mont Castre but was stopped early in the day. Toward evening some progress was made. However, during the night, the Germans gained some reinforcements. The German artillery on Mont Castre continued to dominate the battle.

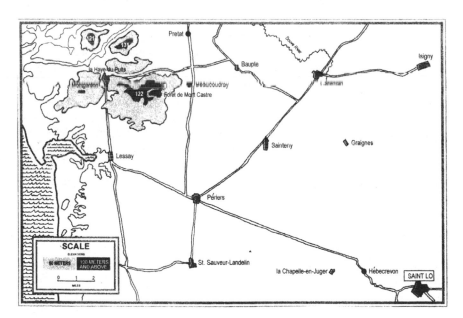

La Haye-du-Puits and the High Ground

On July 5 the 325th Glider Infantry Regiment (82nd) captured La Poterie after a five-hour battle and joined with the 90th Infantry Division to hold the town and surrounding area. The 82nd Airborne Division, meantime, held its position.

The 357th Infantry Regiment (90th) was committed on July 5 but made little progress. However, the rain subsided and with air support, the 359th (90th) made significant progress and by the evening of July 6 had four battalions on Mont Castre including Hill 122, the highest point. Progress was slow and tough. Roads were minimal and trails hardly passable. Evacuating the wounded and maintaining a supply line were severe handicaps because they had to be accomplished on foot as the tanks were limited by the terrain. Many severely wounded soldiers were delayed for long intervals for removal, many needing blood, plasma, and control of blood loss. Medics did their best to relieve pain with morphine, but they were often overwhelmed by the numbers of wounded, with no means to evacuate them.

Rain began in the evening of July 6 and the Germans launched a counterattack, but the 90th Division, now becoming more seasoned, held Hill 122 tenaciously. As took place many times in the ETO during World War II, engineers were converted to infantry and utilized as such until the battle situation improved.

Beaucoudray was the objective for the 357th Infantry Regiment (90th), which was still trying to fight through the corridor. On July 6 three infantry companies advanced to just south of Beaucoudray; one company was north of the village. The battalion was thus well positioned to take Beaucoudray. The Germans counterattacked and isolated two of the infantry companies. A task force of tanks and infantry was organized to rescue them but all officers and noncoms in the reserve party became casualties and the remnants of the group had to fall back. One of the trapped companies surrendered to escape annihilation. Escapees from this vicious battle reported that most of the two companies were captured or killed. Because of the desperate situation, more support personnel were converted to infantry. Because of the tough terrain and well-concealed German defensive positions, the 90th Infantry Division had made little progress and had sustained 2,000 casualties. Some infantry companies were mere skeletons of their full complement. It must be remembered that antibiotics were in their infancy, blood and plasma were in short supply, repair of blood vessels had not been developed, and specialist such as neurosurgeons and thoracic surgeons were scarce and only in major service hospitals. Heart wound repair was nonexistent. Helicopter evacuation was rare. These factors all contributed to a high percentage of deaths from severe wounds. Many of the soldiers wounded in World War II could have been saved with today's technology.

Maj. Gen. Ira T. Wyche, commander of the 79th Infantry Division, had been given the assignment to clear the western sector down to the Ay River estuary. First Montgarden and hills 84 and 121 near La Haye-du-Puits had to be cleared. The 314th Infantry Regiment (79th), commanded by Col. Warren A. Robinson, accomplished this on July 4, and then advanced to within two miles of La Haye-du-Puits where they linked up with the elements of the 82nd Airborne Division.

LA HAYE-DU-PUITS

By July 7, Middleton's forces, which included the 79th Infantry, the 82nd Airborne, the 90th Infantry, and the newcomer 8th Infantry divisions, had surrounded La Haye-du-Puits. After eight days of hard fighting, they finally secured the heights and moved five miles. Steady rain eliminated air support. The 79th Infantry Division sustained 2,000 casualties during this struggle.

The 315th Infantry Regiment (79th) advanced at a very slow pace toward Montgarden. When the Germans launched a counterattack, General Wyche ordered the 314th Infantry Regiment (79th) to enter La Haye-du-Puits on July 7. To aid in this assault, the 313th Infantry Regiment (79th) reached the north slope of Hill 84. On July 6 the 313th and 314th Infantry regiments (79th) joined the attack and were successful so by the morning of July 7 the hill was in American hands with its excellent position from which to control La Haye-du-Puits. General von Choltitz held La Haye-du-Puits in spite of the advantage gained by the Americans and launched a counterattack during the afternoon of July 7 but this was stopped by the Americans.

On July 8 the 8th Infantry Division passed through the 82nd Airborne to attack La Haye-du-Puits. The 82nd Airborne then passed into corps reserve and would soon be shipped back to England for reorganization and training for their next mission. On their way back to Normandy Beach, they passed the 82nd Airborne cemetery near Ste. Mère Église. The white crosses stretched as far as they could see and brought tears to the eyes of even the toughest among them. The 82nd Airborne Division had 46 percent casualties in Normandy.

During the fighting on the high ground, the Americans had lost 1,000 men killed, wounded, and missing. For the five-day battle, there were 2,000 casualties and the 79th Division was depleted and demoralized. The combination of rain, no air support, poor visibility for the artillery, no truck transport, flooded and boggy terrain, and constant shelling from the Germans overwhelmed the infantry. The infantry soldier in these conditions was constantly wet as there was no way to get dry. Hot food was unusual as the mess trucks could not maneuver in the constant rain. Added to this was sleep deprivation and exhaustion. In spite of all of this, they plugged along doing their duty. Courageous young soldiers. The fighting in and around La Haye-du-Puits was vicious and casualties were high but this battle has been given little notice in books and other reports on World War II.

Meanwhile, on the eastern sector General Montgomery decided to attack the area of Caen again in a mighty effort to provide a pathway for his tanks to gain open country. A massive aerial bombardment was planned with the cooperation of Air Marshall Sir Arthur Trevers of the Royal Air Force. On July 7 460 Wellington bombers dropped 500- and 1,000-pound bombs on a designated carpet area 4,000 by 1,500 yards. The ground troops rushed in behind the bombardment and finally captured Caen.

VII CORPS ENTERS THE OFFENSIVE

As soon as Cherbourg fell, General Bradley ordered the VII Corps to move to Carentan on June 30. They were to take a position east of the VIII Corps between the Prairies Marecageuses de Georges and the Taute River. There was a highway linking the forces on each side of the Taute River. Carentan needed a strong defense as a successful counterattack by the Germans to take Carentan would split the American forces. The VIII and VII Corps would both advance south to the Coutances–St. Lô highway, beginning their attacks on July 3 and 4 respectively.

General Collins, commanding the VII Corps would keep the 4th and 9th Infantry divisions and take on the 83rd Infantry Division. The 83rd Infantry Division would attack towards Sainteny, which would require passing through the two-mile-wide Carentan-Périers isthmus. Again, the hedgerow country favored the defense. In opposition was a German Panzer division and a parachute regiment, both formidable foes. Rain, fog, and mist ensued, eliminating air support and much of the artillery support An attack under these conditions in the terrain of hedgerows and muddy trails would be slow and costly. Tank and truck movement could not be counted upon.

By midday on July 4, the 83rd Infantry Division, under very adverse conditions, had advanced only 200 yards. Col. Martin D. Barndollar Jr., commander of the 331st Infantry Regiment (83rd), was killed. Communications failed, as did tank support. A battalion commander on the right flank of the 83rd Infantry Division called for a withdrawal, which infuriated General Collins. He demanded the attack restarted. Gen. Robert C. Macon, commander of the 83rd Infantry Division, resumed the attack on July 5 although the division sustained 1,100 casualties.

General Macon continued to prod his commanders forward although each unit was paying dearly with casualties. General Collins kept the pressure on, which went down the line to each basic company. The 4th Infantry Division relieved the 83rd Infantry Division of some of its territory to bolster the attack. All units continued to battle against fierce resistance and General Collins called a halt to the attack and called for help from the IX Tactical Air Command. This battle is one of many during World War II which exemplifies the high cost that our country has had to pay to retain freedom. Infantry, slugging it out in terrible terrain and inclement weather with no tank or air support and very little artillery support. Lest we never forget. The beaches of Normandy were only the beginning of a very difficult journey to Germany.

On July 7 rain began and the air support was not available. The attack began again but progress was little to nil with a high casualty rate. The 83rd Infantry Division was stalled in the Carentan-Périers isthmus but the XIX Corps to their east was making progress.

FIERCE FIGHTING ALONG ENTIRE FRONT

On July 7 the entire advance was stalled, which gave the Germans more time to strengthen their defense with reinforcements and supplies. General Bradley was frustrated as he was anxious to get out of the Cotentin Peninsula and into Brittany to secure the Brittany ports. His immediate objective was the Coutances-Caumont line from where he could launch a mobile offensive into Brittany.

The 79th Infantry and 90th Infantry divisions were still three miles apart so General Middleton committed the 8th Infantry Division. On July 9, after a fierce battle, the 79th Infantry Division turned La Haye-du-Puits over to the 8th Infantry Division, which was new to combat, and the division made little initial progress. Lt. Gen. Courtney H. Hodges, the deputy Army Commander, visited Maj. Gen. William McMahon, the commander of the 8th Infantry Division, and two regimental commanders were relieved. Shortly thereafter, General Middleton relieved Major General McMahon and placed Brig. Gen. Donald A. Stroh in charge of the 8th Infantry Division. This is an example of the relentless pressure put on our troops to advance, thus allowing the Germans little time to strengthen their defenses. These were critical times during the war when the outcome depended so much on each advance no matter how small. The soldiers were young guys slugging it out against great odds. Discipline was supreme and any lack of it was not acceptable. Commanders were sometimes relieved through no fault of their own but this served as a selective process to find the high achievers. The VIII Corps moved seven miles and sustained 10,000 casualties. Again in this campaign the Americans had to pay a high price for freedom. The Germans continued to resist fiercely but on July 13, there was the hint of withdrawal. Under General Stroh the 8th Infantry Division improved and by July 14 they were on the banks of the Ay River, as was the 79th Infantry Division. On July 14 the badly depleted 90th Infantry Division reached the Seves River and made contact with the VII Corps on their left.

German General von Choltitz suffered a minor brain concussion and his reserve forces were depleted. He was badly discouraged as there were no reinforcements to send to him. General von Kluge gave him permission to withdraw from his present position. The Americans were fourteen miles from Coutances and continuing to press the Germans.

Meanwhile the VII Corps in the Carentan-Périers isthmus was progressing slowly with the 83rd and 4th Infantry divisions. There was no room on the narrow isthmus for the 90th Infantry Division. The forward American troops were a mile short of Sainteny and thirteen miles from the high ground between Coutances and Caumont, which was their objective. Finally on July 9 the 331st Infantry Regiment (83rd) took Sainteny and the 4th Infantry Division advanced toward Périers.

Middleton's progress was so slow, 12,000 yards in twelve days, that General Bradley discontinued the attack toward Coutances. The minefields and German resistance were too strong. Because of this and the difficult progress of Collins's VII Corps through the Carentan marshes, General Bradley decided to abort the Coutances–St. Lô road as a starting point and settle for some other vantage point from which to break out. The American position remained tenuous.

Bradley was regrouping after halting the attempted advance to Coutances. An alternative route had to be selected to put the Americans in a suitable area to launch a breakthrough into Brittany. Much to Bradley's chagrin, the only plausible approach would be through the marshes around Carentan. However, he considered this breakout from Normandy as "the most decisive battle of our war in western Europe." In his opinion, if the Americans could break out, it would eliminate any doubt that the Allies would win the war. The Germans, realistically, could not expect a victory and essentially would not be able to contain the Allied forces. However, resistance remained strong and nothing could be taken for granted.

The St. Lô–Périers road was selected as a substitute for the St. Lô–Coutances road as the departure route. Bradley marked off a rectangle a few miles out of St. Lô that measured 3.5 miles in length and 1.5 miles in depth. Two roads ran south through this rectangle, which was to be designated as a "carpet."

On July 15 the 4th and 83rd Infantry divisions were placed under the VIII Corps as part of a reorganization. The 4th Armored Division, recently arrived, and the 83rd Infantry Division would begin replacing the 4th Infantry Division, which had suffered 5,000 casualties in twelve days and remained operational only by a generous supply of replacements. Again this casualty rate in a little-known battle shows what price we pay for freedom and how many crucial battles were fought with little or no acclaim. Thousands of young G.I.s were killed or wounded in this campaign to break out into Brittany.

On July 11 Panzer Lehr counterattacked from Hauts-Vents in order to disrupt the 9th and 30th Infantry divisions but their gains were minimal. The 90th Infantry Division quickly recovered the territory lost. The 3rd Armored Division took Hill 91 and Hauts-Vents where the Germans were on the offensive. Panzer Lehr paid a price of 25 percent casualties. This was one of Hitler's best Panzer units.

The Germans stopped the VII Corps on the Carentan-Périers isthmus on July 15. The battle for both sides had been a bitter one. By the end of July 15, the 9th Infantry Division had advanced only six miles. The 30th Infantry Division had 3,300 casualties in nine days and was exhausted but had secured an important bridge at Pont-Hebert. Combined with the attached combat command, they had become a threat to St. Lô from the west while the XIX Corps was threatening from the east.

The 9th and 30th Infantry divisions finally gained positions that overlooked the St. Lô–Périers highway, their final objective. VIII Corps dominated the highway between Lessay and Périers. XIX Corps took St. Lô on July 19. The city had become a memorial to the thousands of soldiers who died in the battle of the hedgerows with the objective of breaking out of the Normandy beachhead. Elements of the First Army were now along the Lessay–Périers–St. Lô–Caumont line. The casualty rate had been high. The First Army sustained approximately 40,000 casualties of which 90 percent were infantrymen. Young soldiers fighting viciously and tenaciously to defeat our enemy—we should never forget them.

THE REPLACEMENT

It is evident from the foregoing that the fighting on the Cotentin Peninsula was intense and that casualties were high (90% of which were from infantry units including the airborne infantry). Very few units from the corps down to the rifle squad escaped a significant attrition.

The major source for these replacements was those soldiers completing an infantry basic training course in the States and from the cannibalization of infantry divisions of soldiers who had some additional training since leaving basic training. Most were eighteen or nineteen years old. Smaller numbers were obtained by dissolving various units not essential to the war in Europe. Some engineer and cavalry units were given "on-the-job training" in Europe and used as infantry as long as they were needed and then reverted back to their primary duties.

If anyone ever walked down "lonely street," it was "the replacement," who is due our respect and gratitude. He took the long trip punctuated by stops at multiple replacement depots ("repo-depo") without a family (squad, platoon, company). Ordinarily a group of replacements would be placed on trucks or trains and carried to a "repo-depo." The replacement might know some of the group or he might know none. Soldiers of this age make buddies easily and by the time the trip ended, most would have a buddy or two. However, at each "repo-depo" (five or six along the journey) the arriving group would be split into groups and parceled out to other "repo-depos." The new buddies usually were sent in another direction so the replacement had to make new ones on each leg of the trip. Finally, he would arrive at the headquarters of an infantry or armored division (those were the units with the greatest need because of their high casualty rate). There, smaller and smaller groups would be sent to regiments, battalions, companies, and platoons, in that order. It was unusual to still be with a buddy of long standing. War is a depressing event and the thing that bolsters a young soldier most is to have a good buddy.

Finally, the replacement reached his destination, such as a rifle squad. There he met his sergeant, who would be his primary commander. Sergeants vary considerably in intelligence, compassion, fairness, and combat efficiency. It is really the "luck of the draw." He would be referred to as a "replacement" until he survived long enough to be considered a veteran. If he was lucky, he formed some meaningful friendships and experienced acceptance by the group. Fortunately, usually that was the case. Unfortunately, his lack of a long training period and no combat experience added to his vulnerability until he could acquire combat savvy.

Most often, when we reflect on our soldiers in a war, we dwell mostly on the dangers they face and the physically uncomfortable environment they are subjected to. The replacement should be remembered for his additional sacrifice for our country for enduring the loneliest trip of his life.

6

Breakout

GENERAL BRADLEY HAD deliberated long and hard about solving the major problem of getting off the Normandy beaches. To do this, the Allies would first have to traverse the terrain of hedgerows, marshes, and swamps crossed by very poor roads. The Germans had a formidable defense. They continued to bring up reinforcements while contemplating a counterattack to push the Allies into the sea. The Allies needed solid dry ground in order to turn their armor loose.

Bradley concluded that if the proper area was found, a designated well-defined area approximately three by seven miles could be bombed intensely, effecting an obliteration of the forces and equipment therein. This might effectively produce a gateway through which the infantry and armor could rapidly advance to dry land. Once reaching such a platform, the attack on Brittany should not be too difficult.

OPERATION GOODWOOD

Operation Goodwood, planned by General Montgomery, was scheduled for July 18 on a plain southwest of Caen. Seventeen hundred planes of the Royal Air Force Bomber Command and U.S. Air Force, plus almost 400 medium and fighter-bombers of the U.S. Eighth Air Force, dropped more than 8,000 tons of bombs to open the path for the British. The 8th Corps of the British army, with three armored divisions, followed closely behind the bombardment and advanced three miles in a little more than an hour. Tactical surprise and the effect of the bombardment allowed this advance. During the four-day attack, 8th Corps secured 34 square miles and the Canadian Corps had captured the remainder of the city of Caen and part of the plain immediately southeast of the city. The British 8th Corps lost 500 tanks and had over 4,000 casualties, 36 percent of all British tanks on the Cotentin

Peninsula. Eisenhower had expected Goodwood to accomplish more than it did. He thought the advance would carry through Caen, across the Orne River, and to the Seine River and Paris. Montgomery was satisfied but Eisenhower thought him too cautious. On July 20 Montgomery directed General Dempsey to withdraw his armor and replace it with infantry. Lessons were learned from Operation Goodwood and Bradley felt that with an intense air bombardment that saturated a given piece of land completely with an overwhelming ground attack, the Americans might smash the German ring of containment.

Eisenhower wrote to Montgomery on July 21 expressing his disappointment and inquiring if he and Montgomery were in agreement on the big issues. Eisenhower stressed the importance of the Breton ports increasing their acquisition of space, administration, and airfields. He did not feel that had been accomplished and now he was hoping that Bradley's attack would bring the Allies the objectives they needed, that is, the Breton ports. He urged General Montgomery to have Lt. Gen. Sir Miles Dempsey's Army launch an offensive coordinated with Cobra.

General Montgomery made it clear to Eisenhower that he had no intentions of slowing the offensive on the east flank. After instructing General Dempsey to continue operations "intensively" with infantry to make the enemy believe that the Allies were contemplating a major advance toward Argentan and Falaise. Eisenhower was reassured but began to place his hopes on General Bradley.

COBRA PREPARATION

Operation Cobra was one of the most important undertakings in World War II in the ETO. Its success or failure was of monumental importance. Success would be the breakthrough essential to gain the open ground for a mobile war which the Allies should dominate. Securing Brittany would neutralize large German forces and give the Allies access to the Breton ports. Failure would give the Germans more time to wall off the Normandy beaches, which would turn the conflict into trench warfare until one side or the other could prevail. Brittany was the goal. The first step was to advance to the Périers–St. Lô highway.

The two commanders most intimately associated with Operation Cobra were generals Bradley and Collins. Bradley had spent an inordinate amount of time planning Cobra and had chosen Gen. Joe Collins to execute the ground war. Collins would need his sobriquet "Lightning Joe" to be successful.

The requirements for a successful outcome for Cobra were:

1. The Americans needed to be in contact with the main line of resistance.
2. The enemy line could not be so strong that penetration would be delayed.
3. The ground beyond the Cotentin marshes needed to be firm enough for armor transport.

4. The roads had to be sufficient for large number of troops to exit.
5. The Allies needed to get their armor committed before the Germans recovered.

A concentrated saturation bombing was the first part of the plan. Bradley requested that the bombers fly parallel to the carpet in order to avoid dropping any bombs short on the Allied forces. Two infantry units would break through and hold the shoulders on either end. The motorized infantry would push through to Coutances, fifteen miles to the southwest, in hopes of subduing remnants of seven divisions blocking the VIII Corps progress. Phones were attached to the outside of the tanks for direct communication with the infantry. The armored units would turn south to Avranches, the gateway to Brittany.

The bombing was planned to be so intense that the Germans who were not killed would be so stunned and disorganized that the immediate onslaught of infantry and armor would overwhelm them. General Bradley chose the Lessay–St. Lô highway as the starting point as the Coutances–St. Lô plateau was just south of this highway. This was the battleground, bounded on the west by the ocean and on the east by the Vire River. The First U.S. Army had eleven infantry divisions and three armored divisions committed to Operation Cobra. In addition, there were several divisions in reserve. Bradley wanted a six-to-one attacker against defense to tackle the bocage country that greatly favored the defender. The Americans began adding additional automatic firepower to the infantry rifle squad. Traditionally, the twelve-man infantry squad had only one Browning automatic rifle and eleven rifles or carbines. With superior communications, the infantry began to use their reinforced artillery to great advantage. An infantry squad leader often called for and directed the artillery to the desired target.

That July a certain gloom had settled among the newsmen in Normandy. They perceived a stalemate and were worried about the Allied troops being bogged down to almost trench warfare reminiscent of World War I. They were not privy to the plans for Operation Cobra, as for security purposes this plan remained highly classified. Bradley was frustrated because he knew, although there was a slow, methodical advance among all sectors, the open, firm, and dry ground necessary for a breakout had not been secured. Weeks of rain had hampered the air force while the enemy continued to bring up reinforcements without duress.

The 4th, 90th, and 30th Infantry divisions would lead the way with the initial objective of securing Marigny and St. Gilles. They would create an open corridor for exploiting forces to come through while they guarded the shoulders.

The air bombardment would begin eighty minutes before the ground attack. The Air Force was enthusiastic about their part in this carpet bombing and they were anxious to get it done and assess the effect. The order of attack was as follows:

350 fighter-bombers: 20-minute strike

1800 heavy bombers: 1-hour strike

350 fighter-bombers: 20-minute strike

396 medium bombers: 10 minutes following the above

In addition, 500 fighter planes would fly bomber cover, for a total of 2,500 planes bombarding the enemy with 5,000 tons of high explosives, jellied gasoline, and white phosphorous for two hours and twenty-five minutes.

OPPOSITION

General Bradley and his staff tried to analyze the German position in an attempt to predict what the enemy would do following Cobra. Because of their anticipated lack of support and the destruction of men, vehicles, equipment, guns, food, and water as a result of the bombardment, it was logical to believe that they would withdraw to a favorable defense position in an attempt to reorganize. The American strength in men and tanks was estimated to be five times that of the Germans. The strength in opposition was estimated to be 30,000 men. Panzer Lehr, part of the opposing force, was reduced 60 percent to 2,200 men and 45 armored vehicles. Its line of defense extended for three miles along the Périers–St. Lô highway.

Seemingly, the Germans were aware of the preparations for an attack but still unsure where and when this would take place. They still thought that Patton and his army would attack from Pas de Calais and heavily reinforce their troops in that area as well as the other sectors of their line. The Allied armor was at a standstill with no place to go while the infantry bore the brunt of the fight and continued to slug it out, advancing small increments at a time. Losses were heavy. So many of our soldiers there were in their late teens and early twenties, many having been in the army a year or less. Here, as well as in the entire campaign, they were up against soldiers who had much longer training periods, many veterans of combat in North Africa and Sicily. The courage and obligation to duty by these wet, hungry, and exhausted soldiers was unprecedented and our country should never forget them. Many performed deeds of heroism warranting the Medal of Honor but no one was there to witness their deed when the heroic soldier and his buddies were found dead on the battlefield. It reminds one of a passage in James Dorian's book, *Storming St. Nazaire*: "The courage and fortitude of ordinary men is all that ever really keeps us from tyranny." The major battles in Normandy and Brittany were fought by ordinary men of the Allied Forces, which resulted in the liberation of France from the Germans.

General Bradley stuck to his plan as he knew the infantry obtaining a proper springboard was essential before the armor could be vaulted into the open country. The Carentan marshes had to be traversed to reach dry ground. One British correspondent ventured that this slowdown was a ploy to allow the Russians to exhaust themselves fighting the Germans alone.

Major General Quesada of the Air Force became one of General Bradley's greatest assets. He had developed bombing tactics for fighter planes and was anxious to use this in the support of ground troops in a close cooperative venture. He continued to experiment with heavier bomb loads and with the technique of having his fire directors on the ground actually riding with the tank columns so that very close and safe air support could be delivered immediately. Unlike many of the high-ranking Air Force officers, Quesada was eager to participate in the ground war in close support of the armored and infantry advances.

It was Major General Quesada's plan, once the breakout occurred, to put up a dawn-to-dusk fighter-bomber umbrella over the advancing armor, which would reconnoiter what lay ahead of the tanks and deliver air strikes immediately when opposition was encountered. The Air Force fire directors actually rode in the tanks.

General Quesada had been in the ground forces and had a great appreciation for their needs. The 9th TAC (Tactical Air Command) had 400 combat aircraft and performed preplanned missions and immediate-response missions. Preplanned missions were usually requested a day in advance. Immediate missions were requested by air-support parties attached to army formations. The superior American air force provided timely reconnaissance to allow current disposition of troops and guns. The French Resistance supplied much information about troop location and strength.

On July 17 Field Marshall Rommel was eliminated from this battle when he was severely wounded by an Allied fighter-bomber that attacked his staff car. General von Kluge took over Rommel's duties. By July 18 plans for Operation Cobra had been completed and approved by General Montgomery. The Périers–St. Lô road was to be the front border of the carpet rectangle. The troops would be withdrawn 1500 yards behind the Périers–St. Lô road to protect them from the bombardment.

The plan for this attack was well coordinated with saturation bombing of the front of the carpet along a narrow strip and the Périers road. The heavy bombers would follow. When they departed General Collins would launch his attack with 500 guns and three infantry divisions. The fighter-bombers would come in and the medium bombers would saturate the back edge of the carpet. This would require split-second timing for the coordination of this massive air attack. The aerial bombardment would be followed by artillery bombardment.

OPERATION COBRA

On July 24 the skies were overcast and dictated postponement of Cobra. Unfortunately, some planes were en route and could not be called back. Mistakenly, some of the bombers unloaded their bombs over the troops of the

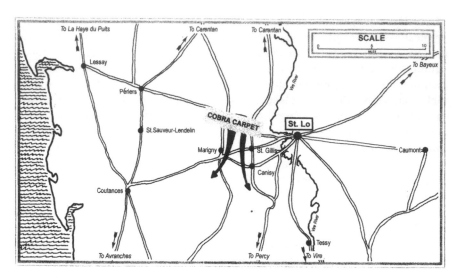

Operation Cobra

30th Infantry Division, killing twenty-five soldiers and wounding 131 more. The bombs had fallen almost one-half miles short of the Périers–St. Lô highway. General Collins, not knowing whether the air assault would continue, ordered the 9th, 4th, and 30th Infantry divisions to move forward and reoccupy the ground yielded when they pulled back in order to create a buffer zone between them and the bombardment.

General Bradley was shocked at this news of the short bombing and especially that the bombers approached the carpet area in a perpendicular fashion. He was positive that the air force had agreed with him to utilize a lateral approach so as to avoid such a tragedy. The air force denied that such a firm agreement had been finalized as they did not believe that many bombers could get through the narrow lateral approach of the carpet quickly enough to be effective. Discussion had to wait as now that the Germans were alerted, it was essential that the attack resume the next day, weather permitting.

On July 25 the attack was resumed. P-47 fighter-bombers were followed by B-17s and B-24 heavy bombers in successive waves. Later B-26 medium bombers followed. Approximately 4,700 tons of bombs were dropped into an area 3.5 miles long and 1.5 miles wide. Unfortunately, the bombers repeated the perpendicular pattern and again dropped their bombs short, resulting in numerous casualties in the 30th and 9th Infantry divisions.

Smoke markers delineating the foremost ground troops failed due to wind and dust. creating difficult recognition of the troop forward line. General Leslie McNair, chief for procurement of U.S. Ground Forces, an observer, was killed. He was buried secretly as he had been used as a decoy in the Pas de Calais threat. General Eisenhower decided that he would never use heavy bombers in a tactical role again.

One battalion was so decimated that it had to be replaced. A fire-direction center for the artillery was obliterated. All four assault companies of the 8th Infantry Regiment (4th) were bombed. Furnishing enough ambulances was a major problem as 164 cases of shock and combat exhaustion occurred in addition to the wounded.

General Collins had picked the 9th and 30th Infantry divisions for the initial Cobra attack. The 9th Infantry was a veteran of North Africa and Sicily and had taken 3,500 casualties in the bocage fighting. The 30th "Old Hickory Division" was commanded by Maj. Gen. Leland "Hollywood" Hobbs. The 1st Infantry Division, "The Big Red One" commanded by Maj. Gen. Clarence Huebner, would be in reserve. The 1st Infantry Division fought in North Africa where it was commanded by Maj. Gen. Terry de la Mesa Allen. General Allen was commander of the 104th Infantry Division which would fight with the VII Corps in Germany.

General Collins's VII Corps had also the 2nd and 3rd Armored divisions. The 2nd Armored fought in North Africa and Sicily and the 3rd Armored fought in Normandy. The 4th Armored Division in Middleton's VIII Corps began its fighting in Cobra and was destined to cut a swath through Brittany although it was stopped at the gates of Lorient, its objective, by concentrated artillery from the fortress. In addition, there were thirteen separate tank battalions attached to the infantry. The First Army had a 10–1 advantage over the Germans in medium tanks. The First Army's composition was:

VIII Corps with the 79th, 8th, 90th and 83rd Infantry divisions and the 4th and 6th Armored divisions

VII Corps with the 9th, 30th, 1st, and 4th Infantry divisions and the 2nd and 3rd Armored divisions

XIX Corps with the 35th Infantry Division

V Corps with the 2nd and 5th Infantry divisions

General Patton had crossed the Channel on July 6 with the advanced guard of the 3rd Army headquarters, which set up on the Cotentin Peninsula. He was to await commitment until August 1, a week after First Army's breakout. General Bradley's and General Patton's roles would be reversed, as in Sicily Bradley was second in command to General Patton. General Patton, thirteen years General Bradley's senior, would now be under General Bradley's command. General Patton was greatly relieved to get back into the fight and was very cooperative with General Bradley's plans and orders. He was on his best behavior. They remained good friends. It was General Bradley who befriended a much-dejected General Patton when he was relieved as commander of the Third Army after the war during the occupation period. The U.S. VIII Corps had begun its offensive in the western sector and took Périers. German General Hausser feared an entrapment of his 84th Corps. General von Kluge finally received permission from Hitler to transfer three infantry divisions from Pas de Calais.

PAUL "PAPA" HAUSSER

Paul Hausser was born October 7, 1880, in Brandenberg an der Havel, Germany, to a Prussian military family. His father was a major in the German Imperial Army. Hausser entered the army in 1892 and until 1896 was in a cadet school, moving from there to a cadet academy where he graduated as a lieutenant in 1899. Noted as a gifted soldier, he attended the War Academy in Berlin, October 1908 to July 1911. This was followed by several general staff assignments and by 1927 Hausser had risen to the rank of colonel. During the interwar years he became very involved in the Waffen SS troop movement in the German army and became one of its leaders.

In World War II Hausser served in Poland and was commander of an SS motorized infantry division in the French campaign in 1940. His next assignment was to Russia in the early days of Operation Barbarossa. For service in Russia, Hausser was awarded the Knight's Cross in 1941 and the Oak Leaves in 1943. He continued his service in Russia as commander of an SS Panzer corps, which was eventually re-formed and sent to Normandy. In late June 1944 Hausser was placed in command of the depleted Seventh Army. He was seriously wounded in August 1944 during the escape of his army from the Falaise pocket. In post war Germany, Hausser became the leader of an organization of Waffen SS veterans. Serving in that capacity, he acquired the sobriquet of "Papa" Hausser.

General Hausser received the Swords to his Knight's Cross in 1944. Other significant decorations were the Iron Cross, First and Second Classes in 1917, Cross of Honor in 1934, Wound Badge in Silver in 1942, SS Honor Ring, and Waffen-SS Long Service Award.

General Hausser was seriously wounded twice, losing one eye. He was the author of two books, *Waffen SS in Action* and *Soldiers Like Any Other*. He died December 21, 1972, in Ludwigsburg, West Germany.

GERMANS LOSE GROUND

General Collins ordered an attack toward Coutances. A regiment of the 1st Infantry Division took the town. On July 27 portions of the 3rd Armored Division advanced toward Coutances. One group was ambushed and lost three tanks but overall gained four miles in four hours.

The Germans continued to strengthen their defense positions but, fortunately for the Americans, five of their Panzer divisions stayed on General Montgomery's front. Field Marshall von Rundstedt had been replaced by Field Marshall Guenther von Kluge. The German 15th Army was held at Pas de

Calais as Hitler still thought that General Patton would launch the major attack there. He knew that if this was true, there would be a good chance that General Patton's forces would break through to open country where they would gain the terrain and mobility to reach Paris. Von Kluge was desperate to organize resistance on the right or west wing in the Panzer Group West sector if Hitler would allow him some free movement. This was granted.

Lt. Gen. Fritz Bayerlein, commander of Panzer Lehr, thought that the Americans had been dispersed on July 24, not realizing that the first attack on that date was aborted due to weather. General Hausser shared the same opinion but von Kluge disagreed. Hausser then warned von Kluge that he feared a major attack.

The results of the bombardment were devastating. Many tanks were destroyed as were communications. Panzer Lehr, what had been left of it, was effectively eliminated. Approximately 1,000 German soldiers were killed. The Americans had penetrated three miles in width and three miles in depth.

The Germans were not faring well. Bayerlein informed Hausser that his division was on the verge of collapse and that he had no infantry left. Two reserve infantry regiments were committed to reinforce a road junction at Chapelle-en-Juger. A couple of Panzer companies of the 2nd SS Panzer Division were also committed. Hausser had failed to build a reserve and von Kluge did not correct the error. Von Kluge requested transfer of the 9th Panzer Division from southern France.

GROUND ATTACK

The VII Corps infantrymen moved out at 11:00 A.M. with the towns of Marigny and St. Gilles as the main objectives. Securing these two towns would establish a three-mile corridor through the carpet and reach a vantage point from which to launch the armor.

The 330th Infantry Regiment (83rd), on the right (west) flank, was stopped by German artillery several hundred yards short of the objective. German troops offered stiff resistance but only in places where bombing had been sparse. In other areas, due to the intensity of the bombing, the Germans were in shock and offered little or no resistance. A battalion of the 8th Infantry Regiment (4th) moved in rapidly for a mile and a half. Another battalion of the 8th Infantry Regiment (4th) could not advance at all until eighteen tanks came to their support. After advancing 700 more yards, they were stopped again.

General Collins repaired his line where it had been damaged by the short bombing and closed the gap in the Périers–St. Lô road. His corps advanced rapidly and found almost total destruction in its path. Carcasses of men and animals and burned-out tanks and vehicles littered the way. The initial crisis had passed. The VII Corps gained only a little during the first day. General Collins had to decide whether to maintain the infantry attack or turn more aggressively to the mechanized forces. He chose the latter. Counterattacks did not materialize.

The 30th Infantry Division recovered quickly from the short bombing but as they began to move forward, friendly planes bombed and strafed them again, driving them into ditches and craters. The planes departed and these brave infantrymen were up and at them again.

After a critique of Operation Cobra, American commanders were grossly disappointed in the effect on the enemy. First of all, the bombing had not saturated the designated area. Second, it was believed that the enemy artillery remained effective following the bombardment. The German infantry remained ready to fight.

This view was not shared by many of the German commanders who were subject to the relentless bombardment. General Bayerlein protected his tanks as best he could but later stated,

> The planes kept coming over as if on a conveyor belt and the bomb carpets unrolled in great rectangles. My flak had hardly opened its mouth, when the batteries received direct hits which knocked out half the guns and silenced the rest. After an hour I had no connection with anybody, even by radio. By noon, nothing was visible but dust and smoke. My front lines looked like the face of the moon and at least seventy percent of my troops were out of action—dead, wounded, crazed or numb. All my forward tanks were knocked out and the roads were practically impossible.

Essentially, the VII Corps had advanced the line about a mile south of the Périers–St. Lô highway. The 330th Infantry Regiment (83rd) had not crossed the Périers–St. Lô highway. The 90th Infantry Division was short of Marigny and the 4th Infantry Division had not secured La Chapelle-en-Juger. The 30th Infantry Division was having difficulty taking Hébecrevon.

General Collins did not know for certain that his troops had crossed the German first line of resistance. He considered that the aborted attack on the twenty-fourth may have caused the Germans to pull back to another defensive line so in effect, it was possible that no headway had really been gained. He finally decided to go on and commit his units of exploitation and turn the armor loose on July 26. He had determined that the roads to Marigny and St. Gilles were cleared well enough to commit the armored units.

BREAKTHROUGH

Generals Paul Hausser and Dietrich von Choltitz committed their reserve forces to help defend Chapelle-en-Juger, which was a vital road junction. In assessing the damage from the American attack, they found that many of their units were decidedly weakened and not capable of significant defense, much less any counterattack. Hausser proposed a withdrawal to Coutances of the coastal units.

Field Marshall von Kluge insisted on restraint as he envisioned the possibility of a rout. He ordered all available personnel to the front. He also

A German machine-gun emplacement at Utah Beach.

A navy communication emplacement on Utah Beach. Its mission was to maintain contact between ships and ground forces.

Soldiers of the 4th Infantry Division landing at Utah Beach on D-Day. Their mission was to head for Cherbourg, a much-needed port.

Gliders deliver supplies and equipment to the beachhead.

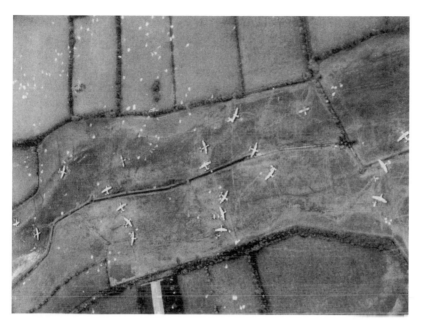

Gliders land near Ste. Mère Église, June 7, 1944. The hedgerows caused numerous crashes.

An American paratrooper stops to offer gum to two French children.

Battle in the hedgerows near St. Sauveur-le-Vicomte.

American soldiers pass out gum and hard candy that they had saved from K and C rations.

Negotiations for the surrender of St. Nazaire in a small café on the waterfront.

America's greatest ambassadors: a GI holds court near St. Malo.

A U.S. patrol on the outskirts of St. Malo.

A German soldier digs his way out of sand that buried him to his neck during the carpet bombing that was part of Operation Cobra. He was taken prisoner when the American infantry poured through the gap.

American soldiers examine a German "jeep" that was captured at La Haye-du-Puits. The vehicle is probably a Volkswagen.

A German soldier dead at his post in Fort du Roule, June 27, 1944.

German General von Schlieben (*right foreground*), covered with dust and dirt, surrenders the Cherbourg bastion.

German soldiers captured in and around Cherbourg before the fort surrendered.

Soldiers of the 83rd Infantry Division firing on Germans from a captured strongpoint in St. Malo, August 9, 1944.

Searching for dead bodies, two infantrymen emerge from the ruins in the streets of Brest.

General Ramcke, commander of Fortress Brest, is escorted to an American headquarters shortly after his surrender on September 9, 1944.

Soldiers of the 2nd Infantry Division advance under machine-gun fire on the outskirts of Brest, August 9, 1944.

German prisoners of war await transport to the mainland from Ile de Cezembre after the fortress's surrender.

Infantrymen of the 83rd Infantry Division fight from house to house in the streets of St. Malo.

With their sergeant still in charge, this platoon surrenders to the Americans near St. Malo on August 7, 1944.

Two exhausted infantrymen, a few yards from the front lines, sleep in their foxholes surrounded by grenades and other weapons.

Weary infantrymen leave La Haye-du-Puits after the vicious battle that led to the town's capture.

A German casualty somewhere on the Cotentin Peninsula, July 11, 1944.

An American M-4 tank drives through the rubble of Cherbourg, cleaning out German snipers.

Gen. Omar Bradley (*left*), commander of the U.S. First Army, listens as Gen. J. Lawton Collins, commander of the U.S. VII Corps, describes the battle for Cherbourg, June 30, 1944.

Gen. Dwight Eisenhower (*front passenger seat*) and Gen. Omar Bradley (*back seat*) say goodbye to Maj. Gen. Ira Wyche, commander of the 79th Division.

Gen. Matt Eddy talks to a highly decorated German officer in Cherbourg, June 28, 1944.

Infantrymen and tanks advance through the village of St. Fromond, July 8, 1944.

U.S. Army trucks roll across the beach from LSTs at Morlaix, on the way to deliver supplies for the siege of Brest.

requested of the Oberkommando der Wehrmacht (OKW) that they allow him to bring the 9th Panzer Division up from southern France to reinforce his 7th Army.

The Germans were trying to retreat south, fearing encirclement, and their forces were so oppressed by the advancing Americans that dissension began to appear and escalate. General von Choltitz, commander of the German 84th Corps and soon to become well known for failing to destroy Paris in spite of Hitler's orders to do so, realized that his forces were in danger of being captured and planned to exit down the west coast road. Hausser disagreed with this plan and von Choltitz protested. Hausser instructed him to follow orders. Von Kluge objected strongly to Hausser's plan and instructed Hausser to follow von Choltitz's plan to retreat south.

Actually, the Americans were expecting a counterattack and one column of thirty German tanks tried to break through a crossroad near Notre-Dame-de-Cenilly but the Americans held. Another German group overran an outpost of the 4th Infantry Division at La Pompe. Although a few of the German groups slipped out in the night, the Americans held most of the important road junctions, leaving many of the German troops trapped near Roncey.

ACROSS THE PÉRIERS–ST. LÔ ROAD AND BEYOND

The 330th Infantry Regiment (83rd) crossed the Périers–St. Lô road during the afternoon of July 26 and at the end of that day, the 90th Infantry Division was 2.5 miles south of the Périers–St. Lô road. The 8th Infantry Regiment (4th) took La Chapelle-en-Juger during the morning of the twenty-sixth. At that time, they committed their reserve, which gave them the momentum to advance to five miles from the Périers–St. Lô road by evening of the twenty-sixth. Similar progress was made by other units, so by evening General Collins was secure in believing that the 30th Infantry Division was three miles south of the Cobra starting line. During the night all units advanced except the 330th Infantry Regiment (83rd), which was detained on the right (west) flank.

On July 26, during the afternoon, Combat Command A (CCA) of the 2nd Armored Division rolled through St. Gilles and thereby launched the exploitation phase of Cobra. Penetration of the German defense was ascertained. The VII Corps had achieved its breakthrough, another significant contribution to World War II by Gen. "Lightning Joe" Collins, who had gained important victories in both the Pacific and European theaters.

On July 27 the 1st Infantry Division broke into Coutances and Middleton picked his way through the minefields on the Cotentin front. At the same time German units were trying to disengage and head south. This caused some traffic jams on the roads south and more than 500 vehicles as well as many German soldiers were destroyed in one day by American fighter-bombers. There were also some vicious close-quarter battles along these same routes as the Germans were desperate to break out. Another German force of 2,500 tried to overrun the Americans on a roadblock near Coutances but they were defeated by an American infantry unit that killed 450 Germans and captured 1,000 with 100 vehicles.

July 27 had been a good day with all units advancing. Germans were surrendering and fleeing south. Many of the retreating troops would find their way to Brittany ports such as St. Malo, Brest, Lorient, St. Nazaire, Bordeaux, and La Pallice, and once again offer resistance from these vantage points. On July 28 the 330th Infantry Regiment (83rd), which had been held up, finally was able to advance and catch up with its parent unit, the 83rd Division.

The 9th, 4th, and 30th Infantry divisions had completed a difficult and vicious battle, one of the most important and costly of the ETO. This corps of aggressive officers and brave and determined infantrymen had gained their objective having endured exhaustion, incessant artillery bombardment, and a paucity of hot food and inclement weather, in addition to the hazards of battle. This was a major turning point in World War II as it vaulted the Allied forces into terrain where they would dominate a mobile war.

The 90th Infantry Division went into a short reserve period for rest and rehabilitation. The 9th Infantry mopped up isolated pockets and moved south. The 30th Infantry advanced south along the west bank of the Vire River and passed from VII Corps control. For the infantry units Operation Cobra was over. All would continue to distinguish themselves in other battles toward Germany.

General von Choltitz's plan for retreat down the coast began early by the German 91st Division and this unit remained intact. One of General Hausser's units, the 2nd Panzer Division, was virtually destroyed. Field Marshall von Kluge tried desperately to establish a defensive line with the coastal road at Granville and running east. The 2nd SS Panzer Division was positioned in this line by July 28 and stopped Corlett's XIX Corps near Troisgots but failed in its attempt to stop the U.S. infantry units. On July 30 the German 116th Panzer Division was committed to the line southwest of Collins' forces.

The battle for the Cotentin Peninsula was at an end. The Americans had soundly defeated the German 7th Army and captured 20,000 German soldiers. Hitler's crazed belief that he could contain the Allied forces in Normandy fell far short of reality as his officers had so informed him. He had underestimated the mighty production of war machines by the United States and, above all, of the courage and determination of the Allied soldiers. The growth, training, and equipment of the American units in such a short period of time was one of the most remarkable events in U.S. history.

GERMAN DEFENSES DETERIORATE

Generals Hausser and von Choltitz now feared encirclement as they were well aware of the deep penetration in their defensive line by the Americans, especially punctuated by the armored columns moving through the Marigny–St. Gilles corridor. To attempt to thwart encirclement, they formed a north-south defense line facing eastward. Although this north-south line was effective in slowing American columns that were heading south, von Choltitz discovered during the afternoon of July 27 that the 3rd Armored Division was headed for Coutances with little or no opposition.

General Hausser wanted permission to withdraw further toward Coutances but could not contact Field Marshall von Kluge as he was over near Caen trying to stem the tide of the British and Canadian forces to the east. Finally Hausser and von Choltitz decided to withdraw to Coutances, which would be an anchor point for a new line in the configuration of an arc through Cambernon, Savigny, and Cerisy-la-Salle. They were hoping that Panzer Lehr could hold the line at Pont-Brocard, but in truth, Panzer Lehr had been reduced to near ineffectiveness.

Field Marshall von Kluge was informed of the rapid deterioration of their defenses when he returned from Caen during the afternoon of July 27. General Hausser now wanted to withdraw further to the Soule and Seine rivers. This worried von Kluge as he was fearful that this would expose the west flank of the defense lines around Caen. He decided to try to move an armored division to the Cotentin from Caumont. He requested four infantry divisions and the 9th Panzer Division for support. Hitler finally relented and sent him the 9th Armored and three infantry divisions from southern France. German units began to slip by the American units on the west coast during the night of July 27 and this continued the next day. These units had escaped encirclement. The Allied attacks on June 28 disrupted the German withdrawal. General Middleton placed the 4th and 6th Armored divisions on the offensive and Gen. John Wood's 4th Armored Division was in Coutances by nightfall.

To thwart the northward movement of German troops as reinforcements on the west coast, General Collins ordered the 3rd Armored Division to attack through the Marigny–St. Gilles gap, secure Montpichon, cut the north-south highway south of Coutances, and establish a blocking element on the high ground that overlooked roads leading to Bréthal and Gavray. On July 29 elements of the Third Army reached the Coutances-Gavray highway but were too late to encircle the retreating Germans.

Meanwhile, Middleton's VIII Corps was applying pressure on the Germans from the north. The plan was to tie the Germans down and give the VII Corps a chance to set up south of Coutances to block the retreating Germans. General Middleton was well positioned with four infantry divisions, one armored division, a two-squadron cavalry group, plenty of artillery, and sufficient ammunition for a major attack.

The Germans, well experienced in detaining the Americans in the hedge-row terrain, fought well and kept the Americans from making much progress on July 26. The VIII Corps sustained 1150 casualties and made only a small penetration in the Lessay-Périers highway. General Middleton was actually accomplishing his mission of tying the Germans down while the VII Corps was trying to encircle them. General Middleton kept his units patrolling continuously as he wanted to be aware of any German withdrawal.

On July 27 units advanced more rapidly, an indication of German withdrawal. They left the terrain and roads well mined to slow the Americans. The Germans were able to escape encirclement. On July 28 the 79th and 8th Infantry divisions moved to Coutances, encountering little resistance as they found the Germans had slipped out.

ENEMY WITHDRAWS

The Americans now were making good progress as the German defenses began to disintegrate. General Bayerlein stated that all calls for help had been ignored and he blamed higher headquarters for the failure. It was his belief that higher headquarters did not realize the seriousness of their position.

A large German force was encircled on July 28 near Montpinchon and Roncey. There was at this time a difficulty in communications between Hausser, von Choltitz, and von Kluge. However, when they could communicate, withdrawal versus counterattack was discussed. With most units in a state of depletion, some attacked to the southeast as per their original orders, while others withdrew along the west coast. A large group banded together near Roncey to try to break out to the southeast.

A fierce battle occurred in the early morning hours of July 29 when a group of thirty German tanks and vehicles led by a self propelled 88mm cannon approached a crossroads near Notre-Dame-de-Cenilly. The Germans withdrew, having lost seventeen dead and 150 wounded. The Americans had fewer than fifty casualties. Another unit of fifteen tanks overran an outpost of the 4th Infantry Division and the American commander was killed. The remaining infantrymen fell back to an artillery position. The artillery unit held off the Germans for thirty minutes until armored infantry arrived and re-established the outpost line. They found seven destroyed Mark IV tanks and 125 dead Germans.

Enemy stragglers and demoralized remnants of small units began surrendering to the Americans, many without food and ammunition. Other small units of Germans continued to slip through American territory and would find their way to Breton ports to fight again. The American fighter-bombers bombed and strafed many of the larger groups.

The IX Tactical Air Command found a large German traffic jam near Roncey on July 29. For six hours the planes attacked while American artillery units, tanks, and tank destroyers added to the decimation. Approximately 250 vehicles were disabled or destroyed, many after having been abandoned.

During the night of June 29, Maj. Gen. Edward H. Brooks, commander of the 2nd Armored Division erected a defensive line designed to ensnare the retreating Germans. Some fought fanatically to escape, while others surrendered after exploring the defensive line, and yet others surrendered having made no effort to escape.

The Americans were driven back temporarily at St. Denis-le-Gast by a well fortified German force but the Americans quickly regrouped and recovered control of the town. The German casualties were high. Small but vicious attacks continued through the night of July 29 as the Germans were desperate to free themselves and withdraw. This night, however, was the Germans' last main effort to flee the Cotentin battleground where hundreds had died, especially during the last twelve hours. The 2nd Armored Division killed approximately 1,500 Germans and captured 4,000. Its own loss was 100 dead and 300 wounded.

During the night of July 30, small sporadic fights took place but essentially the battle of the Cotentin Peninsula was over. In Operation Cobra, the forces east of the Vire River played a supporting role by tying up German forces and keeping them from opposing the VII and VIII Corps west of the Vire. Major generals Charles H. Corlett and Leonard T. Gerow commanded the XIX and V Corps respectively. They were left much on their own during Cobra to plan operations independently. On July 27 General Bradley moved XIX Corps to the west of the Vire River. A new operation was about to begin.

CLEARING THE COTENTIN PENINSULA

The German forces north of Coutances had to be destroyed. It was essential to pursue those retreating to the south immediately so as to give them no time to establish another effective defense line. Efforts were made to run down as many as possible before they reached Brittany ports. General Gerow was directed to move toward Vire as General Bradley thought it was necessary to secure the town. Gerow had to overcome rear-guard pockets of Germans and more hedgerow terrain to reach Vire. Word reached Gerow that the Germans were withdrawing and that on July 29 the British were planning to attack. Therefore, he ordered his division commanders to make an all-out attack simultaneously.

The 35th, 5th, and 2nd Infantry divisions encountered a strong German defensive line near Torigni-sur-Vire and sustained 1,000 casualties. The V Corps regrouped and prepared to attack again the next day only to find that the Germans had fallen back. The V Corps made good progress and then during the afternoon of July 31 was slowed again by resisting forces. If the British on the left (east) and the XIX Corps on the right (west) continued to advance, the V Corps would be pinched out near Vire.

Although the XIX Corps was still far from its post-Cobra objective, it had made a major contribution to the final stages of Operation Cobra. By blocking for five days the German attempt to re-establish a defensive line across the Cotentin, XIX Corps had enabled troops of the First Army to make a spectacular end run.

TO AVRANCHES

A week after the start of Operation Cobra, on August 1, the VII Corps was at the base of the Cotentin Peninsula, thirty miles south of the Périers–St. Lô road on August 1. General Collins had turned the entire VII Corps and out-flanked the Germans.

There were still pockets of Germans on the Cotentin Peninsula but these would soon be mopped up by following units. The Americans were in control and could advance toward Avranches, which was the gateway to Brittany. The Allied forces in the eastern sector of the lower peninsula would continue to advance to secure the area surrounding Caen, setting up a breakout to the Seine River and on to Paris.

The Third Army was to be committed on August 1, so General Patton, who was to command the Third Army, had established his headquarters on the Cotentin Peninsula. General Bradley had requested General Patton to supervise the VIII Corps during the exploitation of Cobra. In turn, Patton knew that the quicker the VIII got to Avranches, the sooner the Third Army would be committed for a thrust into Brittany. Needless to say, Patton was very anxious to move.

General Patton immediately chose the 4th and 6th Armored divisions, com-manded by major generals John S. Wood and Robert W. Grow respectively as the leading elements for the advance south. On July 28 General Middleton ordered General Wood to pass his division through the 90th Infantry Division and proceed to Coutances as far as Monthuchon. He was then to continue to Cérences, nine miles south of Coutances.

General Patton did not want to go into Brittany and had a bitter argument with generals Eisenhower and Bradley about it. He wanted his entire Third Army directed toward Germany with no side trip to Brittany. Eisenhower and Bradley finally conceded to allow him to send one corps to Brittany and the rest of the Third Army on toward Germany. Eisenhower and Bradley were still very anxious to secure the Brittany ports. General Middleton's VIII Corps got the assignment to Brittany, which included the 4th and 6th Armored divisions.

General Middleton ordered General Grow to move from his bivouac area north of La Haye-du-Puits to come abreast of the 4th Armored Division on the west side and attack with them down the coast. The division would have to pass through the 79th Infantry Division, bypass Coutances on the west side, and proceed to Granville, twenty-eight miles south of Coutances. The infantry divisions were given the duty to remove the mines from the roads south. Members of the infantry and armored divisions were taught in small groups by the engineers how to find, remove, and disarm the mines.

The 4th Armored Division moved out on July 28. Brig. Gen. Holmes E. Dager, commanding Combat Command B (CCB) (4th Armored Division) moved through Périers toward Coutances. A dense minefield near St. Sauveur-Lendelin held them up for three hours. The armored infantry dismounted and entered Coutances on foot and fought an intense battle for several hours with a German unit. By that evening, Coutances was clear of defenders and secured by evening on July 28. The Germans were too disorganized to set up a defensive line. The tactical aircraft were following the German withdrawal and destroyed many tanks and other vehicles. As the Germans departed, they quickly placed mines along the way.

The American commanders feared that reinforcements would arrive from southern France to attempt to halt the rout. Therefore, they wanted to neutralize all defensive positions and move quickly toward Avranches, their goal. Avranches sits between the Sée and Sélune rivers, both of which flow to the west. Five highways arrive from the north and east and course out of Avranches as one highway leading south.

On the evening of July 28 General Middleton ordered the 6th Armored Division to proceed south and take Avranches. The 4th Armored Division was to take Cérences. Capture of Avranches and of bridges over the Sée and Sélune rivers would make it possible for the Third Army to enter Brittany.

The 4th and 6th Armored divisions were well on their way south by the end of the day on July 29. The enemy was disorganized and seemingly incapable of setting up a defensive position in an attempt to stop the American

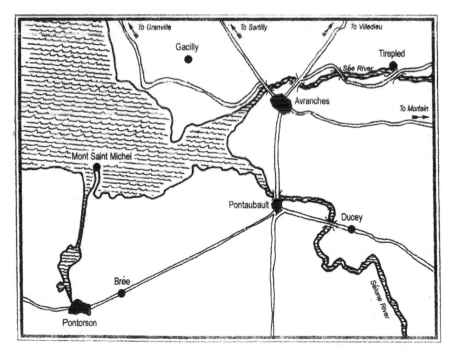

Avranches

advance. Sporadic German fire on bridge construction units was the only show of resistance.

General Middleton directed General Wood to attack Avranches with the 4th Armored Division and General Grow to advance to Bréthal and Granville with the 6th Armored. General Grow sent Combat Command B (CCB) (6th Armored Division) to take Bréthal, which they did against token opposition. General Wood ordered his CCB (4th Armored Division) to move on to Avranches and capture river crossings east of the city. Destroyed bridges at Cérences and Lengrone slowed the advance until engineers erected a crossing. One column of CCB encountered an ambush and was relieved by dismounted infantry and artillery, having sustained forty-three casualties and the loss of five halftracks.

General Dager's western column CCB (4th Armored Division) moved rapidly for ten miles, encountering little resistance. Unknowingly, they passed within several hundred yards of the German Seventh Army advanced command post with General Hausser present. He and other staff officers escaped on foot, continuing after commandeering vehicles. Early in the evening of July 30, troops entered an undefended Avranches. Pilots reported Frenchmen in the VIII Corps zone waving the tricolor flags indicating that the Germans had parted.

It was necessary to secure the main highway from Avranches to the Sélune River crossing near Pontaubault so that the 3rd Army could pass into Brittany. General Dager's CCB (4th Armored Division) was to receive help to hold Avranches and to secure the Sélune River crossings. During the night of July 30 the CCB tank company encountered a column of trucks with red crosses on the coastal road near Granville. The Germans fired on the Americans and the Americans returned fire. Several hundred Germans piled out of the truck and surrendered. The prisoners informed the Americans that a second column was coming. The commander ordered withdrawal, abandoning the prisoners.

Before daylight on July 31 the Germans entered Avranches. Some set up guns. Others with any means of transportation headed to Mortain. A bitter fight ensued with elements of CCB (4th Armored Division) who were serving on an outpost south of the city. The Germans broke off the fight, returned again after daylight and began fighting again. Finally several hundred surrendered.

There was little resistance in the way now. The 4th and 6th Armored divisions had collectively taken 4,000 prisoners. The 79th and 8th Infantry divisions, following on secondary roads, had collected an additional 3,000 prisoners, all seemingly glad to be out of the war. The VIII Corps lost only 100 men between July 28 and 31.

Fighter-bombers pursued the retreating enemy and destroyed so many vehicles that it caused many road obstructions. Disorganization was rampant and abandoned guns and equipment littered the roads. German units fled into Brittany and many sought haven in Brest, Lorient, and St. Nazaire to fight the Americans again when these Breton ports would be attacked one at a time. Many dead animals created a health problem.

The German defenses in the Cotentin Peninsula had disintegrated after a very costly war for both sides. The Americans controlled the last line of defense before entering Brittany. The First Army captured 28,000 German prisoners during the month of July, of which 20,000 were captured during the last six days. The German LXXXIV Corps was decimated. The II Parachute Corp was beaten. The German Second Army had been defeated and badly depleted.

In the VII sector a new combination had evolved. A combat command was attached to each infantry division, imparting the armored characteristics of firepower, mobility, and shock to the infantry, which was capable of sustained action. In all corps sectors west of the Vire River, balanced teams of tanks, tank destroyers, motorized infantry, artillery, and engineers had pushed ahead making generous use of marching fire.

7

Advance into Brittany

AS THE ADVANCE into Brittany began, General Eisenhower wanted to make sure that General Montgomery would operate boldly against the enemy with his armored and mobile columns. He wrote to him, "The ideal situation would be to obtain the entire coastal area from Le Havre to Nantes, both inclusive. With such a broad avenue of entry, we could bring to the Continent every single soldier the U.S. could procure for us." It was important to recall that in 1943 Hitler designated the following ports as fortresses. Each commander had taken an oath to defend "to the last man." The ports so designated were Dunkirk, Calais, Boulogne, Le Havre, Cherbourg, St. Malo, Brest, Lorient, and St. Nazaire. Cherbourg had fallen in late June and efforts to restore it as a usable port were in progress.

REORGANIZATION OF COMMAND

Major organizational changes were being made in the U.S. forces. At noon on August 1, 1944, the 12th Army Group, with General Bradley commanding, became operational. Lt. Gen. Courtney H. Hodges became commander of the U.S. First Army and General Patton's Third Army was committed.

During the transitional period, the VIII Corps remained technically under the command of the First Army but General Bradley had informally loaned the VIII Corps to General Patton, who was to be the Third Army commander. This caused confusion as an order would be given by Bradley and changed by Patton. This confusion lasted for several days during the first week of August. For instance, Bradley told General Middleton that when he went through Avranches to guard his south flank heavily. Middleton was ready to send the 79th Infantry Division to Fougères to block the right flank when Patton came along and said, "Hell no, we're going to Brest."

Another example was an order from General Bradley to General Middleton to capture St. Malo. Just as Middleton was preparing to attack, Patton came along and said, "No, pass it up; there's nothing there anyway; there aren't 500 troops in there." Middleton then asked Patton how many German troops were between their present position and Brest. Patton answered that there were about 1,000. Middleton's VIII Corps captured 10,000 Germans on the way to Brest.

General Middleton's VIII Corps received a lot of shelling from St. Malo as they were passing it. He ordered the 83rd Infantry Division to attack the town, which would turn into quite a battle. The 83rd Infantry Division captured 14,000 Germans and also killed a large number. General Middleton did not put much stock in General Patton's estimates and rightly so. Patton insisted that the 6th Armored Division commanded by General Robert W. Grow and under Middleton's VIII Corps command "just get in the middle of the road and barrel on out to Brest [150 miles or so from St. Malo] and capture the fortified port before the Germans get ready."

Middleton thought this dangerous nonsense. He knew the Germans were ready and had been fortified for all eventualities as Brest, like Lorient and St. Nazaire, was a U-boat fortress. He had studied aerial photographs which showed large numbers of concrete pillboxes housing 90mm cannon. The 6th Armored Division went on to Brest. The 4th Armored Division went to Rennes and General Wood was surprised to find few German units there as it had been anticipated that a bitter battle would take place in Rennes. The 83rd Infantry Division would capture St. Malo on August 17.

General Bradley requested General Patton to include VIII Corps under his command during the breakout period. The plan was to exit the Cotentin Peninsula through Avranches and proceed immediately to Pontaubault and secure the bridges for the advance into Brittany. Avranches was on high ground and commanded the surrounding terrain. The infantry units that had been designated to lead the attack were replaced by the 4th and 6th Armored divisions under Major General Wood and Major General Grow respectively. The 6th Armored Division led out with the 4th Armored Division on its left. Avranches fell quickly and quietly. General Middleton sent General Wood with the 4th Armored Division on to Pontaubault to secure the bridges there. The move through Avranches and Pontaubault was accomplished in one night. The two armored divisions were moved down a single highway during seven hours of darkness so as to escape German planes. This unusual feat was accomplished by placing officers at critical points to keep the flow going.

QUIBERON CONSIDERED AS A NEW PORT

Originally the plan was to make a thrust to St. Nazaire and Nantes and subsequently to turn west to secure Brest. The Germans had fortified Brest, Lorient, and St. Nazaire, so would in all probability defend them to the limit while destroying the port facilities, thereby denying any immediate usage to the Allies should they be captured. Having mad\e this assumption, it was decided to consider making a new port out of Quiberon Peninsula as it jutted out into the Bay of Biscay between Lorient and St. Nazaire. Excellent railroads and roads connected Quiberon to Brest and Nantes. With Brest in American hands, the convoys could sail around Brest to Quiberon without hindrance from German forces in Brest. However, eventually Quiberon was not turned into a port because of the major engineering problems necessary to do so.

The plan was for the VIII Corps to turn west into Brittany toward Rennes and St. Malo. General Bradley ordered General Patton to seize Rennes and Fougères, then turn toward St. Malo, Quiberon Bay area, and Brest. Because the Germans had disintegrated so much, the force entering Brittany was reduced to one corps rather than the three originally planned. Patton was unhappy about having to go to Brittany at all as he wanted to strike for Germany right away. This would have left a large force of Germans in his rear and the Breton ports would have remained functional and denied to the Allies. Generals Bradley and Eisenhower prevailed in the decision to send at least one corps of the Third Army into Brittany.

General Patton planned to send his armor from Avranches to Quiberon in order to cut off the Brittany Peninsula. He would then liberate the central plateau of the peninsula. However, many of the German troops that had escaped the Cotentin Peninsula had headed for the Briton ports as safe haven and in addition strengthened them in the process. Patton dispatched the 4th Armored Division to Rennes and Quiberon and the 6th Armored Division to Brest. A key target was the railroad from Brest to Rennes, which the Allies wanted to capture before it and its several bridges were destroyed. Patton considered St. Malo an unimportant objective that could be bypassed.

A new kind of war suddenly emerged due to the change in terrain from the swamps and hedgerows of the Cotentin to the more open country conducive to armored thrust. Patton recognized that the German forces were in a state of disorganization so he pushed his armor to continue to disrupt the enemy rear areas and to continue their exploits in enemy territory. He granted his division commanders free rein to use their own judgment. To do this, Patton had to remain aware constantly of frontline changes. He transformed the 6th Cavalry Group into the Army Information Service, thus making it a communication service. Reconnaissance platoons were formed to patrol wide and far and to feed back information to G-2 and G-3. This arrangement would provide contact between forces that were beyond the usual boundaries and the army command posts. The two were sometimes separated by 100 miles or more. It was not unusual for the army staff to have more information than the corps staff that was directing the operation. No one could have enjoyed this more than generals Wood and Grow, commanders of the 4th and 6th Armored divisions, respectively, as their units were bashing and slashing their way across Brittany, overrunning their maps and communications systems. They did not want to stop. The 4th Armored Division would eventually run out of fuel at Rennes. General Wood had complained bitterly about having to delay in Brittany and not continue toward Germany while he had the Germans on the run. The type of arrangement that Patton made was an example of his understanding of war and his ability to adapt the previously untried methods of warfare to this new and fast-moving campaign. He relentlessly pursued the enemy, never giving them time to stop and regroup. The armored units overran maps and communications.

THE 4TH AND 6TH ARMORED DIVISIONS ADVANCE BEYOND COMMUNICATIONS

However, with any change of plans or the indoctrination of new concepts comes a certain amount of confusion until the wrinkles are ironed out. General Middleton was confronted with the problems of control of his forces as oftentimes he did not know where all of his units were and in what activity they were engaged. Thus he could not share in decisions that the corps commander should be privy to. He was, after all, the commander responsible for the Brittany campaign. He was an infantryman, methodical and meticulous, and this upset his ideas of orderly and controlled progress to a specific objective. The VIII Corps had been transferred from the First to the Third U.S. Army and from the jurisdiction of General Bradley to General Patton, which in itself was a difficult adjustment. The terrain had changed so the issues for General Middleton were somewhat formidable. His plan was to send the two armored divisions into Brittany abreast with an infantry division following each of them. The 4th Armored Division followed by the 8th Infantry Division would move toward Rennes, and the 6th Armored Division followed by the 79th Infantry Division would advance to Pontorson, Dol-de-Bretagne, and Dinan. The columns would then go on to Quiberon and St. Malo respectively.

General Middleton had his hands full with generals Wood and Grow. Wood was complaining bitterly of his unit's chore in Brittany as he wanted to be turned loose toward Germany and seemed to resent taking orders from Middleton who was an infantryman rather than from General Patton who was a cavalryman with the same hell-for-leather attitude. He actually had sent one of his combat commands on beyond Rennes to Châteaubriant and Middleton made him turn it back toward Lorient, which was the order General Patton had issued. This error was actually picked up by Patton's chief of staff, Maj. Gen. Hugh J. Gaffey, who made it very clear that this move was contrary to Patton's orders.

It was decided that Maj. Gen. Wade Haislip's XV Corps would not be needed so General Middleton had the total responsibility for clearing Brittany. He had a frustrating chore of maintaining an organized campaign. His two armored divisions were at Brest and Rennes, a cavalry group was at St. Malo, and his three infantry divisions were at Rennes and St. Malo with the third guarding the right flank.

On August 6 a report reached First Army Headquarters that a large German force was approaching Brest from the northeast which would place the

6th Armored Division between this force and Brest. Communications were poor, which gave more concern to this problem. If the German force was approaching from the northeast, then the 6th Armored Division was caught between two major forces as it was becoming apparent that Brest was going to be strongly defended. St. Malo was putting up a formidable defense and the 4th Armored Division had run into major resistance at Lorient. General Patton had already ordered a battalion of the 8th Infantry Division to leave Rennes and head for Brest. General Grow reported this new development to General Middleton, who knew from past experience that General Grow was a commander who, when ordered to do something, would always come up with a better plan. Therefore, Middleton decided to let him take care of the problem in his own way, a bit of poetic justice. Fortunately Grow was able to neutralize this force after a brief battle, but of course, this delayed his progress toward Brest. This also raised a red flag of caution concerning one unit getting too far away from the unit to which it was attached.

Communications at this point were dependent upon the cavalry unit that General Patton had converted to a moving communications unit and the air force, which was called in to find the 6th Armored Division. Some system of a courier service back to headquarters had to be established. Small planes, which had no place to land in this hedgerow country, would fly over low and drop a message to a marked panel on the ground, wait for a reply, and snare it from between two poles holding it aloft, an example of "do what you have to do," repeated so many times during a war.

General Middleton had grave reservations about trying to take Brest with the 6th Armored Division. He asked General Patton of his estimates of the German forces in Brest. General Patton told him that he did not know exactly how many were in Brest but there weren't more than 10,000 Germans in the entire peninsula. Again Patton's figures were far from accurate. Approximately 35,000 prisoners would be taken at Brest. Approximately 50,000 German troops collectively were fortifying Lorient and St. Nazaire. Patton seemed to have some denial about the strength of the Germans in Brittany probably because he just did not want to be held up there.

Generals Wood and Grow felt a kinship to General Patton, who was a tank officer, a feeling that they did not have for General Middleton, an infantry officer. The two divisions had not suffered the depressing battles and heavy losses in the Cotentin Peninsula as had the infantry divisions of the VIII Corps and were flush with their victories in the breakout. Their enthusiasm and self-confidence, and their indifference to the corps commander, made it difficult for the corps commander to maintain control through no fault of his own. In spite of these problems and differences, Middleton was one of the better generals the U.S. Army ever had and his record in combat in Europe was one of the longest of the generals engaged there. Middleton wanted to move his corps headquarters deeper into Brittany so as to maintain communication with his armored divisions but Third Army headquarters objected as they wanted to maintain telephone communication with the VIII Corps and could not do so if he were too far removed. As early as August 2, Middleton said that his communication with his two armored divisions was "practically nil."

Postwar, General Middleton wrote, "[T]he expensive signal equipment at the disposal of the Corps was never designed for a penetration and pursuit of the magnitude of the Brittany operation." The 6th Armored Division had just left "in a cloud of dust" toward Brest and far outran its communication capability with Corps Headquarters (HQ). Couriers between Corps HQ and Division Command Post (CP) often ran into pockets of Germans in some small towns who were trying to journey to one of the Breton ports. The French people often told the couriers the location of these German pockets, which they were able to bypass most of the time. Most of the corps artillery planes had been damaged by enemy fire or from rough landings in rocky fields. There had not been ample time to clear fields and make suitable landing areas even for the small planes used for reconnaissance and direction of artillery.

All of these difficulties with communications caused a certain amount of confusion to this rapidly moving war with the "pony express" type of courier systems. The message was often obsolete by the time it reached its destination. The 6th Armored Division was 150 miles from VIII Corps HQ by August 6. General Middleton advised General Patton of the situation and informed him that as corps commander he could not be responsible for the division completely distanced from any type of communication. He would, however, make a continued effort to establish and maintain contact with all units under his command. Middleton never hesitated to be candid. Patton highly respected Middleton.

Confusion, at this time, was certainly generalized. General Wood found the going difficult because his messages to corps headquarters were being ignored and there was no reply and no assistance or guidance. Essentially, the division commanders were left on their own and had to react quickly to fast-changing situations. It was a fluid campaign to which they had to respond on their own authority as under these conditions no orders were received from higher authority. Successful rapid advance created problems.

Supplying these outbound units became a big problem as supply dumps were out of the question. G.I. trucks likened to the old-time stagecoaches would load up and make a run through the country, dodging snipers and pockets of resistance as best they could with the attitude of "the mail must go through." Supply routes were gradually established and guarded with antiaircraft batteries aided by members of the FFI.

Moving essential Allied units out of the Cotentin Peninsula into Brittany was a major problem due to the total devastation along the route of the coastal road through Avranches. Debris, dead animals, mines, destroyed vehicles and the rubble of buildings all contributed to the mess through which a path had to be cleared with bulldozers to establish an exit sufficient for military traffic. High-ranking officers were seen at many crossroads and bottlenecks waving the continuous parade of units through the area in order to speed up the process. Convergence of the two coastal highways at Coutances and Avranches were major sites of confusion and obstruction. Subsidiary roads and bypasses were constructed by the engineers, which helped ease the congestion considerably. The German Luftwaffe made an appearance, trying to destroy key bridges so as to obstruct the flow, but they were hammered by new antiaircraft gunners pleased to go into action.

A GOOD WEEK

In spite of all of the confusion, controversy, and second-guessing by commanders, the initial campaign in Brittany during the first week after the breakout from Avranches was one of the U.S. forces' "finest hours." Generals Middleton, Grow, and Wood were brilliant, hard-driving commanders. Grow and Wood were bold and farsighted and reveled in advancing rapidly deep into enemy territory. Neither agreed with warnings of caution by their superiors. On the other hand, Middleton was dealing constantly with the problems of his corps with its widely dispersed units in a variety of situations, often with poor communication between him and his subordinates. Had things not gone well with the escapades of the 4th and 6th Armored divisions, Middleton would have borne the brunt of it in history as an inept commander who approached his objectives in a reckless manner. Although General Middleton was known for his care and caution, he was placed in an untenable position with the unpredicted lightning advances of the initial campaign in Brittany. However, his equanimity in a tough campaign helped to stabilize a volatile situation. He was truly the anchor for our forces in Brittany. No one could have done it better.

As for General Patton, he seemingly had little interest in Brittany as he was hell-bent on advancing toward Germany with no detours. He wanted to keep the Germans on the run, giving them no chance to set up defenses. This was his modus operandi for which he was famous and his performance during World War II established him as one of the world's most aggressive and competent commanders. He gambled but fortunately these were successful. He loved any challenge and was always present with his troops to overcome any obstacles confronting them.

PREPARING FOR BREST

As the Third Army moved on toward Germany, General Middleton was left in Brittany to take St. Malo, Brest, St. Nazaire, Lorient, Rennes, Vance, and Nantes. There had been much speculation postwar that if Grow's 6th Armored Division could have reached Brest a day or two earlier before German troops from Normandy bolstered the defense, Brest might have fallen. In Middleton's opinion, which seems to be the most logical one expressed, this argument has no merit. Middleton was a scholar and he had considered the problem of taking Brest in much detail and never thought it would be anything but a bitter battle with high casualties on both sides and destruction of the port. Middleton knew from aerial photographs of Lorient that Hitler had fortified all of these ports extensively. Brest was defended by three German divisions and was bristling with 90mm cannon placed in structures with thick impenetrable walls of steel and cement. Middleton believed, and rightly so, that the forces at Brest were waiting for an attack and were prepared to defend the fortress to the last man. There would be no surprises. He thought a head-on attack of a single armored division would have cost Grow every tank in the 6th Armored Division

General Middleton shifted the 2nd Infantry Division to Brest as he knew this was an infantry and artillery battle. The 6th Armored Division left to relieve the 4th Armored Division at Lorient. The 2nd Infantry Division was commanded by Maj. Gen. Walter M. Robertson, whom Middleton knew from prior assignments. The 8th Infantry Division was commanded by Gen. Donald A. Stroh, who had been in North Africa and Sicily. The 29th Infantry Division, a National Guard unit from Pennsylvania, was commanded by Maj. Gen. Charles Gerhardt, a former West Pointer. A cavalry group and two Ranger battalions commanded by Lt. Col. Earl Rudder were brought in as special forces. Middleton was satisfied that he had in his VIII Corps quality commanders and divisions to secure the Brittany Peninsula.

In 1919 Middleton spent a week in Brest waiting for a ship to return to the United States following World War I. He remembered the terrain well. Since then the city had migrated to higher ground and that is where the defensive positions were located. In a defensive position on high ground, the defender has a huge advantage over the aggressor. The defense of the city was commanded by Generalleutnant Hermann Ramcke who had led the airborne assault on Crete and was a hard-core soldier with much experience. He could be counted on to carry out Hitler's orders to defend to the last man.

8

The North Shore and St. Malo

TASK FORCE A

THE BREST-RENNES railroad ran along the north shore of Brittany and would be important to the Allies for transporting supplies away from the port of Brest into the interior of France once Brest was captured. Several significant bridges on the railway were still intact which General Patton was anxious to save. To do this, a new task force was organized of about 3,500 men. Brig. Gen. Herbert L. Earnest was selected to be the commander of Task Force A. This highly mobile unit fortified with armament and armor was actually planned by Patton only a few hours before it was organized and it was assigned to General Middleton's VIII Corps. It had been determined that German troops in the northern half of Brittany were withdrawing and headed for Brest so it was desirable for this newly organized mobile unit to cut off the northern half of the Brittany Peninsula. The 15th Cavalry Group was assigned to Task Force A on August 1, 1944. Other components were the 6th Tank Destroyer Group, the 705th Tank Destroyer Battalion, C Company of the 159th Combat Engineers, and an engineer Bailey Bridge company, as well as the headquarters for the task force. No U.S. infantry unit was available. The FFI, which was becoming very active in Brittany, was to secure the bridges and support the 6th Armored Division in capturing Brest.

Task Force A was to proceed to the vicinity of Brest, along the northernmost route through Avranches, Pontorson, Dol-de-Bretagne, Dinan, St. Brieuc, Guingamp, and Morlaix, and drop off small guard detachments to remain at each town until they could be relieved by elements of the 83rd Infantry Division.

AMBUSH ON THE HIGHWAY

Shortly after Task Force A had passed through the bottleneck at Avranches-Pontaubault on August 3, it struck resistance at Dol-de-Bretagne. Civilians informed General Earnest that Dol was strongly defended so he decided to bypass it to the south. The 15th Cavalry Group was deployed from the assembly area, located between Dol and Dinan, on August 3, 1944. The group commander, thinking that the way was clear and that the 6th Armored Division was in front of them on the same road, was riding at the front of his column and was pushing the column at a speed of 35–40 miles per hour. Troop C led with the 3rd Platoon in front.

Avranches was cleared and the speed of the march accelerated. The leading platoon cleared Baquer-Pican, a small village east of Dol. The highway then led down a hill with a curve at the bottom and woods on both sides of the road. As the 3rd platoon reached the bend in the road, the unit was ambushed by antitank guns, mortars, and machine guns with flanking German troops on each side of the road for several hundred yards.

The group commander's jeep, still at the head of the column, was hit and burst into flames. Members of the third platoon jumped out of their vehicles into the ditches for cover. The assault guns of Troop C were brought to the crest of the hill and fired on the German position in an effort to extricate members of Troop C who were pinned down. Troop A covered Troop C as it pulled out and regrouped. The group commander and four men were not recovered. It was learned later that they were wounded and captured and held on the Island of Jersey until release in May 1945.

A critique of this ambush was held and it was determined that the 6th Armored Division had diverted to the south just beyond Pontorson because of reports of enemy resistance on the route chosen and had not cleared the way ahead on the original route. The critique was critical of the group commander riding at the head of the column and for Troop C not to be leading by a half mile. This would have been a more appropriate formation. Regardless, it emphasizes the vulnerability of a road-bound mechanized unit to an ambush The FFI did this to German units repeatedly.

PROBING THE DEFENSE

General Middleton was concerned about the defenses around St. Malo so he requested General Earnest to probe northward toward St. Malo and try to determine the strength of the defenses. Defensive positions were encountered again near Miniac, several miles to the west of Dol. This was broken and the task force again encountered more intense resistance near Châteauneuf-d'Ille-et Vilaine.

General Earnest put out a call for help to the 83rd Infantry Division and to the 6th Armored Division The 330th Infantry Regiment (83rd) was at Pontorson when it received the call and proceeded on to Dol-de-Bretagne, which it secured after a short battle. The resistance against Task Force A escalated as it continued northward.

Even though generals Patton and Bradley had decided to **bypass** St. Malo to secure later, General Middleton became concerned about the concentration of German forces there and the effect that this force would have on the American lines of communication in Brittany. Middleton wanted the 83rd Infantry Division to focus on the capture of St. Malo. Patton, thinking that St. Malo would offer only token resistance, had wanted the 83rd Infantry Division to continue toward Brest and let Task Force A secure the North shore. Again, Patton had grossly underestimated the opposition at St. Malo.

The American commanders were unaware of the strength of the defense of St. Malo and of the fanatical determination of the German commanders there who had taken an oath to defend this fortress "to the last man," as Hitler had requested of them. Hitler personally chose the commanders of his Atlantic

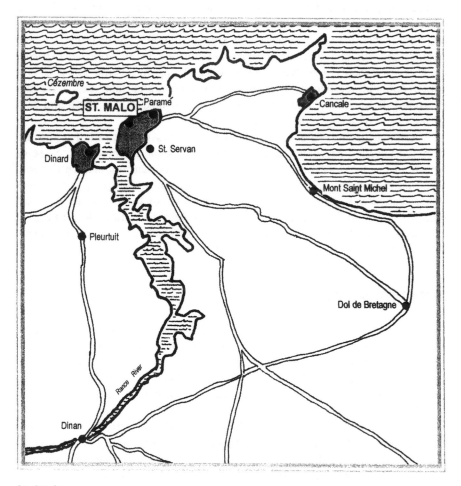

St. Malo

Wall fortresses. Being chosen was an honor and enhanced the devotion that these commanders already had for their Fuehrer. There were three dominant commanders in the St. Malo Complex, each action independently. Each one of them commanded a fortress.

In 1942 Hitler, believing that the place to stop an invasion was on the coast itself, concentrated the three years on having an awesome coastal defense built by the Todt Organization, with both voluntary and involuntary labor. The first phase of the construction was submarine bases, followed by strong artillery coastal positions to defend them. Next were a line of strongpoints along the coast to control landing sites on the beaches. Last were the defensive positions built to defend against attack from the interior. St. Malo was considered to have the most advanced system of defenses on the Atlantic Wall. The fortresses so constructed remained in the normal chain of command until attacked and then each commander of a fortress under siege became independent of any other command other than Hitler, who would control them personally. Each commander chosen had vowed to Hitler that he would defend the fortress unto death.

The Allies did not realize that they were to be confronted by three commanders who were so fanatically dedicated to Hitler. This would be a major factor in the battle to come. Col. Andreas von Aulock, an arrogant Nazi, commanded the Citadel. Col. Rudolf Bacherer was the commander of Dinard. An unknown lieutenant colonel on the island of Cézembre would be the last to fall. Each of these commanders eventually had to make a decision to surrender and each did so in his own way. The concept, however, was that only when nothing else could be done to hurt the enemy was it senseless to continue.

Hitler realized that the beach landings had been successful for the Allies, which infuriated him. He also knew that he had a second chance to defeat the Allies by denying them any port. Logistically, the Allies would need sufficient ports to support a moving Army. The commanders of all port fortresses had been instructed, if attacked, to begin immediately to destroy all port facilities and reduce them to rubble.

Another factor in Hitler's plan was that the garrisons in these port fortresses were static troops without vehicles, tanks, and so on, to carry out an offensive; therefore, their only choice was to stick to their defensive positions, which were well fortified, and to defend them to the last possible moment before annihilation. Although this concept might not defeat the Allies, it would buy time to build up defenses in the approaches to Germany where the final battle would be fought. Hitler's field commanders took a different view as they believed losing so many thousands of troops in Brittany would greatly reduce the manpower needed to protect Germany in the final phase of the war.

As would be expected, Colonel Aulock supported Hitler enthusiastically, announcing to all, "I was placed in command of this fortress. I did not request it. I will execute the orders I have received and, doing my duty as a soldier, I will fight to the last stone." Naturally, Hitler was pleased and Aulock's troops were supportive. The French citizens whom Von Aulock had always treated well were shocked. Von Aulock finally convinced the town fathers that the citizens of St. Malo were in harm's way and should evacuate. They objected at first but finally on August 5 approximately 15,000 citizens left and passed through the American lines with white flags.

Prior to this evacuation, the town council pleaded with Colonel Aulock to make St. Malo an open city to obviate its destruction as it was a splendid medieval city and should be preserved. Von Aulock told them that he had already discussed this with Hitler, who replied that there was no such thing in wartime.

The composite of defenses surrounding St. Malo included Dinan to the southwest and St. Brieuc, thirty miles from Dinan which the FFI had already secured. Task Force A bypassed Dinan and it would be taken later. With the continued help from the FFI, Châtelaudren and Guingamp, both west of St. Brieuc, were secured. Thus far, all of the bridges on the double track railway were found to be intact.

The task force continued on to Morlaix, thirty miles west of Guingamp, where the most important railway bridge was located. It was a stone viaduct 1,000 feet in length and 200 feet high. Fortunately, it was intact. The Germans had vacated Morlaix on August 8 without destroying the bridge. General Middleton then directed General Earnest to proceed northeast to the bay of St.-Michel-en-Grève where cargo was to be unloaded. The task force patrolled the coastal region and captured remnants of German units. Within a week, they had captured 2,200 prisoners. Three LSTs (landing ship tanks) came in on August 11 and began unloading.

The FFI and Task Force A then joined forces to attack coastal forts near Paimpol and Paimpol itself. Through Paimpol, the Germans supplied the Channel Islands with men and supplies. A four-day engagement transpired. which included a strongpoint near Paimpol and the town of Paimpol. By August 17 the mission was complete with the capture of 2,000 prisoners. During this time a battalion of the 8th Infantry Division secured the Cap Fréhel area between Dinan and St. Brieuc.

General Bradley became concerned about leaving such a large German force in St. Malo and also thought that it might be a suitable port to help some of the units in Brittany. The peninsula of St. Malo was bordered on the east by the Bay of Mont-St.-Michel and on the west by the Rance River which ran back to Dinan. The Rance River formed a wide estuary at its mouth and Dinard was immediately west of the river on the coast. When the Americans first bypassed St. Malo, small garrisons were pulled in from the region to help defend the multiple fortresses involved in the conglomerate. Troops also came in from the Channel Islands.

Meanwhile, on August 5, when Task Force A left the St. Malo area to clear the Brittany north coast, the 83rd Infantry Division stayed to complete the task already begun. General Macon sent a battalion of the 329th Infantry Regiment (83rd) across the Rance River to cut the Dinan-Dinard road. Resistance was so intense that the battalion was recalled. It became evident to generals Middleton and Macon that they were going to have a tough fight on their hands so General Middleton committed all three regiments of the 83rd Infantry Division to the battle for St. Malo. General Bradley was in agreement.

On August 6 some Germans were burning codes and documents and inadvertently spilled gasoline. The fire that erupted got out of control. The SS troops took this as an incentive to create more fires and did so aggressively. Someone had suggested earlier to the Americans that they cut off the water to St. Malo. The French mayor of an adjacent town led them to the valves, where the Americans turned off the water. Thus the fire spread rapidly. The following morning von Aulock set off demolitions, which were already in place to be detonated. The port and its facilities were completely destroyed. The city burned for a week. The Germans had plenty of food, water, and ammunition, so the destruction of the city did them little harm.

General Middleton realized that he had a tough fight on his hands as St. Malo was heavily fortified by multiple positions. Associated with specific fortresses were many satellite positions as well as numerous cement bunkers well positioned throughout the area to guard every approach into St. Malo. The fortifications of St. Malo were the most advanced of any of the western fortresses. Von Aulock was a veteran of Stalingrad and vowed to make the St. Malo conglomerate "another Stalingrad." By land, St. Malo could only be entered by a causeway which was entirely exposed with water on both sides.

The Todt Organization used the foundations of an old French fort to build a fortress in 1942 with laborers of multiple nationalities, which became the Citadel. Its wall would deflect most of the artillery shells and bombs fired or dropped upon it. It was dug deeply into the ground and the heart of the fortress complex. Cézembre was a small island a few thousand yards off shore, one half mile long and one quarter mile in width which was in a position to protect St. Malo from all sea approaches. Its numerous guns were pointed landward when the American troops arrived and it continued to shell them constantly. The Channel Islands of Jersey, Guernsey, and Alderney could furnish supplies. In the bay, Fort du Petit Bay, Fort du Grand Bay, and Fort National were active artillery emplacements and would have to be dealt with individually.

General Middleton became increasingly concerned about St. Malo and requested that General Earnest probe its defenses with Task Force A. General Earnest split his command into two columns. One attacked Dol and quickly secured it. The other, probing north toward St. Malo, ran into stiff opposition around Châteauneuf, which were the outer defenses of St. Malo.

THE 83RD INFANTRY DIVISION DIVERTED TO ST. MALO

General Middleton believed it essential to clean out St. Malo so he ordered the 83rd Infantry Division, which was headed to Brest, to divert to St. Malo.

Realizing that the battle would take some time, Middleton instructed General Earnest to disengage and proceed westward on his original mission. General Bradley decided that the St. Malo harbor might be valuable as an auxiliary supply port. General Patton agreed, thinking that the Germans would not put up much of a fight. The battle that developed proved General Patton wrong.

St. Malo was a picturesque medieval city separated from the Cotentin Peninsula by the Bay of Mont-St.-Michel. It was the former base of privateers who had preyed on English shipping. The port is actually on the broad estuary of the Rance River. Dinard lies across the river to the west and was a popular resort for British tourist.

Guarding the land entrance into St. Malo was the fifteenth-century château of Anne of Brittany. Although constructed to withstand a siege, it was further strengthened with thick cement walls and contained a generous assortment of cannon and machine guns. To the east was the town of Paramé, formerly a resort area of bourgeois homes and hotels lined with wide boulevards but transformed into an artillery center. St. Servan, a charming fishing village, was just south of St. Malo and was the port for the ferry to Dinard. Other strongpoints were Fort la Varde, east of St. Malo, St. Ideuc on the eastern edge of Paramé, and St. Joseph's Hill positions on the southeast outskirts of St. Malo. All of these forts and emplacements resisted the American troops bitterly and could be supported by the guns of Cézembre. Between St. Malo and St. Servan was the Citadel. Cézembre was a small island between two and three miles offshore, measuring a half mile by one quarter mile. It was in a position to protect St. Malo from all sea approaches. It was bristling with batteries which could fire toward the sea or landward. Offshore were the islands of Jersey, Guernsey, and Alderney, which provided food for the Germans and used as areas to evacuate the wounded.

The three regiments of the 83rd Infantry Division attacked but progress was slow. General Middleton added the 121st Infantry Regiment (8th), a medium tank company and a battalion of the corps artillery. He also requested increased air support. On August 7 the three regiments continued the attack and concentrated on St. Joseph's Hill in the center. The elevated position with its gun emplacements and troop shelters carved into a granite rock quarry continued to hold. For two days artillery and tank destroyers relentlessly pounded the hill with the resulting surrender of more than 400 Germans on August 9. During the preceding five days, the 83rd Infantry Division had captured 3,500 prisoners.

On August 7 while the 83rd Infantry Division was attacking St. Malo, Col. John R. Jeter was taking the 121st Infantry Regiment (8th) across the Rance River to attack Dinard. He dispatched a small unit to Dinan to accept its surrender, which had been promised to the FFI if the Americans would show. The 121st while approaching Dinard received heavy artillery fire and encountered many camouflaged strongpoints which were generously supplied with automatic weapons. In addition, there were underground pillboxes, barbed

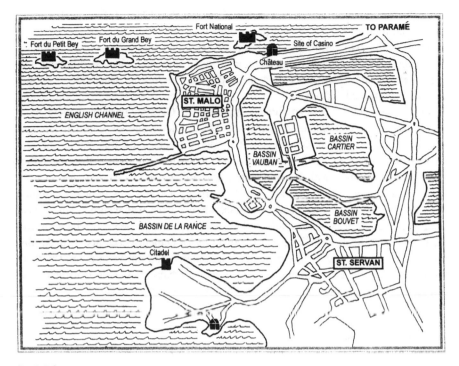

St. Malo

wire, concertina, and extensive minefields. The American artillery was ineffective against the concrete pillboxes.

On August 8 the third battalion of the 121st Infantry Regiment (8th) entered the village of Pleurtuit but were isolated by German forces cutting in behind them. The remainder of the regiment tried desperately to reach them but were unsuccessful. Five small airplanes were destroyed in efforts to drop plasma and in the process of reconnaissance. On August 9 St. Joseph's Hill fell and the 83rd Infantry Division occupied St. Servan and Paramé. Only then was General Macon able to reorganize and send help to the 121st Infantry Regiment (8th). The 331st Infantry Regiment (83rd) crossed the Rance River to support the 121st. Infantry Regiment (8th). Reaching them was painfully slow as the advance was through heavily fortified strongpoints.

Dinard was defended by Colonel Bacherer, who now commanded a veteran group of soldiers. They fought on the Cotentin Peninsula and were remnants of the German 77th Division. When General Macon sent him a surrender ultimatum, he replied: "Every house must become a fortress, every stone a hiding place, and for every stone we shall fight." In spite of this determination, there were overwhelming odds against them, that is, two infantry regiments and the increasing power of additional artillery units. On the afternoon of August 12 the 331st Infantry Regiment (83rd) broke through the German line of defense and reached the isolated battalion of the 121st Infantry Regiment (8th). The men of the 121st had performed well while surrounded.

Finally, the two regiments methodically reduced one pillbox after another. On August 14 both regiments were in Dinard and had cleared adjacent villages. Bacherer's headquarters was captured, including Bacherer. Colonel Bacherer remained defiant.

Once again, the American forces' estimates of German resistance were woefully inaccurate. Throughout Brittany the FFI's knowledge of German strength and positions was quite accurate so the inconsistencies of this battle for and around the fortress of St. Malo are difficult to explain. It is true that the Allies had had little contact with the Resistance and FFI prior to Overlord for security reasons but this was now two and a half months later and this deficiency should have been greatly alleviated. The Resistance knew "what was where." These positions had been in place since 1940 so they were not mobile defenses changing frequently. It is difficult to believe that the quantity of cement necessary to make this segment of the Atlantic Wall essentially impregnable had not been poured without the Resistance and FFI counting cement trucks. Perhaps de Gaulle's arrogance so turned the Americans off that they just did not listen to the French.

ONE FORT AT A TIME

The strongpoints of St. Ideuc and Fort la Varde, small forts on the coast east of Paramé, were next on the agenda. They were attacked by two battalions of the 329th Infantry Regiment (83rd). After three days of artillery bombardment and assault on nearby pillboxes, 160 Germans surrendered at St. Ideuc. The assault immediately switched to Fort la Varde, which surrendered twenty-four hours later with only a force of approximately 100 soldiers. Casino was taken on August 11 but the château less than 1,000 yards away held on tenaciously. Between Casino and the château was an exposed causeway over which the attacking force would have to maneuver without any cover. Bombardment with cannon, even those of eight-inch shells, had little or no effect on the thick concrete walls. The fires within St. Malo had spread and become more volatile and a truce was agreed upon for several hours to allow civilians to escape.

On August 14, following a massive artillery bombardment, an infantry battalion forced its way across the causeway into St. Malo. Although the château garrison continued to fire on the Americans, there was little resistance in the town itself. Finally, in late afternoon of August 14, 150 prisoners surrendered, although the château as a fortress was still intact. The two small offshore islands of Fort National and Grand Bay were approached and Fort National was found abandoned. Grand Bay was seized under a smoke screen with the surrender of 150 prisoners.

Although the Citadel and Cézembre had no value to the Americans, they had to be eliminated to prevent them from shelling Allied shipping to

Granville and Cancal. The Citadel could defend itself against invaders from any direction. Guns from Cézembre and Dinard could help protect it. The interior of the fort was protected by guns positioned to defend the interior. Protection walls constructed of cement, stone, and steel were so thick that they could withstand high-explosive bombs or artillery similar to the U-boat pens at St. Nazaire and Lorient. The interior was well equipped with food, water, and ammunition. The exterior was surrounded by steel rail, barbed wire, and mines. Periscopes provided observation without exposure.

St. Malo was pounded with eight-inch guns, 240mm howitzers, and eight-inch howitzers provided by ten artillery battalions. The lack of effect of all of those guns was demoralizing. The same was true of the air attacks. The walls were just too thick for penetration by modern cannon. Every effort was made to induce Colonel Aulock to surrender his forces so as to avoid more bloodshed on both sides. Loudspeakers were used to urge the German troops to lay down their arms and come out of the fortress. A captured German chaplain was allowed to enter the fortress and appeal to Colonel Aulock to surrender. A young French woman was known to have been friendly with the colonel so the mayor of St. Servan asked her to contact Colonel Aulock and try to persuade him to surrender. This failed as his reply via a subordinate was that he was very busy.

Colonel Aulock was somewhat encouraged by the news he heard from Mortain. A rather strong counterattack there by the Germans initially threatened to break through to Avranches and had that occurred, the American troops at St. Malo would have been between the two German forces. He tried to encourage his troops with this news but it soon became apparent that the counterattack had failed and his troops realized that they were trapped. Colonel Aulock refused to give up because he was "a German soldier and a German soldier did not give up."

On August 11 an aerial attack by medium bombers dropped heavy loads of general-purpose bombs, incendiaries and semi-armor piercing bombs to no avail. Following this bombardment a rifle company accompanied by several engineers and FFI soldiers assaulted the fort. Approximately thirty soldiers scaled the wall and gained the interior court but saw no damage from the air attack. Pole charges were dropped through air vents without effect. Shells from Cézembre began to fall and crossfire from machine gun positions became intense. The assaulting infantry company had to withdraw.

Tank destroyers got into position to bombard with direct fire any gun emplacement opening in the walls with the hope of eliminating some of the guns. They fired on the fort for two days. On August 13 aerial bombardment was repeated. In a twenty-four-hour period, the tank destroyers had fired more than 4,000 shells directly at the fort. On August 15 medium bombers returned for a thirty-minute bombardment. Another infantry assault was driven back by relentless machine-gun fire.

With much frustration, General Macon organized another bombardment by artillery and air force. Guns were placed very close to the fort for direct fire into port holes and vents. Mortars were to fire white phosphorus and high-explosive shells. "Gasoline jell" bombs (the forerunner to napalm) were to be dropped for effect and experimentally.

THE CITADEL FALLS

Just before the bombardment was to begin on August 17, a white flag appeared on top of the Citadel. Aulock was ready to surrender. The bombers, already on their way, were diverted to Cézembre. Four hundred Citadel defenders emerged with Colonel Aulock. The reason that Aulock surrendered was the loss of guns by shells penetrating the apertures at point-blank range and the rapidly progressive demoralization of his troops. They were on the verge of mutiny. Aulock felt that he had done all that he could be reasonably expected to do.

With the exception of Cézembre still to be secured, the St. Malo conglomeration of forts had been neutralized and the north shore cleared of German forces. The 83rd Infantry Division had done a superb job against veteran German troops secured in almost impenetrable fortresses which had been in a stage of defense preparation for four years as a significant part of the Atlantic Wall constructed by the Todt Organization. The division, which had taken in excess of 10,000 prisoners, was then sent to help contain the pockets of St. Nazaire and Lorient, where they would stay for about one month before going on to the eastern front.

While the 83rd Infantry was patrolling the territory around St. Nazaire, German general Botho Elster surrendered 20,000 German soldiers to them with no shots fired. General Elster was leading a large body of German troops out of southern France in front of the advancing U.S. Seventh Army, which had invaded southern France in the area of St. Tropez and were heading north with Elster's group to their front. Feeling the pressure from the trailing Americans and with no vehicles for transportation, Elster realized that his forces could easily be annihilated by the Allied air forces as they marched slowly back toward Germany. Food and water were in short supply. His decision was certainly a humane one.

CÉZEMBRE HOLDS FAST

Attention was now directed toward Cézembre and an opportunity for surrender was extended to the German commander, an unknown lieutenant colonel. He refused, explaining that he was carrying out the orders given him. The small group who delivered the surrender proposal reported that Cézembre was badly damaged. The gun positions and connecting tunnels had been excavated from rock.

On August 18 General Macon, hoping that Aulock's surrender would encourage the lieutenant colonel (he did not give his name) commanding Cézembre to surrender, sent an officer and two enlisted men to the island fortress. An offer to surrender was given him. The lieutenant colonel informed them that the last orders that he had received were to stay and fight. When reminded that Colonel Aulock had surrendered, the lieutenant colonel informed the Americans that his own supply of ammunition was not used up. He was courteous to the Americans and several German soldiers helped the small party launch their boats to return to the mainland. Although the island was a wreck, the coastal guns placed in tunnels of rock were still functioning.

The pursuit to capture Cézembre was delayed for a week. While plans and preparations were being made to capture Brest, a decision was made to eliminate the threat of Cézembre. A sea assault was planned for the 330th Infantry Regiment (83rd), and for this mission the troops of the regiment were given a brief training period. On August 30 and 31 aerial bombardment, including napalm, was carried out. The island was shelled with large-caliber guns continuously. Again, the commander refused to surrender. Another bombardment was carried out on September 1. The HMS *Warspite* fired fifteen-inch armor-piercing shells. The artillery continued to fire salvos to the island with large caliber guns. A third offer to surrender was made and refused by the commander.

On September 2, just as the infantry was loading their amphibious craft, a white flag appeared and was raised. The troops proceeded as planned to the island and accepted the surrender of the fortress. The island's distilling plant had been damaged by a shell or bomb. Three officers and 320 men filed out.

The tenacity of the German troops during this battle of St. Malo is a testimony to the devotion of German troops and their officers to Hitler's orders to fight "to the last man." Each bunker, strongpoint, and fort sustained devastating and relentless bombardment by air, sea, and artillery, yet the troops stuck to their duties as soldiers and time and again stopped the American advances. On the other hand, this battle as much as any other exemplifies the Americans will to win. The soldiers attacked the thick cement walls of the forts time and time again until some small advantage occurred to be quickly exploited by very courageous infantrymen and engineers.

Although the Brittany ports were in shambles and beyond use, their importance at the end of August was much less than considered initially. The war had moved rapidly through Brittany, which was clear of Germans except for those buttoned up in Lorient, St. Nazaire, and Brest. Brest was to be taken and St. Nazaire and Lorient would be contained, thus neutralizing these fortresses as any major threat to the advancing Americans.

It must be evident from the ferocity of these battles, the number of Germans captured, and the American casualty rate that the battle for Brittany was one of the most vicious campaigns that the Allies fought in Europe, yet there has been little recognition given this courageous effort by American troops, these young soldiers fighting against hardened German veterans.

9

Rennes, Lorient, and Nantes

RENNES AND VANNES SECURED

WHEN THE 6TH Armored Division left Pontaubault and headed toward Brest, the 4th Armored Division left Pontaubault on August 1 and headed for Rennes, the capital of Brittany. It was anticipated that Rennes would be strongly defended. As many as ten roads form a hub there. Within sixty miles of Brest are Lorient, St. Nazaire, Quiberon, Nantes, and Vannes. There was some confusion as to whether the 4th Armored Division would stop at Rennes or whether it would proceed to Quiberon. This was the result of conflicting orders between Generals Middleton and Patton. The CCA of the 4th Armored Division covered the forty-mile trip to Rennes by evening. The advanced units ran into stiff opposition and withdrew. The Germans, knowing the value of this road junction to the Americans, reinforced the small garrison with infantry, which was well supplied with machine guns and minefields. The resistance increased and General Wood realized that he needed more of a force than the 4th Armored to take the city. He requested a regimental infantry combat team plus air support. Early on the evening of August 2, the 13th Infantry Regiment (8th) boarded trucks for Rennes. The remainder of the 4th Armored Division reached Rennes on August 2.

General Wood knew that the 8th Infantry Division was headed to Rennes so he made a plan that would extricate his division from Brittany and head eastward. He directed his division around the western part of the city and then sent it toward Châteaubriant to the southeast and then on to Angers on the Loire River. This would block the Brittany Peninsula from Rennes to Angers rather than from Rennes to Quiberon as originally planned. This plan ignored Quiberon Bay. Two columns of the 4th Armored Division circled Rennes on the west by two arcs and proceeded south to the Bain-de-Bretagne and Derval, encountering only token opposition. Seven of the ten roads leading into Rennes had been cut.

On August 2 the 13th Infantry Regiment (8th) moved out of its new command post east of Ducey. The 13th Infantry Regiment was attached to the 4th Armored Division in the drive to capture Rennes and would become a motorized infantry regiment. They set out for the high ground where the 4th Armored Division was in a holding position. On August 3 the 13th Infantry Regiment (8th) moved within two miles of the city. General Wood, 4th Armored Division commander, ordered an attack for 5:00 P.M. The first battalion led the attack and on the outskirts of the city encountered small arms fire and fire from 20mm cannon. An intense battle took place, but finally the enemy began to withdraw. The casualties were high for Company C of the first battalion. By the next morning, the 13th Infantry Regiment (8th) held all positions northeast of the city and prepared to advance into the city proper.

On the morning of August 4 the Germans began to burn installations, supplies, and buildings. By 4 P.M. the 13th Infantry Regiment command post was able to move into the city and the remainder of the advance into the city was more or less an uncontested walkthrough. The civilians took to the streets with tears of joy and appreciation. The soldiers were showered with flowers and fruit and the French shouted "Vive l'America." The mission of the 13th Infantry Regiment (8th) then became one of guarding the main roads and junctions leading into the city and to protecting St. Jacques Airport on the southeastern edge of the city. Immediate preparations were made and troops were positioned to battle a German counterattack.

The 4th Armored Division captured some of the German units trying to escape. The 13th Infantry Regiment (8th) kept the pressure on from the north. The German defenses crumbled and the 2,000 German troops there departed early morning of August 4. They remained off of the main highways and, with motorized units and foot troops, reached St. Nazaire five days later. The remainder of the 8th Infantry Division reached Rennes and the city was secured.

At this point, some confusion arose. General Middleton was tempted to send the 4th Armored Division east to Châteaubriant. Finally, after much thought, he instructed General Wood to block the bridges on the Vilaine River from Rennes to Quiberon. The Vilaine River runs south westward from Rennes so this would essentially cut off the Brittany Peninsula.

General Middleton visited General Wood and Wood almost persuaded Middleton to let him turn eastward unrestricted. The outcome was a compromise, with Wood agreeing to block all the roads south of Rennes but not to disturb the units already headed eastward. At Third Army HQ, Maj. Gen. Hugh J. Gaffey, the Third Army chief of staff, picked up on this and immediately issued messages to Wood and Middleton that General Patton had not changed his plans and was expecting the 4th Armored Division to head for Vannes and Lorient. Adding to this controversy was the fact that the 4th Armored Division was about out of gas. This problem was resolved and on the morning of August 5 Wood ordered CCA (4th) to advance to Vannes, which they did in seven hours. The FFI had secured the airport and guided the 4th Armored

Division to the best approaches to the city. Vannes was so quickly secured that the Germans accomplished no destruction of the city.

4TH ARMORED DIVISION ATTACKED ON OUTSKIRTS OF LORIENT

On August 6, the enemy counterattacked from Auray and drove back the outpost of CCA (4th). Col. Bruce Clarke, commander of CCA (4th), sent a strong task force that cleared Auray and went beyond to seize a bridge across the Blavet River at Hennebont. When they arrived they found the bridge demolished. During this time, General Dager's CCB (4th) had driven directly toward Lorient. They reached the city on August 7 and, finding strong defenses, turned north through the village of Pont Scorf. As the advance guard entered the town, German artillery became overwhelming and they could go no further. What happened there is described in *The Fourth Armored Division: From the Beach to Bavaria* by Capt. Kenneth Koyen:

> The CCB (4th) Headquarters vehicles had just pulled into the two fields when the first shells whistled in. For two hours, the headquarters and attached infantry were held down and blasted by murderous shell fire. At least one battery of German artillery rained high explosive rounds into an area less than 500 yards square. The artillery was carefully observed and corrected. Shells sought out single halftracks and blew them up with direct hits that exploded mines, shells, and gasoline. Men were killed crouching beside and under vehicles. Hedgerows were no protection. Shells hit on both sides and on top of them. Splinters slashed tires, halftrack plates, and flesh. Finally the Germany artillery observers, a lieutenant and a sergeant, were hunted out on a nearby hill and killed. Twenty 4th Armored Division men were killed and 85 wounded. Five halftracks, six jeeps, two trucks, and armored cars were destroyed completely and a score more vehicles badly damaged. The dead were buried one day later where they fell south of Pont Scorf. The French still tend the graves.

There is a beautiful, large granite monument near Pont Scorf where the 4th Armored Division was stopped. This monument honors the 4th and 6th Armored divisions and the 94th and 66th Infantry divisions, as well as several French units. It was erected by the French in appreciation for the combat of those divisions in and about Lorient.

LORIENT CONTAINED

CCA (4th) soon arrived and a thin line around Lorient began to materialize between Hennebont and Pont Scorf. Probing patrols were thwarted by intense artillery fire. It became apparent that Lorient was very heavily defended and General Wood realized that it would take much more than his armored division to take Lorient. General Wood believed that at least one infantry division supported by corps artillery, additional air power, and naval forces would be necessary to take the city. Actually, it would probably have required two or three infantry divisions plus attached artillery and engineer units.

The military forces in Lorient outnumbered the 4th Armored Division five to one. Five hundred field pieces were estimated to be positioned throughout the pocket. The FFI reported that the Germans had large quantities of ammunition and food and could sustain a long siege. Antitank ditches, mines, barbed wire, and numerous automatic weapons with interlocking fields of fire were prevalent. Allied observation planes could not operate because of the heavy flak that immediately obstructed any attempt to use them for reconnaissance or direction of artillery fire. General Wood was relieved to receive orders from General Middleton to hold his armor at a safe distance and not to become involved in a fight unless the enemy attacked.

Gen. Wilhelm Fahrmbacher, German commander of the Lorient pocket, later claimed that if Wood had developed a strong attack between August 6 and 9, the fortress probably would have fallen. Each day, however, the German defense became more organized and Fahrmbacher thought his defensive position was adequate. The number of military personnel had swelled from 12,000 to 25,000 with the influx of German soldiers retreating from Normandy. Most of these were experienced combat soldiers, some of them having fought in North Africa as well as at Normandy. The naval personnel were retrained for frontline defensive and artillery units.

General Wood tried unsuccessfully to get the Lorient garrison to surrender from August 6 to 16. The 4th Armored Division contained Lorient and waited for another unit to take over the containment of the Lorient pocket so the 4th Armored could resume cavalry warfare toward the east. During the first twelve days of August, the 4th Armored Division captured 5,000 prisoners and destroyed or captured 250 vehicles. Their own losses were 98 soldiers killed, 362 wounded, and 11 missing. Fifteen tanks and eleven vehicles were lost. Although quite successful, they did not capture Lorient, their objective. It was subsequently theorized that if Middleton and Wood had been more aggressive toward the Quiberon Peninsula and Lorient, the division might have arrived before the German garrison had strengthened their defenses with the additional troops from Normandy. Generals Patton and Wood remained bitter about the detainment of the cavalry for the Brittany ports. In retrospect, it is dubious that Brest, Lorient, or St. Nazaire could have been taken had the American arrived a few days earlier.

Now that the VIII Corps had a loose hold on the Brittany Peninsula and General Wood was bitterly complaining about having to remain there carrying out an infantry division's duties, some decision had to be made about the immediate strategy in Brittany.

On August 8, Generals Middleton and Patton held a conference and General Patton informed General Middleton that securing the Brittany Peninsula still remained the responsibility of the VIII Corps. Capture of Brest and St. Malo held priority over the capture of Lorient. General Wood would have to continue to contain Lorient until enough forces were available in Brittany to help him take Lorient. General Middleton was in a difficult position as he had too many objectives to be satisfied at one time and his forces were fanned out all over Brittany. He could only proceed with one objective at a time. Wood would have to sit tight on Lorient for the present.

NANTES SECURED

General Patton told General Middleton to send some troops to Nantes to relieve an American task force that was containing the city. Instead of dispatching troops of the 8th Division, which were in Rennes, Middleton instructed Wood to continue to contain Lorient but to send a combat command to Nantes and relieve the unit. On the morning of August 10 Wood sent Colonel Clarke's CCA (4th) to Nantes. The next day, Clarke relieved a battalion of the 5th Infantry Division. That night, heavy explosions were heard, indicating that the Germans were destroying ammunition dumps and installations. French civilians informed Clarke's force that the Germans were withdrawing. During the afternoon of August 12, the FFI led Clarke's troops through the minefields into the city. The city was secured quickly. On August 13 the 4th Armored passed from control of the VIII Corps and was relieved at Lorient by the 6th Armored Division on August 16. The 4th Armored Division departed eastward.

On August 12, 1944, the 6th Armored Division began redeploying its troops to relieve the 4th Armored Division at Lorient. They found Vannes secured by the FFI. CCA of the 6th Armored Division went to Plouay and relieved CCB of the 4th Armored Division. The 6th Armored Division found the line to be naturally divided into three sections. The first was the Quiberon Peninsula. The second was the area between Belze and the Blavet River below Hennebont, which included a section west that lay between the Scorf and Blavet rivers. The third and most important was a section west of the Scorf River extending to a point three miles south to the coast.

The rapid advance from Avranches to Rennes, Vannes, and Nantes involved many additions to prior warfare. One was the tactical involvement with the XIX Tactical Air Command (TAC) of the Ninth Air Force with the Third Army for a spectacular air-ground offensive. The ground-support parties of the XIX TAC turned their vehicles into the leading column of the 4th Armored Division and called in the P-47s to attack targets ahead of the tanks. The P-47s were immediately available as they were maintaining an umbrella of protection over the tank column. When "Egg Cup" (ground control unit) called "Yellow Leader" (air group code name), the response was immediate with a bombing run followed by a strafing run that cleared many German units with hardly any delay for the advancing column of tanks. The planes also preceded the tanks on reconnaissance patrols to take out any obvious targets in front of the tanks.

General Grow, commander of the 6th Armored Division, recalled the relief of General Wood and the 4th Armored Division, and considered it the most informal and briefest that he had ever heard of in military history. Neither got out of their cars when General Grow arrived as General Wood was in his car ready to leave. General Wood said words to the effect: "We're off, its all yours! And we're gone."

10

Battle for Brest

SURRENDER OFFER DECLINED—ATTACK DELAYED

GENERAL GROW DECIDED to offer surrender to the German garrison in Brest on August 8, 1944. A four-man patrol approached Brest in a jeep covered with white cloth. Maj. Ernest W. Mitchell and M.Sgt. Alex Castle were the two emissaries chosen to deliver the surrender offer. They were blindfolded and led to a building in the city. The blindfolds were removed and they found themselves standing before several German officers. Sergeant Castle, who spoke German, read to them the surrender ultimatum. The German commander said that he could not surrender. Mitchell asked him if he understood the surrender offer and the consequences of his refusal. He replied that he understood. Mitchell took back the surrender document and the two Americans were blindfolded and taken back to the line.

General Grow decided to attack the next day, August 9. The ground attack would be led by CCR (6th) on the right, CCB (6th) in the center, and CCA (6th) on the left. The attack would start on the northeast perimeter of the city. However, the attack was not to materialize on that day. Reports began coming in of sporadic firing from the rear. Small groups of Germans in vehicles had appeared and were heading into Brest. Late in the day a field artillery battalion captured Lt. Gen. Carl Spang, commander of the German 266th Division. Documents captured revealed that the 266th Division had supplied troops to Dinan and St. Malo and the remainder were going to Brest to strengthen that garrison. Spang and members of his staff were preceding the main body of the 266th Division so as to prepare for them in Brest. He was completely unaware that the Americans were in front of him.

General Grow called off the attack and a containing force was left outside of Brest. The 6th Armored Division reversed its direction to meet the Germans in their rear. Small firefights began during the night and turned into a full-scale battle the next morning. All three of Grow's combat commands

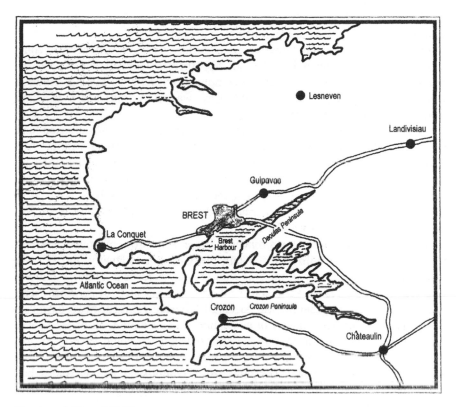

Brest and Tip of Brittany

engaged the enemy. By evening, a thousand prisoners had been taken and approximately half of the unit had been destroyed. An additional day was required to round up the remaining groups of the 266th Division. The 6th Armored then formed a containing ring around the land side of Brest out of artillery range. Brest was thus sealed off. An airfield was cleared and adequate communication facilities were restored.

General Grow decided to secure a good jump-off spot to begin an attack and selected the high ground near Guipavas where his artillery would have an advantage and could support the infantry into the city without having to move their guns. However, efforts to secure the high ground failed and it became apparent that a much greater force would be necessary for the battle for Breast. Additional artillery, air support, engineers, and infantry were all essential to break down the outer defenses of Breast. The enemy artillery was very strong, which General Middleton had predicted after reviewing the aerial photographs of other fortresses in the Atlantic Wall. St. Malo had not yet fallen, so the additional forces needed to capture Brest would not be available until St. Malo was secured. Middleton advised General Grow that it would be unwise to attack Brest until he had a more dominating force with which to assault this strongly defended garrison.

On August 12 General Grow received orders to leave one combat command at Brest to contain it and send the others to Lorient and Vannes to relieve the 4th Armored Division. He completed the relief of the 4th Armored Division on August 14. Left to guard Brest was CCA (6th) and a battalion from the 8th Infantry Division.

General Grow was very proud of the performance of his division and rightly so. The division had cleared a 200-mile corridor through central Brittany, destroyed the remnants of the German 266th Division, and bottled up the remainder in Brest. He remained bitter about his next assignment to contain Lorient and St. Nazaire as he felt that a static war was best assigned to infantry and artillery and that his armored division would serve best in exploitation of new ground toward Germany.

The FFI had become much stronger and General Grow recommended that the French troops be utilized to contain the Germans. Actually, the FFI did just that for the remainder of the war with greater increasing numbers and distinguished themselves as very able soldiers. The question of whether Brest could have been taken had the 6th Armored Division reached it two days earlier remains to this day a matter of conjecture. In considering all of the factors pro and con, it is doubtful that a lone armored division could have taken this well fortified fortress when it arrived on August 6. This cannot be considered a failure. The 6th Armored Division had accomplished an incredible feat which received very little acclaim because of activity elsewhere on a more impressive scale.

During the middle of August, the Germans were withdrawing faster than the Allies had anticipated. The 21st Army Group was pursuing the Germans to the east and the 12th Army Group was advancing toward the west. Although the Allies had planed to stop at the Seine River for about two weeks, General Eisenhower now thought it imperative to cross the Seine as quickly as possible so as not to allow the Germans any time to build up a meaningful defense line along the Seine. For this to happen and to have sufficient logistical support, capture of ports along the Channel and on the Brittany Coast had to be accomplished quickly as only Cherbourg and some minor ports were in service. Troops and vehicles were pouring out of Normandy toward Brittany and eastward toward the Seine and ultimately to Paris. Massive tonnage of supplies was requisite to support this migration with ever-lengthening supply lines. Most of the supplies were still coming in over the beaches. The rapid progress of the 12th and 21st army groups had created a critical demand on supplies. Cherbourg was handling even fewer supplies than anticipated. There were American divisions in the United States awaiting transfer to the ETO. Eisenhower wrote to Montgomery to impress upon him the necessity for capturing and preparing ports to receive them.

PREPARATION FOR THE ATTACK

In the last week of August, the initial attack on Brest coincided with the pursuit of the Germans beyond the Seine. Generals Eisenhower and Bradley expected the Breton ports to fall within a relatively short period of time. Unfortunately, the defense of these ports was grossly underestimated. A plan formulated to construct a port complex on Quiberon Bay became too much of an engineering problem. Therefore, Brest was elected as a prime target.

General Middleton's VIII Corps were widely dispersed and he found himself responsible for guarding a southern flank of 250 miles. He did not have available to him the sufficient troops to attack Brest. General Bradley transferred the 2nd and 29th Infantry divisions to Middleton from the First Army as well as two Ranger battalions. The Communications Zone took on the responsibility of Rennes and released the 8th Infantry Division to Middleton. General Middleton knew that the battle for Brest would depend heavily upon infantry, artillery, engineers, and air force so he was elated to gain these three infantry divisions. He released the 4th and 6th Armored divisions to return to the direct control of General Patton. He considered the 2nd Infantry Division a first-class unit commanded by Maj. Gen. Walter M. Robertson with whom he had served on the Fort Leavenworth faculty. The 8th Infantry Division was commanded by Gen. Donald A. Stroh whom Middleton admired as a fine combat soldier who had a splendid record in North Africa and Sicily. The 29th Infantry Division was a National Guard unit from Pennsylvania, commanded by Maj. Gen. Charles Gerhardt, who had been a quarterback for West Point in 1916. Additionally a cavalry unit and two Ranger battalions commanded by Col. Earl Rudder were to join Middleton's forces. Rudder became president of Texas A&M postwar. Middleton considered him one of the finest combat soldiers he had ever known. Task Force A and FFI units were available and on sight so Middleton had gathered experienced forces with which to attack Brest but had to wait for sufficient supplies to arrive before he could launch his attack.

Finally, all was in order and General Middleton launched his attack on August 24, 1944. It was necessary to suspend operations after three days for lack of artillery ammunition. Arrangements were quickly made to speed up the supply line to Brest but it was not until September 7 that enough ammunition was on hand to renew the attack. General Bradley gave this attack high priority on artillery ammunition, so essential for this type of ground war attacking formidable defensive positions.

General Middleton's VIII Corps passed from Third Army to Lieutenant General Simpson's Ninth Army on September 10. The Ninth Army was responsible for protecting the southern flank of the 12th Army Group and for the operations at Brest. General Simpson wanted to send the 6th Armored Division back to the eastward moving Third Army so he brought in the newly arrived 94th Infantry Division, commanded by Maj. Gen. Harry J. Maloney to take over the responsibility of containing Lorient and St. Nazaire.

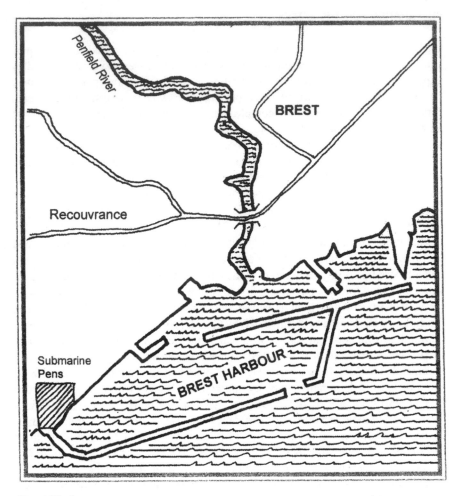

Brest Harbor

The terrain around Brest was ideal for defensive positions with its many streams and rolling hills. The Germans took full advantage of ground prominences to construct pillboxes and gun emplacements. Barbed wire, minefields, and antitank ditches surrounded the inner city. Ancient French forts constructed in the seventeenth century were reinforced with outer walls and inner partitions of thick concrete.

Approximately 30,000 troops were in the Brest Fortress, many more than originally estimated. General Ramcke became commander when he came in with his 2nd Parachute Division, a unit of veteran soldiers who had made the airborne assault on Crete in 1940. They represented the best that Hitler had to offer. Col. Hermann von der Mosel, former commander of Brest, became second in command with Ramcke's arrival.

HERMANN-BERNARD RAMCKE

Hermann-Bernard Ramcke was born January 24, 1889, in a rural area of Germany where his family had a farm. He enlisted in the German navy when quite young and subsequently transferred to the marine infantry during World War I. He was awarded the Iron Cross, 2nd and 1st class, as well as the Military Cross. After being promoted to ensign, he transferred to the army in 1919 and earned the Badge of Gold for being wounded five times. Rising quickly through the ranks, Ramcke was promoted to lieutenant colonel in 1937. With the help of an elder German officer, he was able to transfer to the Luftwaffe, which controlled the paratroops in 1940. Following a rigorous training period at age fifty-one, he parachuted into Crete with his unit and again distinguished himself. He was awarded the Knight's Cross and promoted to major general.

In North Africa, while under General Rommel's Afrika Corps command, Ramcke formed the "Ramcke Brigade" which fought at El Alamein. His unit was cut off by the British during an attack and he led his men through the British lines and across the desert to their own line. In the process, he and his men captured a British supply convoy, which they used for their own transport. For this venture, Ramcke was awarded the Oak Leaves to his Knight's Cross. He subsequently transferred to the Russian front where he was involved in numerous actions.

General Ramcke and his paratroop unit were chosen by Hitler to defend Brest in June 1944. He, like other commanders of Hitler's fortresses on the Atlantic Wall, took an oath to defend "to the last man." General Middleton offered him an opportunity to surrender several times, which he refused. He finally surrendered on September 19, 1944, after becoming convinced that further opposition was useless. Having been an enlisted man, he held his troops in high esteem and thought it inhumane for any more to be sacrificed in battle. While in prison, he was presented the Swords and Diamonds to his Knight's Cross through the Swiss Red Cross. While a prisoner in Mississippi, he sneaked out one night, bought stamps, and mailed a letter to a U.S. congressman complaining of the poor treatment the German prisoners of war (POWs) were receiving. He sneaked back in, undetected by the guards. His letter created an uproar in Congress, but thereafter the POWs received better treatment.

General Ramcke was sent to a French prison and escaped to Germany to object to so many Germans being held without formal charges. He returned to prison voluntarily, was tried and sentenced to five years, but given credit for having served all but three months. In 1957 he was released and entered business in Germany.

It is somewhat ironic that Generals Middleton and Ramcke opposed each other in the battle for Brest. There were certainly similarities in their lives and professions. Both grew up in farming country and both enlisted in the service of their country. Neither had an advantage of upper-class status nor the opportunity to go to West Point or to the German equivalent. Both progressed rapidly through the ranks. Both had long combat records in both world wars and both were decorated numerous times. They respected each other as professional soldiers and maintained a correspondence postwar. During Ramcke's trial in France, General Middleton issued a statement to the effect that he did not understand why the French had him on trial. As far as General Middleton was concerned, Ramcke always conducted himself according to the rules of war. "Papa" Ramcke, as he was called by some of his men, died of natural causes July 5, 1968.

On August 18, the VIII Corps moved its command post to Lesneven, fifteen miles from Brest. General Middleton expected a stiff fight just as he had encountered at St. Malo. The Allies expected Ramcke to make a strong stand in defense of Brest. He was a hard-core German soldier and would obey Hitler's orders to fight to the last man.

A rather strange correspondence between Generals Ramcke and Middleton began on August 19 and continued throughout the campaign. Ramcke opened this with a letter to the American commander, whom Ramcke thought was General Grow. In this first letter Ramcke complained that German prisoners were being turned over to the FFI, who had taken their personal belongings and threatened to shoot them. Ramcke implied that if his soldiers who were captured were not treated well, he would change his method of treating the Allied prisoners of war.

General Middleton wrote back the next day and stated emphatically that Americans did not mistreat prisoners of war and allowed no one else to do so. He stated that Americans took prisoners from the FFI whenever possible. He added that he was not aware of any mistreatment of German prisoners by any of the Allied countries. There was no further discussion on this issue between the two.

TASK FORCE B COMMITTED

General Middleton made a preliminary move to protect his flanks, seal off any escape across the harbor, and attack Hill 154, which would give the VIII Corps a vantage point to ward off approaches to Brest from the south. For these missions a new Task Force B was formed under Brig. Gen. James A. Van Fleet.

Task Force B began the attack on August 21 but after a few miles was stopped by a deadly barrage from Hill 154 and batteries north of the Elon River. As usual, the defenders were well dug in and surrounded by barbed wire, minefields, and reinforced pillboxes, typical of those in St. Malo. This initial thrust was indicative of the difficulty that could be anticipated in trying to take Brest.

A battalion of the 38th Infantry Regiment (2nd) assaulted the hill on August 23 and with the support of tank destroyers and artillery finally gained the crest of the hill. S. Sgt. Alvin Casey alone destroyed a pillbox with grenades but lost his life in this heroic deed. Task Force B pushed on to take the remainder of the hill. Pillboxes and gun emplacements were destroyed with flame throwers, artillery, and demolitions.

On August 27 General Ramcke wrote to General Middleton again and with the letter sent back to Middleton one medical officer and eight corpsmen personnel, adding that he assumed that Middleton would need them. He further stated that Fortress Brest was so well supplied with medical personnel that American prisoners of war who were wounded were receiving excellent medical care. A little "one-upsmanship" had entered the picture.

His request with this letter was for the Americans to quit shelling their field hospital, which was apart from any military targets. He enclosed a plan showing where each medical facility was located and each marked with a red cross. He called attention to the Geneva Convention, to which he strictly adhered, and requested that Middleton remind his subordinates of the articles of the Geneva Convention. He continued to explain the protection and care he was giving the American wounded. The ships traversing the harbor with red crosses were only for the transportation of the wounded and should be spared bombardment. In closing he asked for a reply.

General Middleton knew that General Ramcke was a sly old fox and that he had mixed medical buildings in with other buildings so that military targets could not be bombarded without hitting a few buildings with red crosses. He answered the next day, acknowledging the receipt of the letter and the medical personnel. He made it clear to Ramcke that although he appreciated the return of the medical personnel, they were not needed by the American command. Middleton advised Ramcke that the buildings with red crosses were widely dispersed throughout the area and it would be impossible to miss some of them, although any hits would be unintentional. He advised Ramcke to cluster the medical buildings in one sector removed from military installations. He assured Ramcke that the German prisoners were receiving excellent care and that any damage to medical buildings in Brest would be entirely unintentional.

By the last day of August, the entire Daoulas peninsula was cleared and 2,700 prisoners taken. Task Force B was dissolved and Task Force A was positioned to guard the approaches to the Crozon Peninsula. The last remaining unit of the 6th Armored was sent to Lorient to rejoin its own division.

TASK FORCE S FORMED TO CLEAR THE TIP OF BRITTANY

General Middleton next formed Task Force S, commanded by Col. Leroy H. Watson, to clear the tip of Brittany between Brest and Le Conquet. The newly formed unit cut the highway between the two cities on August 27. Moving west, the radar station at Ponte de Corson was taken. Lochrist and Le Conquet fell on September 9. The German commander surrendered his fortress and a thousand men. Task Force S had completed its mission and was dissolved.

The main attack on Brest was scheduled for August 25. General Middleton's three infantry divisions, the 2nd, 8th and 29th, would lead the attack abreast. These units first engaged the German defense perimeter which formed an irregular semicircle around the mouth of the Penfeld River. Two defense lines had been formed by the Germans. The outer line was newly constructed during the few months preceding this attack. The inner circle, much stronger than the outer one, was fortified with permanent defenses built or reinforced in the early 1940s for protection of the naval base. The Germans were mainly dependent on the outer line as the inner one, although very strong, lacked depth.

BOMBARDMENT BY SEA AND AIR

General Middleton arranged for a heavy air bombardment as well as a barrage from the sea by the British battleship *Warspite*. The latter was to fire on the coastal batteries near Le Conquet. Flying Fortresses attacked Brest and started a large fire in Recouvrance. The *Warspite* bombarded the coastal guns at Le Conquet and Recouvrance in sequence. The Corps battalions joined the fray and added significant destruction to the German defensive positions. Several ships were sunk in the harbor. In spite of this intensive bombardment, the ground attack made little progress.

Royal Air Force (RAF) bombers bombarded Brest on the night of August 25–26. The following morning, the U.S. Air Force made a similar attack. Again, the German defense held the three American divisions at bay. This lack of progress made it clear to the American commanders that the Brest defense had been clearly underestimated. This realization rung true time after time during the battle of the Cotentin Peninsula and Brittany. Commanders realized that tactics must change from a purely frontal assault. Another detracting factor was the supply of artillery ammunition had been much less than Middleton thought necessary for this battle. This accentuated the necessity of capturing Brest or some other significant ports so this failure of supply would not slow the progress of the ground units.

The commanders of all units, large and small, began to study the German defenses in detail to try to detect soft spots that might be exploited. They began choosing smaller objectives and concentrating on them one at a time. These weak spots were found and exploited. Pillboxes, weapons, and gun emplacements were identified. A concentrated bombardment would address each one and the infantry would follow with demolitions and flamethrowers. It was a battle of study, patience, and surprise attacks that gradually gave the intended result. During the remainder of August air support and delivery of supplies were curtailed by rainy weather.

On August 28 a regiment of the 29th Infantry Division advanced two miles and on the following day the 8th Infantry Division had made a significant gain in one sector of its line. Unfortunately, the Germans cut off and isolated two infantry companies and marched them off as prisoners. The 2nd Infantry Division made slow progress and casualties were high; that division had been assigned the largest sector.

On September 1 the supply of ammunition improved as did the weather. General Middleton organized another joint attack. A strike by medium bombers was followed by a forty-five-minute artillery barrage. In spite of almost continuous bombardment by artillery, only the 8th Infantry Division was able to made a small gain.

General Middleton was very discouraged about the quality of his troops, late replacements, inadequate ammunition supplies, and lackluster air support. The Germans remained strong and gave no indication of weakening. Middleton requested more and bigger guns and an improvement in the quality of air support. In response, both generals Eisenhower and Bradley conferred with Maj. Gen. Hoyt Vandenberg and urged him to increase the quality and size of the air support to Middleton's VIII Corps for the battle for Brest.

THE NOOSE TIGHTENS

Fortunately, a break came on September 2 when Hill 105 southwest of Guipavas was captured by the 2nd Infantry Division, a key terrain east of the city for Brest's defense. There followed an advance by the 8th Infantry Division to take a similar hill.

The three divisions carried on their individual offenses for five days supported by daily attacks of medium and heavy bombers. The noose around Brest was gradually and progressively tightening. The siege area became small enough that heavy bombers could no longer attack without endangering the Americans with scattered bombs.

On September 8 Middleton launched a coordinated attack with the three divisions, six surveillance planes per division, and strong artillery barrages preceding the infantry assault. With this attack force, all three divisions advanced. One thousand prisoners were taken. American casualties were light. Middleton was optimistic for the first time.

On September 9, following the arrival of two trainloads of ammunition, the artillery bombardment pace was stepped up and advances were accomplished on the entire line. The 2nd and 8th Infantry divisions reached the streets of Brest. The 29th Infantry Division entered the village of Penfeld. During that one day 2500 prisoners were taken.

Thus far the battle was going well. However, once the American troops entered the city of Brest, the difficulty for them increased rapidly. House-to-house street fighting ensued with the Germans holding on to each building tenaciously. The German cannon and machine guns were well concealed and there was no way to see them until they fired their guns, often too late for the advancing American soldiers. Progress was slow as often it was necessary to blast a hole in the wall of the exit house as well as the next house to be entered and secured. It became a squad- and platoon-type warfare with each small unit mapping out its own way of getting the job done, slowly clearing a small segment of a city block. Finally, the 8th Infantry Division reached the old wall on September 11.

The 8th Infantry Division was moved to the Crozon Peninsula to silence artillery guns and to block any escape of the German garrison across the harbor. To cover the absence of the 8th Infantry Division, General Gerhardt attacked near St. Pierre on September 11. On September 12, units of the 29th Infantry Division advanced toward Hill 97 and toward French forts Keranroux and Montbarey.

OFFER FOR SURRENDER REFUSED

On that same day General Middleton sent a messenger to carry a proposal to General Ramcke for surrender so as to stop the unnecessary killing. Middleton listed all of the negatives associated with the present position of the German garrison. He went on to inform General Ramcke that the German soldiers as prisoners of war would be treated humanely and with respect. He also told Ramcke that the port of Brest had lost its significance with the acquisition of other ports.

General Ramcke's reply the following day was brief and to the point. He merely stated that he had to turn down the proposal. Middleton then ordered that a copy of this exchange be copied and reach every Allied soldier in the Brest campaign. An accompanying note read, "General Ramcke has been given an opportunity to surrender. Since he has declined what is believed to be a humane and reasonable request, it now remains for the VIII Corps to make him sorry for his refusal. Therefore, I ask the combat soldiers of this command to enter the fray with renewed vigor—let's take them apart and get the job finished."

A 29th Infantry Division battalion advanced on Fort Keranroux on September 13 as the air force and artillery units bombarded them. Two infantry companies crossed open land and secured the front entrance. One hundred Germans surrendered.

Fort Montbarey was next on the agenda but was more strongly constructed with very thick walls and surrounded by a moat. The fort was surrounded by an outer perimeter of defense. This line included many gun positions and extensive minefields at its front. The engineers, recognizing a very difficult approach to the fort, requested a unit of flame-throwing tanks. A squadron of the British 141st Regiment responded with fifteen Crocodiles, a Churchill tank with a flamethrower and a trailer of fuel.

On September 14, four Crocodiles advanced through a path cleared of mines by the engineers. Two of the tanks wandered off course and were destroyed. The attack was aborted. For a day and a half the fort was bombarded. At dawn, September 16, Crocodiles advanced through the cleared path again and were within eighty-five yards of the fort. A breach was made in the main gate with cannon firing from 200 yards. The hole was enlarged by the engineers with demolition charges. The German garrison, having been battered relentlessly for several days, surrendered.

Resistance began to disintegrate in the old city as combat patrols began to enter. The 5th Ranger Battalion captured the fort at Pointe du Petit Minor and Forts de Mengant and de Dellec. This thrust by the Rangers cleared the western shoreline on the harbor. By the end of September, the submarine pens and Fort du Portzie were the only positions that remained and these capitulated the following morning. By September 16 the 2nd Infantry Division had reached the city wall and quickly scaled the wall and advanced rapidly to the water's edge. The German capitulation soon followed on September 18. Von der Mosel surrendered the troops in Recouvrance to the 29th Infantry Division Colonel Erich Pietzonka surrendered the eastern portion of the city to the 2nd Infantry Division in President Wilson Square. Nearly 10,000 German troops surrendered. Ramcke had escaped to the Crozon Peninsula.

RAMCKE SURRENDERS

The Crozon Peninsula had been contained since August 27 when a cavalry squadron cut across its base. After Task Force B had secured the Daoulas Peninsula, Task Force A moved into Crozon. The 8th Infantry Division moved onto Crozon in mid-September and General Stroh directed an attack that overran the defenses of the German 343rd Division. General Ramcke surrendered this section on September 17. On September 19, the final action on Crozon took place. Only a few diehards remained with Ramcke. Remaining arrogant, Ramcke, in preparation to surrender, sent a message to Brig. Gen. Charles D. W. Canham, assistant commander of the 8th Infantry Division, requesting his credentials. General Canham replied that his troops were his credentials. Thereafter, on the afternoon of September 19, Ramcke surrendered. Between September 15 and 19, the 8th Infantry Division had taken 7635 prisoners while losing seventy-two men killed and 415 wounded.

The last German station surrendered on September 20 when Task Force A drove down to Douarnencz to demand the surrender of an isolated group of 300 Germans. They refused at first but when given "an offer they couldn't refuse," they decided to surrender.

Like most of the fortresses on Hitler's Atlantic Wall, there were massive thick walled forts that had been standing but reinforced with additional concrete walls and partitions by the Todt Organization beginning in 1940. At

Brest these were mostly located on high ground, giving an excellent observation of the surrounding terrain. The Americans had to find weak spots between these strongpoints and exploit any avenue to gain access to them. Aerial and artillery bombardment then followed and one by one these defensive positions fell but it was a slow process, small victories coming one at a time. In the long run, the Germans in the remaining strongpoints became demoralized from the relentless pounding by the artillery and air support so they were only too eager to surrender after a brief show of force. The air bombardment usually focused on gun emplacements behind the main line of resistance, thereby preventing reinforcements from coming in. Also, it tended to force the gun crews to leave the guns and seek cover. From August 25 to September 19, air support was continuous except during bad weather.

During the battle for Brest, the Americans captured 38,000 Germans. The 2nd Infantry Division had 2,314 casualties and the 29th Infantry Division had lost 329 killed and 2317 wounded. The 8th Infantry Division had approximately 1500 casualties in the month of September.

On September 19, General Middleton wrote an end to the siege of Brest:

TO: All Officers and Enlisted Men who form a part of the VIII Corps

In the capture of Brest and adjacent territory by the officers and enlisted men who form a part of the VIII Corps, a chapter in history is made. By the elimination of approximately forty thousand troops from the German Army our future task has been made easier. By securing Brest, an important Atlantic seaport is made available to the Allies.

To single out the achievements of one unit in the task which has just ended would be difficult. The performance of all units has been magnificent. There has been no shirking of duty or responsibility. Each organization has shared in the undertaking. In the Second Parachute Division of the German Army, you met the best. You will meet no better troops in your future battles. We are better soldiers today than we were when we entered this engagement because of the fact that we have met and eliminated the best Germany has to offer.

We have paid a price in casualties for the job we have done. Many of our comrades have died in the struggle for Brest, in order that we who live can share in the satisfaction that the job has been well done—we regret their passing—it is the fortunes of war that they should die while we carry the torch to other battlefields.

I desire to take this means of thanking all of who have shared in this campaign for their fine work. It has been a privilege to command and work with you. Each officer and enlisted man should take pride in the fact that, as a result of your work before Brest, three German divisions and many other German troops have been erased from the troop list of World War II.

Troy H. Middleton
Major General, U.S. Army, Commanding

The VIII Corps turned over Brest and the prisoners to the Communication Zone on September 19 and the combat troops moved into assembly areas for rest, supplies, and reorganization. The 29th Infantry Division returned to the

First Army. Task Force A was dissolved. The VIII Corps Headquarters and the 8th and 2nd Infantry divisions began to move to Belgium and Luxembourg, remaining under the Ninth Army control.

Ramcke had been thorough in denying the Allies a usable port. All of Brest's port facilities were in shambles. Bridges were destroyed. Scuttled ships blocked the harbor and river. The necessary Allied air bombardments had added to the destruction. The homes, schools, hospitals, churches, stores, government buildings, and hotels were gone and only remained as rubble on the ground.

SHAEF planners recommended that Lorient, Quiberon Bay, St. Nazaire, and Nantes not be pursued as potential ports. Plans to capture Lorient and St. Nazaire were aborted and the Germans in these fortresses were contained until the end of the war. The capture of Brest remains a controversial issue as in the long run; it was not needed but this is in hindsight. At the time Brest was attacked, the Allied port facilities were very inadequate to supply the demand necessary to carry the war to Germany. Although Brest was not used as a port, it did give a lot of security to have it in Allied hands, one to remove the large German garrison in the rear of the advancing Allied armies, and two, to rehabilitate it as a port should it become needed.

The battle for Brest had continued for twenty-six days, night and day. Two other generals and a colonel surrendered with Ramcke, 36,389 Germans became prisoners, 2,000 wounded German soldiers were evacuated. and 800 German graves were found.

General Ramcke was sent to a prisoner of war camp in Mississippi not far from General Middleton's birthplace. Later he was transferred to prisoner of war camps in England and France. He was tried for offenses committed during the occupation of France. Having been found guilty, he served a total of five years in prison. After returning to Germany as a civilian, he went into the concrete business. He pursued a correspondence with General Middleton for fifteen years. Middleton replied out of respect for another professional soldier. Greetings were exchanged during holiday periods. Postwar General Middleton speculated that there would be considerable controversy about the wisdom of the battle for Brest and for having to take a month to capture the port. He defended the necessity of capturing Brest even though it was a costly battle. When the battle began, Cherbourg was the only port available to the Allies and it was operating far below capacity. The submarine pens were in Brest and as far as the Allies knew, they were still operational. The submarine pens and all of the machine shops were in good condition and well protected from bombardment. Brest was well organized to support submarine warfare.

LORIENT AND ST. NAZAIRE TO BE CONTAINED

General Middleton was also of the opinion that the Allies could not afford to leave so many German troops in Brest. He was ordered to capture Lorient but objected, knowing that a battle there would be costly and not worth it as there were only 20,000 Germans there. He suggested that when a new division came in, it should be sent there to relieve the existing division. His plan was adopted. No mention was made of St. Nazaire, which was much larger in area, contained approximately 30,000 German troops, and was more heavily defended than Lorient. However, the plan to contain both fortresses was a wise one as casualties were light among the divisions involved and no major effort was made by the Germans to break out. The 94th Infantry Division relieved the 6th Armored Division in September 1944. The many FFI units fighting there were gradually taken under the wing of the Americans for supplies and training.

WHY TAKE BREST?

It is very interesting how the questions of taking Brest have lingered. In March 1960 Maj. Martin Blumenson, U.S. military historian, published an article in ARMY "The Decision to Take Brest." He considered the battle for the port of Brest one of the most controversial issues of the European campaign during World War II. Blumenson posed three questions:

> Why did 50,000 U. S. troops undertake a strenuous battle for a city on the western tip of Brittany 300 miles behind the front? Why did they fight for more than three weeks and suffer almost 10,000 casualties to reduce defenses that by then were 500 miles behind the main combat forces? Why were these men and their equipment and supplies (and air support as well) diverted—at the height of the pursuit across France, when transportation facilities and gasoline were at a premium—to seize a port that was never used?

There has been an ongoing debate over this issue since World War II and some of those critical of this battle thought the decision to take Brest incomprehensible. Blumenson's article was an attempt to set the record straight and establish this as a reasonable decision. In mid-August 1944, the Germans were fleeing toward the Seine River and the Allies were keeping them on the run in order to prevent them from setting up a defensive line on the Seine.

However, logistics were not in the Allies' favor. Although Normandy had been secured, pressing forward was curtailed by a lack of supplies, men, and equipment. Cherbourg was the only major port in Allied hands and it was operating well below capacity. It had been estimated by this time the Americans would be in possession of St. Malo, Brest, Quiberon Bay, and Nantes, and the British would be in possession of Rouen and Le Havre. However, the Quiberon Bay area (Brest, Lorient, and St. Nazaire) was still held firmly by the Germans. All supplies were still coming in over the beaches. The approaching winter weather would soon curtail the transfer of supplies across the beaches. If the territory between the Seine and Loire rivers was occupied by the Allies, then it would have to become not a mere lodgement but a base from which to launch an attack on Germany. This base would have to be sufficient to support the Allied advance. While the British could anticipate relieving their supply problems by quickly capturing the Seine ports and the Channel ports of Boulogne, Dunkirk, and Calais, the Americans held only Cherbourg and the destroyed, nonusable port of St. Malo. Strong German opposition held Brest and Lorient, which controlled the Quiberon Bay area. The occupied St. Nazaire controlled the entry into the Loire River thus cutting off Nantes as a usable port.

Second, when the Allies broke out of the beaches, the orderly supply system that had existed no longer prevailed. Supply distances had greatly increased. The depot system used while the Allies were confined to the hedgerow terrain was no longer efficient and deliveries had to be made directly to the individual units, requiring much more manpower and time.

If the Allies were going to pursue the enemy, they would have to gamble on the ability to supply the various advancing units with a greatly strained delivery system. Because of the inclement weather anticipated in September, which would slow or terminate unloading on the beaches, acquiring another major port such as Brest became a critical issue.

Brest was an ideal port and much used by the Allies in World War I. It was the largest landlocked port in Europe and serviced France by a very good railway system. However, it was anticipated that the port facilities might well be destroyed so Allied planners intended to utilize the Quiberon Bay area as a large port facility although it would be a complicated engineering project. For the protection of this proposed Quiberon Bay port, Brest would have to be neutralized to clear the shipping lanes around the Brittany tip. Lorient and St. Nazaire, likewise, would have to be captured to obviate the artillery bombardments from the highly fortified ports. This would be a difficult venture.

The American troops entered Brittany during the first week of August with the plan to capture St. Malo, Brest, and Lorient. These ports had received an influx of German troops who retreated from Normandy and all were indoctrinated into Hitler's concept of defending these fortresses to the last man. The 6th Armored Division raced to Brest but was thwarted in their efforts to seize it. Likewise the 4th Armored Division was halted in its tracks when it tried to take Lorient. Therefore, the sum of the German forces in Brest, Lorient, and St. Nazaire approximated 80,000 Germans. Having found that St. Malo, Brest, Lorient, and St. Nazaire were virtual fortresses, well supplied with food, guns, ammunition and veteran soldiers, there was no alternative but to try to take them one at a time. The commanders of each fortress were dedicated to defending them to the last man.

In early August, the battle for St. Malo began. The 83rd Infantry Division fought a vicious battle there against well-entrenched, tough German opposition. Casualties were high on both sides and the battle lasted for two weeks, ending on August 17, 1944. This occurred at the same time Eisenhower gave the commanders in the eastern part of Brittany permission to pursue the enemy beyond the Seine River.

General Middleton moved his VIII Corps westward to Brest. The 2nd, 8th, and 29th Infantry divisions began the attack on Brest on August 25 as the Allied forces were crossing the Seine. The Allies anticipated an early victory at Brest as they mistakenly thought that the Germans would be disinterested in a strong defense in view of the recent setbacks they had encountered at St. Malo and in the failed counterattack on Mortain. Unfortunately, that was not the case, as we know from the foregoing account of the battle.

The Supreme Command decided against using Brest as a vital port as the cost, time, and utilization of personnel would be so great to restore the massive destruction there. The surge toward Germany in the east had been moving so rapidly that the seizure of the Channel ports, Rotterdam, and Amsterdam were becoming within reach of the advancing Allies. On September 3 SHAEF planners decided against using the ports of Lorient, Quiberon Bay, and St. Nazaire. Antwerp was secured on September 7, 1944.

Le Havre was taken by Canadian troops, adding another port for Allied use. Marseille also became a usable port for the Allies on August 28, 1944. Antwerp was in Allied possession in September but because the Germans continued to control the Schelde estuary, it was blocked and out of use until November of that year. In conclusion, Blumenson raised several questions:

"Since the Brittany ports, on which the Allies had counted upon so heavily, were not put to use, what had the siege of Brest accomplished?" His answer was the elimination of the strong garrison of veteran soldiers there. According to General Bradley, containing Brest would have required more troops than could have been spared on an active front. The VIII Corps and its attached units were free to move on to the east and by the end of September joined the Allied forces at the Siegfried Line.

"Had the employment of three divisions and valuable transport and supplies adversely affected the pursuit operations at a time when troops, vehicles, and supplies were desperately needed on the main front?" Blumenson thought not, qualifying this answer by stating that the expenditures at Brest were minimal compared to the expenditures on the main front.

Blumenson compared the taking of Brest to insurance that everyone hoped he would not have to collect. It was a question of being safe rather than being sorry and was at a time when the demand for supplies was much greater than the supply and every avenue that might relieve this critical shortage must be explored. No one had a crystal ball to look into the future. Blumenson sided with the commanders who chose to secure Brest as a matter of caution so as to have in hand the port of Brest should it be needed as the war continued toward Germany.

It seems that Blumenson's analysis was accurate and fair. Securing Brest certainly relieved the American commanders of the uncomfortable feeling of having the additional garrison of 40,000 Germans in Brest added to the 40,000–50,000 contained in St. Nazaire and Lorient in their rear.

11

Reflection on the Breton Ports

IN JANUARY 1995 A. Harding Ganz published an article in the *Journal of Military History* critical of the inability of the high command to adjust operation plans to comply with knowledge gained by contact with the enemy. The last paragraph of the article states:

It is a military truism that operation plans seldom survive contact with the enemy. Therefore, commanders must be mentally flexible to adapt their objectives to changing circumstances. This is especially true with armored warfare, given the pace of operations, if the initiative and momentum are to be maintained. Too late was it acknowledged that the Brittany Ports were no longer a relevant objective.

Ganz raised the following questions:

1. What role did the Brittany ports play in Allied strategy?
2. After the breakout from Normandy in July, should Patton's armored spearheads have been directed eastward to destroy the German forces and possibly bring the war to an end more quickly or be turned back westward into Brittany, to ensure logistical support for a delayed but sustained advance later?
3. Were the needs of the supply services well comprehended by the combat commanders who were to attain these objectives?
4. Were, in fact, fortified port cities appropriate tactical objectives for armored units?
5. Would the capture and utilization of the Breton ports have alleviated the logistical crisis that paralyzed the Allied advance in September? (This refers to the last day of August, the Third Army ran out of gas just as it established bridgeheads on the Meuse River.)

The initial planning for Overlord was undertaken in the spring of 1943 by a joint Anglo-American staff. Eisenhower had not been designated at that time so Lt. Gen. Frederick Morgan prevailed. A prime issue was the proximity of seaports for building up forces and supplies necessary for the future inland

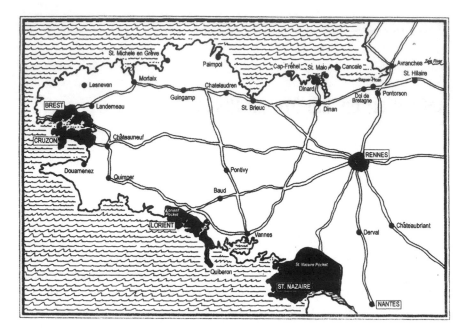

The Breton Fortresses

campaigns. The ports from Cherbourg to Nantes, especially Lorient and Brest, were considered to be secured as soon as possible. It was assumed that the Germans would do much damage to the port facilities as they either withdrew or were captured. Decisions would then have to be made as to how feasible it would be to restore a port based on repair time to make it functional.

In January 1944, with General Eisenhower present as Supreme Allied Commander, planning was accelerated. Phase lines were developed as general guidelines for planning. The First U.S. Army with Lt. Gen. Omar Bradley in command was to advance south to the line Avranches-Domfort by D+20. At that time the U.S. Third Army with Gen. George Patton commanding would be committed and both armies would clear Brittany and capture its ports. The next phase line would be bounded by the Loire and Seine rivers east to the Paris-Orléans gap by D+90. (Actually Patton was beyond that gap by August 25 and by September the Allies were beyond the Meuse River.)

Logistical planning was necessary to support each unit in the field. In addition, reserves had to be built up to provide for future supplies of food, ammunition, transportation, reconstruction and development material, equipment, and personnel. It was estimated that it would require 45,000 long tons of supplies be landed per day by D+90 to sustain a force of over a million men which included twenty-one American divisions.

The Allies planned to capture Cherbourg early and hoped that it could be rehabilitated as they assumed it would be damaged. The prefabricated harbors

(Mulberries) would provide docking facilities initially. Even if Cherbourg was functional, Normandy could provide only 28,150 tons a day of the necessary 45,000 tons. Therefore Brest, St. Malo, and Lorient would have to be captured and functional by D+60, yielding a potential 17,550 tons daily. Additional possibilities were using Vannes and Auray. If these two ports were viable they could ultimately reach a capacity of 10,000 tons a day.

The breakout from the Normandy beaches lagged behind schedule, making the Breton ports less significant because of a time factor to capture and rehabilitate them before autumn weather moved in. Other factors included the American Mulberry destroyed by storms on June 21 and Cherbourg demolished when captured on June 29. Fortunately, adequate supplies had been built up for major offensive operations.

On July 25 the Americans broke out of the Normandy beachhead in Operation Cobra and on August 1 Patton's Third Army was committed with the mission of capturing the Breton ports. The 4th and 6th Armored divisions made unprecedented advances. Combat Command A (CCA) (4th) was on the outskirts of Rennes on the evening of August 1. The 6th Armored Division was headed to Brest, 130 miles away, and the newly formed Task Force A was to sweep the north shore and take St. Malo.

At this time, there was the potential for a deep penetration eastward to destroy the Germans west of the Seine. There was seemingly a good possibility of a decisive victory if the opportunity was seized. Gen. John Wood, meanwhile, derived a plan to swing west of Rennes and circle to the southeast of the city while poised to drive east, having in effect, in his opinion, cut off the Brittany Peninsula without going to Quiberon. On August 3 he started his columns eastward and at the same time notifying General Middleton of his plan of action.

Two very different schools of thought now came into play, which not only caused confusion but would begin a series of "Monday morning quarterbacking" that still exist in military studies to this day. Generals Eisenhower, Bradley, and Middleton were infantrymen and thought in terms of phase lines and geographic objectives. Generals Patton, Wood, and Grow were cavalrymen from the mobile armor tradition and were nauseated by those who "state that all human virtue depends on knowing infantry tactics." As the armor raced out of Normandy, notes the Army official history, "A naturally headstrong crew became rambunctious in Brittany." Actually, Patton's chief of staff, Maj. Gen. Hugh J. Gaffey, found out what Wood was doing and told him in no uncertain terms to turn around and head to Lorient as he had been ordered to do. Patton subsequently backed up the reprimand.

Patton had his deputy chief of staff, Gen. Hobart Gay, pay an official visit to Wood telling him to comply with orders issued. General Wood was to tell the historian Sir Basil Liddell-Hart postwar that it was one of the most stupid decisions of the war. Actually, the 4th Armored Division hit a stone wall when their advanced units tried to enter Lorient. Twenty men were killed and eighty-five wounded from German artillery in a two-hour period in a field near Pont Scorf. The attack stopped only after the German artillery spotters were searched out and killed on an adjacent hill. This should have been a warning to all that though these rapidly advancing armored units had a very successful run across Brittany, they were not invulnerable to the concentrated forces at strongpoints along the way which could have trapped them. This happened to the 6th Armored Division as it approached Brest. The German 266th Infantry was advancing toward them from their rear. Generals Bradley and Middleton were concerned with the lack of control when the mobile units were extended too far from the main body of troops.

The U.S. high command did not realize what they were up against in these port cities that Hitler had converted to fortresses. These were German U-boat bases built by the Todt Organization as part of the Atlantic Wall to withstand any kind of concentrated bombardment. The cement bunkers and submarine pens deflected all of the bombs dropped on them (177 bombardments of St. Nazaire alone). The pens at St. Nazaire and Lorient appear untouched to this day. They were heavily fortified with cement bunkers, strongpoints, extensive minefields, antitank obstacles, and interlacing fields of fire. Some 25,000 troops occupied Lorient and 30,000 defended Brest. St. Nazaire was equally protected from attack. All were packed with gun emplacements.

It has been a criticism by military men postwar that General Grow lost a day getting to Brest because of the delay caused by orders from generals Middleton and Patton. Similarly Middleton and Wood were criticized for the one-day delay in getting to Rennes. The premise for both was that during those one-day delays, many troops escaping from Normandy sought the protection of these fortresses, swelling the ranks of the existing garrisons.

The author, having spent four and a half months with the 66th Infantry Division containing the Germans at St. Nazaire and Lorient, does not agree that attacking either Brest or Lorient one day earlier would have made that much difference. Hitler had made them into fortresses long before D-day and both, as well as Brest and St. Malo, were riddled with gun emplacements and protected with every conceivable defense mechanism. It is true that the German troops seeking safe haven poured into these bases, but the guns, minefields, and defensive lines had long been established. Lorient, for instance, had six defense lines. Throughout the whole campaign, generals Eisenhower and Bradley were aggressive yet cautious. Both pushed commanders and troops to the limit but categorically were not reckless.

It is true that the 4th and 6th Armored divisions could have been more effective in spearheading a thrust to the east if they could have been relieved earlier by infantry divisions. However, the battle in Brittany was very volatile at that time and probably not the appropriate time to replace battle hardened veterans with any units with less experience.

St. Malo was the learning experience. General Patton greatly underestimated the number of German troops in Brittany and their tenacity in "holding the fort," as was evidenced by his estimates given to General Middleton when asked. It is worrisome that he was so far off the mark. It suggests that either our own G-2 misinformed him or General Patton did not bother to ask. Fortunately, the French Resistance fed the U.S. forces much information about the Germans as they made it their business and duty to secure accurate information for the Allies.

In retrospect, it might have been prudent after the learning experience at St. Malo to have contained Brest rather than fight the costly battle to capture it. Subsequently, one division at a time contained both St. Nazaire and Lorient, successfully utilizing the 40,000–50,000 FFI troops generated in Brittany. Maybe it would have been reasonable for the same to have been done at Brest. However, ports were badly needed at the time, which in all probability influenced the decision to take Brest. Although these larger garrisons of German troops were in the rear of our armies advancing to the east, without hundreds of vehicles they could have gone nowhere even if they had decided to break out. However, they could have broken through the thin line of the containing forces to create a major distraction at a critical time.

The logistics of transportation of fuel and supplies became a monumental problem, more so than lack of port facilities. By the end of August, 90–95 percent of supplies in the ETO lay in depots near the invasion beaches. Railroads had to be repaired. The pipeline under the ocean was largely a failure. The "Red Ball Express" from St. Lô to Chartres was expensive and tough on personnel. Had Breton ports been usable, the round trip would have been more than 500 miles. The battle for Brest at its peak took first priority. Marseille, the Riviera ports and the double-track railroad from Marseille to Lyon became a valuable means of supplying 10,000 tons a day. By October, one third of the total tonnage arriving in France was transported by this route. Antwerp became a very valuable asset but was not accessible until late November. The German U-boats continued to sink Allied merchant ships although the losses had been greatly reduced with better defense against them and a greater number of U-boats sunk.

Ganz considered the sending of the 4th and 6th Armored divisions hundreds of miles to the west to Brittany, when the decisive maneuver was eastward, faulty strategy. Ganz's premise might be true, but sending these units eastward without proper support could have resulted in their isolation and destruction. They would be bypassing thousands of heavily armed German troops which possibly could have created a mousetrap situation for them before our infantry could arrive to help them. Some of the Panzer units facing Montgomery could have rolled in behind and cut our supply lines. The Allied estimates of the German strength in Brittany were grossly in error. However, critiques and analyses are very important to future strategy and Ganz has broached some salient points. The war in Europe was a new mobile campaign that none of our commanders had previously experienced and they were in a learning process as was the soldier in the field. It is to their credit that they beat the Germans at every turn. Our generals outcommanded the veteran German commanders and our army of civilians, recently turned soldiers, outfought the veteran German counterpart. Although war is the ugliest of conflicts, World War II was poetic justice for the Allied countries and for the United States, its finest hour.

12

St. Nazaire and Lorient—Prime Military Targets

BOMBARDMENT OF BRETON PORTS

THE DEVASTATION OF the war in Brittany actually began in June 1940 when the Germans occupied the Breton ports. A background of these early years beginning in June 1940 explains much of the strength and resistance of the Germans in Brittany. They had four years to build up their defenses along the coast and were well supplied to ward off the Americans. The massive aerial bombardments of the U-boat pens did little more than kill French civilians and destroy their homes. There was virtually no interruption of the U-boat activity. The war had preceded the advancing American troops by three years. In June 1940 St. Nazaire and Lorient, two of France's largest naval installations, became mini-Dunkirks during the attempt of large numbers of French and British soldiers to escape before being captured by the Germans. The ships evacuating soldiers and civilians were bombed and strafed. The Germans dumped many mines into the harbors in an attempt to destroy ships that were leaving. In addition, hundreds of cement bunkers and gun emplacements were constructed to protect the submarine bases from sea or land attack The U-boats were probably Hitler's most effective weapon so he could not afford to lose them.

Hitler chose St. Nazaire and Lorient for conversion into formidable U-boat fortresses. Large submarine-pen complexes were constructed by the Todt Organization with walls of cement and steel measuring up to nine feet in thickness. They were impenetrable fortresses on the Atlantic Wall.

As soon as the Germans occupied Brittany, construction of the U-boat pens at St. Nazaire and Lorient commenced. Hitler placed a lot of emphasis on these two bases as the U-boats were proving to be his most destructive weapon and he was anxious to move the flotillas to the west coast of France. This would shorten their trip to the hunting grounds by 400–500 miles and greatly decrease the downtime of returning to home base. By the end of World War II, the U-boats had sunk 8,000 Allied ships with the loss of 890,000 men.

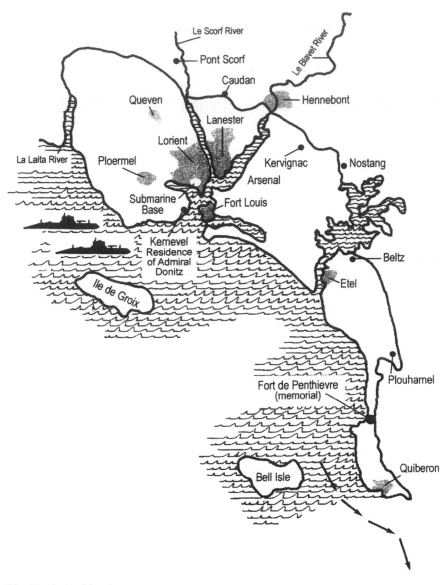

The Pocket of Lorient

MASSIVE LOSSES TO GERMAN U-BOATS

During the first year of the war, approximately 1,000 Allied merchant ships were sunk with the loss of their valuable and essential cargoes of fuel, ammunition, tanks, and planes. By mid-July 1940 the Royal Navy was down to a

The Pocket of St. Nazaire

two-month supply of oil. By September 1941 25 percent of the entire British Fleet had been lost.

Adm. Karl Donitz was given command of the German U-boats. As a young submariner in World War I, he was captured by the British but never quit studying U-boat tactics. He visited St. Nazaire and Lorient on June 21, 1940, and personally supervised the construction of the U-boat pens. The U-boats moved from the Baltic ports such as Bergen and Tronheim. This change brought about an increase in Allied tonnage sunk. U-boat U-30 arrived in July 1940, followed by U-334, U-52, and U-99 in August. Lorient became

TABLE 1. Top Five U-boat Aces

	Tonnage sunk	Ships sunk
Otto Kretschmer	266,629	44
Wolfgang Luth	223,712	43
Erich Topp	193,684	34
Karl-Friedrich Merten	186,064	29
Viktor Schütze	171,164	34

headquarters for the Atlantic fleet of U-boats. Lorient became Donitz's headquarters where he had the facilities to communicate with each U-boat personally.

Hitler, Admiral of the German Navy Erich Raeder, and Sir Winston Churchill all thought that the German battleships such as the *Tirpitz* and *Bismarck* would be the commanding German naval force so the U-boats were initially confined to coastal waters for the leftovers. It became apparent very early that Germany's most destructive force was Donitz and his U-boat flotillas. The U-boats would attack convoys in "wolf packs." When a U-boat spotted a convoy, the commander would inform Lorient of the position, speed, course, and number of ships and escort vessels. Other U-boats nearby would be notified and they would immediately bond together to attack the convoy. Early in the war, neither Great Britain nor the United States had very good defensive mechanisms to counter these attacks successfully. The United States, unfortunately, was slow to adopt the convoy system. An example of these attacks occurred on October 16, 1940. The commander of U-48 spotted Convoy SC-7-30 with only three escort vessels. A pack of U-boats responded to his message and joined him for the attack. As a result, only fifteen of thirty-five ships reached port and no U-boats were lost. Otto Kretschmer, Germany's top ace, sank six ships. The next night this same "pack" repeated the attack on Convoy HX-79, resulting in the loss of twelve ships.

From September 1939 to June 1940, 2,300,000 tons of Allied shipping were lost. From July 1940 through December 1940, 2,500,000 tons of ships and supplies were lost. The Germans lost only two U-boats between July and October 1940. The U-boat crews called this "The Happy Times." (See Table 1 for a list of the five top aces and their records.)

What is so amazing is that Otto Kretschmer was sunk and captured in 1941 so his record of forty-four ships was accomplished before 1942. However, Kretschmer was luckier than most German submariners. Germany lost 28,592 of its 41,000 submariners and 753 of its operational U-boats. Donitz lost his son on a German submarine.

The U-boat destruction continued throughout 1942 but the United States and Great Britain, during that time, produced many more escort vessels, utilized radar on planes to detect submarines, closed the mid-Atlantic gap with long-range Liberators, and developed new technologies such as centimetric radar and resonant cavity magnetron. In May 1943 the Germans lost forty-three U-boats, twice the number that they produced that month.

Although the German "Happy Times" were over, the U-boats continued their devastating attacks until the end of the war. On Christmas Eve and Christmas Day 1944, six ships were sunk just out of Cherbourg harbor. One troop ship, carrying units of the 66th Infantry Division to Europe, was torpedoed six miles out of Cherbourg with the loss of 802 young American soldiers. The 66th Infantry Division was sent several days later to contain the Germans at St. Nazaire and Lorient and did so with a vengeance.

RETALIATION BY ALLIED AIR FORCES

In an effort to in some way counteract the U-boat war, the British began bombardments of the U-boat ports in 1940. The United States joined them in 1942. The British would bombard during the night and the U.S. Army Air Forces would bombard during the day. These bombardments continued for three years and only stopped when the invasion of France necessitated the deployment of the planes to Normandy and to targets that were vital to the Germans in support of their defense of Normandy. In November 1941 Lorient was subjected to fifteen days of intense bombing.

Bombardments on April 15 and 16, 1942, at St. Nazaire killed nineteen civilians and damaged 650 homes. The worst bombardments of St. Nazaire occurred November 9, 10, 14, and 17, 1942. At this time a decision was made to close the schools and try to evacuate all of the children. The Americans first bombed St. Nazaire in daylight on November 9, 1942. Three waves of bombers killed 186 people, including 150 shipyard workers. In spite of these bombardments, business went on as usual and there was no evidence that they produced any inhibitory effect on submarine activity.

On January 14 and 15, 1943, the glow of fires seen by Nazariens were those of Lorient, burning. Much of the city was in ruins. The same fate would befall St. Nazaire. At the Casablanca conference Churchill and Roosevelt decided to step up these bombardments of Lorient and St. Nazaire. In January 1943 Lorient was attacked repeatedly with explosives and incendiaries, which destroyed the town hall and 500 homes. Many civilians were killed and three-fourths of the town was in ruins. In February multiple attacks on Lorient finished the destruction of the city. The newspaper *La liberté de Morbihan* reported:

104 people killed the night of January 14 and 15, 1943

60,000 incendiary bombs dropped in one month

5,000 explosive bombs dropped in one month

3,000 buildings destroyed, not counting the ones that had to be condemned

It was ironic that none of the U-boat pens or the German buildings which were military targets were damaged. February 28, 1943, was considered the Apocalypse for St. Nazaire and surrounding villages. Three hundred B-17s dropped several hundred tons of bombs over a twenty-six-minute period. Thousands of incendiary and phosphorous bombs consumed the city. More than 600 fires were burning at one time. Thirty-nine civilians died and thirty-six more were injured. During the years 1940 through 1943, 177 bombardments befell St. Nazaire, killing 479 civilians and wounding an additional 576.

The foregoing lists only a small number of the bombardments to exemplify their violence and destruction. Also, a large scattering of the bombardments consumed and damaged many small peripheral villages, especially around

Lorient, such as Hennebont, Caudan, Etel, Pont Scorf, Port Louis, and many others. There were no "smart" bombs. The weather was often bad, with thick cloud cover and the antiaircraft fire was so intense that St. Nazaire was referred to by the airmen as "flak city."

THE FRENCH RESISTANCE AND THE FFI

As soon as France was occupied, a small percentage of the population began to resist. As time went on this number would gradually increase and when the invasion of France became eminent, the ranks of the Resistance and the FFI began to swell to become a large effective combat force in Brittany. To fully understand this development, one must go back to the beginning when Germany invaded France and occupied three-fifths of the country in June 1940.

Gen. Charles de Gaulle, who opposed any agreement with the Germans, moved to England to attempt to reform a new French army and a new government for France. Other Frenchmen moved to the unoccupied zone where a new French government would be formed at Vichy. This government was a product of defeat and occupation and became a collaborationist government.

At the time of the capitulation, Paul Reynaud was the leader of the government and he appointed Marshal Henri Philippe Pétain, French hero of Verdun in World War I, as vice president. On June 16, 1940, the Council of Ministers met in Bordeaux and after much disagreement concerning signing an armistice, Reynaud withdrew and Pétain was appointed to run the government. Pétain called for an end to hostilities and approached the German government for an armistice. At this time, large numbers of French and British soldiers were trying to escape France at St. Nazaire and Lorient.

De Gaulle broke from Pétain's government and made a speech from London on June 18, 1940, appealing to the French people to continue to fight and not to sign an armistice. Three-fifths of France was occupied and Pétain brought Pierre Laval into the French government, which moved into the free zone to Vichy. Pétain and Laval had autocratic control and became collaborationists. Under Laval's direction, France became a police state and eventually would ship out of France 641,000 Frenchmen to German labor camps and more than 250,000 Jews to concentration camps. They drew up very severe laws of punishment for anyone aiding the Resistance movement, which was gaining momentum. A "baby army" of 100,000 men was allowed by the German government to maintain order in the free zone. Eventually this would become a hotbed for the recruitment of Resistance leaders and many would join the FFI when the "baby army" was dissolved in 1942.

French citizens began to resent the Vichy government and local officials began to ignore orders from Vichy when they were in disagreement. Local groups of resistance began to form locally and have secret meetings. These groups were formed much like those of the militia during the American Revolutionary War and for the Confederate Army during the War Between the States. Young boys and men from small villages and farms would volunteer as soldiers, be given a few days training and an armband, and be assigned to a local unit. When the ground war developed after the invasion, many of these units were given training by U.S. divisions, which further enhanced their value as soldiers. As time went by, a group from one village would combine with a group from a nearby village and this became the grassroots of what was to become known as the Free French of the Interior (FFI). There were many different factions and some were antagonistic to others. However, cooperation between groups was the norm and was invaluable in returning downed Allied aviators to England and for the information furnished to the Allies regarding German troop movements, location of Panzer divisions, and much other information about the enemy. Prior to Operation Chariot, the daring British commando raid to destroy the Normandie Dock in St. Nazaire, March 28, 1942, the Allies received drawings to scale of the entire area around the dock including gun positions, winding huts for the caissons on each end of the dock, and other facilities associated with the function of the dock.

At this time de Gaulle appealed to French loyalists to build a new French regime. He had not really become part of the Resistance movement but knew that because of its growth, there would be French people who would join him in his fight for a new government for France. De Gaulle was as much at war with the Vichy government as he was with the Germans. Eventually de Gaulle would become the leader of all French forces. The Resistance, a very brave group, began to do as much harm to the Germans as possible, from harassment to overt murder. There were many reprisals against the population for the deeds of the Resistance. In many small villages in Brittany, monuments are erected to honor either members of the Resistance who were killed or hostages who were taken from the population and killed as punishment for the activities of the Resistance.

General de Gaulle began to get more information about this brave, small group of volunteers who were scattered around France. At the end of 1941, he sent Jean Moulin, one of his principal lieutenants, back into France in an attempt to organize the Resistance so that it would become a force to be reckoned with to defeat the Vichy government. Moulin united the movements of factions in different sections of France and acquainted them with Gaullism. De Gaulle soon became recognized as the leader of all forces Français.

Now that the Resistance in Brittany had a leader allied to the British and Americans, through him they attempted to get the Allies to stop bombing the ports in Brittany so as to quit killing French people and destroying their homes. They volunteered to sabotage the submarine bases if provided with appropriate explosives. They were probably right. In spite of the repetitious and frequent bombardments by the Allies, the submarine pens remained intact and fully functional.

FRENCH FORCES OF THE INTERIOR—ORIGIN

Sensing that the invasion of France by the Allies would occur in 1944, the year 1943 became a formative one for the FFI. A growing intolerance to the Vichy government, especially in villages and small towns, accelerated enlistments in the FFI. The Resistance increased its efforts toward sabotage and gathering information.

In November 1942, when the Germans occupied the free zone, all of the units under the Vichy government were dissolved. A great number of the members of this army were recruited by the Resistance and became prominent in the pockets of St. Nazaire and Lorient where the FFI was swelling its ranks. Col. Raymond Chomel (later to become general) was made responsible for the liquidation of the Army of the Armistice so he was able to stay in touch with the members of the organization. He himself had joined the Organization Resistance de l'Armée (ORA), which gave him the responsibility of recruiting officers and men for Resistance groups and for units of the FFI.

In July 1943 another group appeared, the First Regiment of France (1st RDF). Officers and noncommissioned officers were carefully chosen for this elite unit. Many young people were attracted to this unit and half were military students. Thus, the 1st RDF contained many future officers who would become important when the FFI units would be absorbed into the regular French army.

Colonel Chomel moved quickly in another direction and recreated the 8th Cuirassiers by unifying two cavalry squadrons of the 1st RDF and two squadrons of the former 8th Cuirassiers, France's oldest cavalry unit, which had fought in Belgium in 1940 and was now trying to get organized again to fight the Germans south of the Loire River in St. Nazaire. At this time, many of the French soldiers who fought against the Germans in 1940 began volunteering for the new French units so as to fight again in the St. Nazaire and Lorient pockets. Colonel Chomel was made general and became commander of the French 25th Division. One of the most revered French officers to fight with the Americans at St. Nazaire, he had previously served as liaison officer in the French 4th Armored Division under General de Gaulle during the Battle of Montcornet in 1940. After the Normandy invasion, Chomel was put in charge of all French troops south of the Loire River in the St. Nazaire pocket. His leadership became legend. He was at General Kramer's side when the Germans surrendered to the 66th Infantry Division at St. Nazaire May 11, 1945.

In 1944, the Resistance movement became more militarized and units of fifty or more, sometimes reaching numbers of 1,000, formed locally in villages and towns and in regions. They began to unite as the Forces Française de l'Interieur (FFI), reaching a conglomerate of 30,000 before the invasion. They began to play a very aggressive role to defeat the Germans and the Vichy government. They wrecked the railway system, destroyed road communications systems, destroyed minefields, and obstructed German troops moving to defend Germany, often catching the Germans in a withering machine-gun ambush along a road where they were hiding behind the hedgerows flanking the road.

According to General Eisenhower, these troops proved to be worth fifteen divisions and shortened the war by two months. In no other area in France was their presence more effective than in the pockets of St. Nazaire and Lorient. After the Americans broke out from the beaches, these units kept the Americans supplied with information as to the German forces ahead. Preceding the Americans, they had run the Germans out of many small villages. Their knowledge of the German minefields enabled the Americans to avoid them.

THE RESISTANCE MOVEMENT IN MORBIHAN AND IN THE LOIRE ATLANTIC

The Department of Morbihan and the adjacent Department Loire Atlantic are large sections in Brittany similar, but greater in size than the counties in the U. S. Lorient is in the Department of Morbihan and St. Nazaire is the Department Loire Atlantic. Saint Marcel is a small village in the eastern end of the Department of Morbihan. It had two streets and 500 people. The village is located near the larger town of Ploermel and the city of Vannes. Redon is not far away. The location of St. Marcel was ideal for a drop zone as there were visual landmarks which made it easy to locate from the air, even at night. Between St. Marcel and Sérent, there was an open area surrounded by thickets, where supplies could be dropped and quickly hidden. The La Nouette farm was the center of this drop zone.

The FFI began to organize rapidly in the Department of Morbihan just before the invasion. The movement was greatly damaged on May 31, 1944, when more than fifty Resistance leaders were arrested. The encampment at La Nouette was inspected several times by high-ranking officers of the FFI just before the Americans and British landed at Normandy. They found it a satisfactory training area for units of the FFI to visit for a few days' training and a depot to distribute guns, ammunition, and food that had been parachuted in by the British. Orders were given to begin certain coded plans that involved cutting German communications and damaging railway lines. Supplies of arms were not yet sufficient for a major attack but smaller sabotage procedures were begun.

Orders were sent out for local FFI units in surrounding villages and towns to rally at La Nouette and to establish additional larger drop zones. Two forward units of nine men each were dropped in on June 5 and 6. Additional parachutists were dropped, making the total approximately 150 men. This coincided with the Allied invasion of France.

The buildup of forces reached 2,000 men and La Nouette became a very busy training center. Food was brought in from surrounding farms. Bakeries, cobblers' workshops, a clothing workshop, and a vehicle repair shop were set up. On the morning of June 6, local and departmental FFI and Resistance leaders arrived with their wireless operators. Instruction for the newly formed FFI units was given by the now 150 paratroopers who had jumped in to La Nouette.

Commandant Pierre Bourgoin parachuted in on June 9 with some of his men. Bourgoin immediately urged FFI battalions to come in for the weapons dropped in by the British each night. Approximately 700 containers and parcels were dropped June 13, by twenty-five planes, the largest parachute drop in occupied France. Between 3,000 and 4,000 men were armed at this camp. Pistols, machine guns, mines, grenades, antitank weapons, clothes, and tinned food were furnished by the British. Each day, new units would arrive, receive two to three days' training, pick up weapons and instructions, and return to their communities. As many as 2,000 men would be present at any one time, which put a strain on local farmers to supply sufficient food. The women living in and about La Nouette worked diligently sewing armbands, preparing food, and repairing clothes.

Although the Germans were suspicious of an increase in activity, they had no idea of the size and nature of the operation at La Nouette. They were busy trying to move troops to Normandy to support the Atlantic Wall. They were harassed by the many small Resistance groups intent on their destruction.

On the night of June 17–18, 1944, five planes dropped the containers off the mark and they were discovered by the Germans. This discovery initiated more Germans patrolling the area. Commandant Bourgoin and his staff were well aware that this would eventually happen and became anxious about the increased activity at La Nouette. They decided to dispense the groups and let the activity quiet down. They had been ordered not to become involved in a pitched battle. Unfortunately, it was too late.

THE BATTLE OF LA NOUETTE FARM

Early in the morning of June 18, 1944, two cars carrying eight German soldiers appeared on the road where one of the FFI outposts was located. The French opened fire, killing three, capturing three, and wounding one more. One escaped and alarmed the Germans nearby. At this time, there were 2,400 men at La Nouette including 150 French parachutists, many of whom had fought in Libya.

A unit of 500 Germans arrived at La Nouette at 8:15 A.M. Using the hedgerows for cover, they approached an FFI group and killed some of them at close range. Thinking they were dealing with only a small group of Resistance fighters, they became careless and began crossing open fields. The French waited until they were very close and opened fire, killing many of them.

The Germans retreated but a larger force returned and another attack began. Many soldiers on both sides were killed or wounded. At 2:00 P.M. the Germans, with reinforcements, launched a third attack. At 3:30 P.M. Allied aviation was called in and bombed and strafed the enemy. As soon as the planes departed, the battle continued.

At 8:00 P.M. the French command post learned of an approaching convoy of German troops. They realized that the German numbers would soon be overwhelming and so they decided it best to disperse the base before being surrounded. Their mission was sabotage in small groups and to avoid pitched battles of this magnitude. The retreat began at 10:00 P.M. A company of parachutists remained as a rear guard for several hours. One parachutist described the event: "As a bloc of gelatin, the camp seems to liquefy, to lose little by little its structure and is soon only a devastated site." Thirty Frenchmen were killed during the battle and sixty more wounded. The German losses were estimated to be 300 or more killed.

The Germans were angry the next morning to find the camp evacuated and murdered all of the wounded in the vicinity. The population was terrorized and arrests and murders of civilians carried out. The Germans were notified that any prisoners falling into the hands of the Resistance would suffer the same fate.

Often battles were started by the Resistance and FFI thinking that the Allies would soon reach them but unfortunately, in most cases, the French were not supplied or prepared for an open battle. The Allies could not inform them of plans for the invasion for security reasons so these French forces were not aware of the invasion plans and could not be supplied for full-scale attacks. Their performance in furnishing the Allies with information and their destruction of railways and communications was invaluable.

FRENCH FORCES MOBILIZE FOR WAR

Now that the plans of the invasion were no longer a security issue, the Allies made an all-out effort to include the Resistance and FFI into the concerted effort to defeat the Germans as the Allies knew the French units could make many contributions to bring the war to an end. On June 17, 1944, French general Marie Koenig was placed in command of all FFI by the Supreme Headquarters Allied Expeditionary Forces (SHAEF). He would be under General Eisenhower's command and would form a staff of twenty to twenty-five officers.

After the breakout from Avranches, the 4th and 6th Armored divisions of Patton's Third Army liberated Vannes on August 15, 1944. The Germans evacuated Nantes on August 14 and the 4th Armored Division was in the suburbs of Lorient on August 7. Between August 4 and September 7, 1944, the *maquis* (a term used for Resistance fighters) had formed a line south of the Loire River in the St. Nazaire sector. Jedburgh teams were helpful in this effort. The first French unit formed south of the Loire River was the First Ground Mobile Reconnaissance Squadron commanded by Lt. Guy Besnier and was based at Arthon. This was the beginning of thousands of French soldiers joining the battle to contain the Germans in St. Nazaire and Lorient.

By August 18, the line began to stabilize between the Germans and Allies. Hitler had given orders to the commanders of the garrisons at St. Nazaire and

Lorient that there was to be no surrender. Leaving Pénestin the line at St. Nazaire passed Vilaine, Saint Dolay, Fégréac, the Nantes-Brest Canal then south along the Vilaine River to the coast in the vicinity of Frossay.

During the first week of September 1944, the Germans began to launch attacks against the FFI and elements of the 4th Armored Division in the St. Nazaire pocket around Blain. The Americans responded quickly with a barrage of nearly 25,000 shells. The Germans attacked again on September 16 in the Foret de Gavre and the Americans pushed them out of the forest by October 2, 1944. The French and Germans exchanged numerous raids across the Nantes-Brest Canal.

Lieutenant Besnier (later to become captain) was one of the most outstanding and resourceful French soldiers opposing the Germans south of the Loire River. His patrols and attacks against the enemy caught them repeatedly off guard and he quickly subdued the German counterattacks. He had fought them in 1940 as a cavalry officer. He took a group of mechanics to Normandy, rehabilitated fifteen disabled, vehicles and brought them to Brittany for his First Ground Mobile Reconnaissance unit (1st GMR). Colonel Chombart de Laure, with the help of the residents of villages near the St. Nazaire pocket, recruited approximately 12,000 young French soldiers and organized them into twenty battalions, most being used in the zone south of the Loire River. The U.S. 94th Infantry Division would soon replace the armored units and the 83rd Infantry Division. Its commander, Gen. Harry Maloney, would work diligently to further train and equip these newly formed French units.

1944—OCTOBER, NOVEMBER, DECEMBER

By the beginning of October, 1944, the 94th Infantry Division, having relieved the 6th Armored Division and the 83rd Infantry Division. became the controlling unit. The French forces were present in significant numbers and were assigned the eastern section of the Lorient pocket and the area south of the Loire River in the St. Nazaire pocket. The campaign would now be an infantry and artillery affair. The enemy occupied approximately 100 square miles in the Lorient pocket and 680 square miles in the St. Nazaire pocket. The Lorient pocket and surrounding terrain was hilly whereas the St. Nazaire pocket tended to be flat. Both were crisscrossed with hedgerows. The Scorf, Blavet, and Laita rivers ran through the Lorient pocket. The Loire estuary and river coursed through the St. Nazaire pocket. It was estimated that the Allies were opposed by 25,000 German troops in the Lorient pocket and 35,000 in the St. Nazaire pocket. Sabers were drawn for a daily struggle between two large ground forces, both determined to yield very little to their adversary. There were approximately 500 artillery pieces in each of the pockets ranging from 20mm to 340mm cannon. In addition to the two U-boat bases, the Germans occupied the islands of Re, Groix, Belle, and the Quiberon Peninsula, all heavily defended by coastal and antiaircraft cannon.

THE 94TH INFANTRY DIVISION TAKES OVER

When General Maloney and the 94th Infantry Division took over the pockets they were pleased to find the thousands of FFI soldiers already positioned against the Germans. General Maloney seized the opportunity to obtain supplies, weapons, ammunition, and uniforms for them and to schedule training programs with the cooperation of the French officers to upgrade greatly the quality of their units. Rifles, machine guns, mortars, and howitzers were supplied and the artillery attached to the 94th Infantry Division trained them in the use of these weapons.

At first language and political issues made for poor coordination but on October 2, 1944, a conference was held in Châteaubriant with the ranking French officers present From then on cooperation between the Americans and French improved progressively. Shortly thereafter the French navy began using small boats and began to gather much important information which was turned over to American G-2 (intelligence section). Also, Group Patrie, a French air squadron, joined the ground forces with eleven A-24 dive-bombers which were used effectively for reconnaissance and bombing missions.

On October 26, 1944, Gen. Edgard de Larminat, overall French commander in this sector of Brittany, placed Col. Raymond Chomel (to become a general) in charge of French forces in the St. Nazaire sector and Brig. Gen. Borgnis Desbordes in command of the French forces in the Lorient area. When the 94th Infantry Division was relieved by the 66th Infantry Division in December, twenty-one battalions of French infantry were fighting at St. Nazaire and thirteen were fighting in the Lorient pocket.

The 301st Infantry Regiment (94th) relieved the 6th Armored Division on September 9, 1944, at Lorient. Their assigned sector was between the Blavet and the Laita rivers, the line running south to Quimperlé to Rédené, Pont Scorf, Hennebont, and Nostang. K and E companies were immediately attacked by the Germans and the two companies repulsed these attacks. Two American soldiers were killed. Their bodies were placed on a haystack to be burned but were retrieved before the burning occurred. The 307th Infantry Regiment (94th) arrived September 15 and occupied the sector between the Scorf River and Nostang. Numerous small firefights erupted as the Germans tested the 94th Infantry Division troops as soon as they took their place in the line. Private First Class Dale Proctor of Company K, 301st Infantry Regt (94th) was awarded the first Distinguished Service Cross as a telephone operator for an artillery observer. He was severely wounded but refused to leave his post while the medics attended him. The phone literally had to be pried from his hands. This brave soldier died the next day. The price of freedom is high.

The mission for the 94th Infantry Division was extended to include the St. Nazaire pocket. This was in preparation for the 83rd Infantry Division to withdraw and head eastward. General Maloney shifted the majority of his infantry to St. Nazaire and split the artillery between the two pockets. On September 17,

1944, the 376th Infantry Regiment (94th) relieved the 331st Infantry Regiment (83rd). K Company of the 376 Infantry Regiment (94th) was attacked that night, sustaining several casualties. The twenty-two-mile section assigned to the 376th Infantry Regiment (94th) stretched from the Loire River to the Foret de Gavre, running through Le Temple, Fay-de-Bretagne, and Blain. A request was made for a limited advance to put these towns behind the front and to straighten out the line. This was granted and the mission was accomplished.

The 94th Infantry Division commander was next informed that his line of responsibility would be extended east to Auxere. Elements of the 15th Cavalry Reconnaissance Group were obtained to patrol this segment of the line. Again, the responsibility of the 94th Infantry Division was extended to protect the right flank of the Third and Ninth armies from Quimper to Auxere resulting in a front of 450 miles from Quimper to Nantes, then along the Loire River to Auxere. During November, French units began relieving elements of the 94th Infantry Division for a short stay in reserve, which had not been possible until these French units had been properly trained.

On October 2, 1944, K Company of the 301st Infantry Regiment (94th) sent out a combat patrol of fifty men. They ran into an ambush with a relentless machine-gun crossfire. A patrol was sent out by I Company but to no avail as they could not reach them. Five men were killed and twenty-six wounded. The entire patrol was captured. This is an example of many similar attempts to breach the German lines. Their defenses for patrol oriented infantry warfare were virtually impregnable.

On October 6, 1944, elements of the 3rd Battalion, 376th Infantry Regiment (94th) advanced to Bouvron to shorten the line between them and the 307th Infantry Regiment (94th). The battle took place along the Brest-Nantes Canal near the village of La Pessouis. Although small arms and artillery from the Germans was relentless, the Americans took La Pessouis. They finally had to withdraw and the Germans reoccupied the village. Two days later, the Americans pushed the Germans out, never to lose the village again.

Early on October 20, a group of approximately 100 members of the Kriegsmarine attacked positions of the 301st Infantry Regiment (94th). The same day a German force of 100–200 German soldiers penetrated the French line but was beaten back by the FFI. On October 28 the attack on the FFI was repeated and the Germans simultaneously bombarded the first battalion of the 301st Infantry Regiment (94th) in the Hennebont sector. Again they were beaten back. Another German force of battalion strength attacked the FFI at St. Hélene south of Nostang and occupied high ground after driving the French back from the Etel River.

During the first few days of October, the 12th Army Group Headquarters alerted the 94th Division to place a battalion in reserve to counter a possible German offensive of approximately 25,000 to 30,000 troops from the islands of Guernsey and Jersey. Constant patrolling of the coast found no evidence of any landing.

A force of infantry and engineers was formed to weaken the German position on Quiberon Peninsula by separating it from Lorient. On a cloudy night, the engineers cleared a minefield and this was followed by an intense artillery bombardment. With perfect coordination, elements of the 301st and 376th Infantry Regiments (94th) took all objectives in fifty minutes. Fifty-nine prisoners were taken, nine bunkers reduced, and the desired positions obtained. American losses were low.

On December 15 an outpost between St. Nazaire and Belle Isle was attacked by a force estimated at eighty German soldiers. The four men on the outpost were captured as was a supply sergeant on his way by boat to supply the island outpost.

During November and December a series of prisoner exchanges were made which had been initiated and orchestrated by Andrew G. Hodges, an American Red Cross field director. On his own, Hodges approached the Germans and suggested exchanges be made, man for man, rank for rank with equal physical fitness. The Germans agreed to the exchange but kept trying to change the rules of exchange in their favor. Hodges would not give an inch and succeeded in retrieving all but one of the Allied prisoners of war. This included 105 American, 32 FFI, and 3 British soldiers.

FRENCH BATTLE GERMANS SOUTH OF THE LOIRE RIVER

During the fourth quarter of 1944, the French units in the two pockets became very aggressive toward the Germans. General Maloney and his staff had done a superb job of organizing and equipping the FFI units and the soldiers of the 94th Infantry Division had given them intensive on-the-job training. General de Gaulle became involved and placed Gen. Edgard de Larminat in charge of these forces but they would remain under the overall command of General Maloney. The French divided their assigned territories into sectors and placed a commander in each sector. The sector south of the Loire River was held tenaciously by the French.

The French 8th Cavalry Regiment (8th Cuirassiers) was assigned to secure the frontline. The 1st Ground Mobile Reconnaissance Unit (GMR) assisted when the Germans tried to take eighty-five square kilometers of the front but were unsuccessful. On December 21, 1944, in response to Von Rundstedt's offensive in the Ardennes, the Germans attacked La Bernerie, La Sicaudais, and the region of La Rogere. They were assisted by three gunboats of the Kriegsmarine and took Chauvé, which is near the coast. The Germans were opposed by two French battalions flanking the 1st GMR in the center. The French had been taken by surprise and lacked sufficient artillery.

General Chomel met with all of his commanders and then placed himself in the middle of the battle and directed it personally. The two infantry battalions were driven back to Chauvé and Sicaudais. Lt. Maurice Pollomo attacked with a mechanized patrol. His vehicle was demolished by intense artillery fire and he and several other French soldiers were killed. The 1st GMR and the 8th Cuirassiers were persistent with their combat patrols. On December 22 and 23 reinforcements arrived and the front stabilized. The French had approximately fifty casualties.

The 8th Cuirassiers Regiment (8th Cuir.) was an outstanding French cavalry unit. It was formed in 1635 at the king's request and ordered by Cardinal de Richelieu to wear the *cuirass* (armor). The unit had fought in numerous wars since then and in 1940 were the first French army unit to cross the Belgium border, May 10, 1940. They distinguished themselves before France and Belgium capitulated. Many of the members were evacuated at Dunkirk. They eventually reformed at Châteauroux. General La Fayette of Revolutionary War fame had been a member and one of his direct descendants Lieutenant (the Marquis) de Lafayette was killed near Chauvé while fighting there. There is a monument there where he is buried.

SINKING OF THE *LEOPOLDVILLE*

It was ironic that the 66th Infantry Division in Dorchester, England, destined to relieve the 94th Division, was packing its bags for the trip across the Channel. Five to six thousand troops of the division were placed on two small ships at Southampton on December 23 and departed for France early morning December 24, 1944. The two ships had Belgian Congo crews and British gunners. They were overcrowded, dirty, and beset with plumbing that did not work. The weather was stormy and a large percent of the soldiers became seasick. Life vests were issued but no evacuation drills took place. The ships were named the HMS *Leopoldville* and the SS *Cheshire*.

As the two ships departed from Southampton, they were joined by a few small escort vessels and one British destroyer, *The Brilliant*. At approximately ten minutes to 6:00 P.M., December 24, 1944, a torpedo struck the *Leopoldville* and it immediately began a slow sinking process. The G.I.s awaited orders but none were issued. The crew lowered the lifeboats and the soldiers cheered, thinking this was for them. Instead, the crew got into the lowered lifeboats and departed. There was a complete failure of communications from the ship to rescue services at Cherbourg, which was only six miles from the stricken ship. *The Brilliant* pulled alongside but the sea was so rough that it could not be tethered to the *Leopoldville*. Officers of the 66th Division on the *Leopoldville* managed to form jumps at the appropriate time from the *Leopoldville* to the *Brilliant*. This saved approximately 600–700 soldiers. Some mistimed the jump and fell between the two ships to be crushed.

Finally, the *Brilliant* had to depart as it had sustained damage due to the constant banging against the *Leopoldville*. As the ship was in its last stages on the surface, some 66th Infantry Division officers still on the ship urged the men to abandon. The many life-rafts on the deck were lashed down with cable and the G.I.s could not free them. They caught on to any piece of debris or what few rafts were available and tried to stay afloat. The description of the scene in the water at this time was heart-rending.

As the ship sank, more than two hours after being struck by the torpedo, word was received in Cherbourg. Numerous small boats were directed to the site, which was now about three miles from Cherbourg, and in the dark the crews of the small boats worked desperately to rescue as many soldiers as they could. The frigid water took its toll in hypothermia and the darkness made the search difficult. There were many heroes who risked their lives to save others only to lose their own lives from the exhaustion of such efforts.

The tragedy and surviving soldier's accounts can be found in this author's book, *Hitler's U-Boat Fortresses,* as well as several other books listed in the bibliography. There was a lot of blame to be spread around. The tragedy was kept classified for fifty years. That night 802 young American soldiers lost their lives that night. The cost of freedom is high.

A few days after the *Leopoldville* disaster, units of the 66th Infantry Division began relieving the 94th Infantry Division on the Lorient and St. Nazaire pockets. The 66th Infantry Division was short approximately 3,000 men, counting both the dead and wounded. When leaving Dorchester, members of the 66th Infantry Division believed that they were headed for "The Bulge." Whether the original plan was for the 66th Infantry Division to relieve the 94th Infantry Division or go to the Bulge has never been settled. Some are of the opinion that the 66th Infantry Division was sent to relieve the 94th Infantry Division because of its crippled condition and the 94th Infantry Division sent to the Bulge because of its full strength. A moot point at this time.

TWELFTH ARMY GROUP COASTAL SECTOR

On December 27, 1944, the 66th Infantry Division was assigned to the 12th Army Group under Gen. Omar Bradley. On January 1, 1945, the 12th Army Group Coastal Sector was divided into four areas of command. Lorient West Sector was commanded by an American, Brig. Gen. Francis Rollins. Brig. Gen. Borgnis Desbordes of France commanded the Lorient East Sector. St. Nazaire North Sector was commanded by Brig. Gen. George Forster, another American, and St. Nazaire South Sector was commanded by Brig. Gen. Raymond Chomel. Gen. Herman Kramer, commander of the 66th Infantry Division, was the overall commander of all Allied forces in the 12th Army Group Coastal Sector. Needless to say, the soldiers of the 66th Infantry Division were pretty distraught over the U-boat sinking and killing so many of their comrades and were ready to fight. They were well trained and the transition into combat was treated as a natural process. The soldiers immediately took an aggressive approach to the Germans contained in the two pockets. Some of the G.I.s who had been plucked from the frigid waters of the Channel found themselves in combat several days later. General Maloney and the units of the 94th Infantry Division had done their part well in training the FFI units and maintaining an aggressive campaign against the enemy. The 94th Infantry Division would continue its dedicated service on the eastern front. Because of losing so many comrades on the *Leopoldville,* the mindset of the 66th Infantry Division soldiers was "Try to escape and we will even the score."

CONTAINING THE POCKETS

When the 66th Infantry Division assumed responsibility for the pockets at St. Nazaire and Lorient in late December 1944, there was a fairly static line. Both sides were entrenched in dugouts, foxholes, and bunkers, all of which were extremely well fortified and protected by mines and booby-traps. Both were supported by multiple artillery units. The use of tanks was uncommon. Firefights and artillery duels were a daily process. The St. Nazaire pocket spanned the Loire River estuary. Approximately 28,000 Germans contained there fought tenaciously to protect the fourteen submarine pens. They were commanded by Gen. Werner Junck, who had supplied his fortress well for a long siege. Hundreds of artillery pieces were involved in the defensive perimeter, which focused on the land and sea approaches. The area defended was approximately 680 square miles and contained more than 100,000 civilians.

The heavy bombardments had reduced Lorient to little more than rubble with most of its buildings destroyed. Approximately 22,000 Germans defended their base and the pocket contained 9,000 civilians. The area was 100 square miles. Lt. Gen. Wilhelm Fahrmbacher, a fifty-seven-year-old artillery officer, was commander of the German garrison.

The Quiberon Peninsula with its many gun emplacements, including a battery of 340 mm cannon, guarded the entrance to the harbors of Lorient and St. Nazaire. Belle Isle and Ile de Groix were occupied islands off the coast with small civilian and German populations. These two outposts were well equipped with coastal and antiaircraft guns.

Operating under the control of the 12th Army Group, the 66th Infantry Division took over the mission of containing the German garrisons of Lorient and St. Nazaire. Major General Kramer assumed operational command of the French forces. This placed approximately 44,000 American and French soldiers under General Kramer's command.

The Germans knew that a new division had taken over, and on New Year's Eve, 1944, they opened up all of their guns in an effort to draw fire that would expose the American positions. The GIs of the 66th Infantry Division sat it out and let the Germans shoot. However, the next morning, they dug their holes a little deeper. This was the beginning of a great deal of respect for the German 88mm cannon.

The Germans were operating under Hitler's "hold to the last man" pledge, making the opposition a formidable foe. They were well dug in with strongpoints connected by trenches and surrounded by minefields, barbed wire, and booby-traps. Many machine guns in the hedgerows were well concealed with the brush and trees. Many of the German soldiers were seasoned veterans of prior campaigns. They were not inclined to surrender. The German artillery and mortar fire was very accurate and their units had the American line well zeroed in. The 104th and 107th Cavalry units were brought in to join the 66th Infantry Division and retrained as infantry. In all respects, they performed these new duties well. The 283rd Engineer Combat Battalion was also converted to infantry and took their place on line. They were trained to blow up things so did so at any opportunity. The unit later departed and began spanning the Rhine with pontoon bridges.

The defensive lines around the two pockets were composed of was a very thin line with few units in reserve. The Germans could have broken through the Allied line, but without vehicles and supply lines they would have been stopped before making any significant gain. Also their mission was to defend the U-boat bases, which were still operational. The average U.S. battalion segment of the line was three miles. Strongpoints were placed anywhere from 50 to 200 yards apart and each was manned by four to eight men. A squad usually was responsible for two or three positions, depending on the number of personnel in the squad. It was unusual for a squad to have a full compliment. Outposts and listening posts were placed in front of the line to detect any infiltration attempts by the enemy. The outposts were lonely duty, usually with two soldiers manning them. An extremely low profile was maintained, especially during daylight hours.

Anxiety increased during the dark hours as the Germans patrolled aggressively at night. They would pinpoint a position and approach it by stealth to a distance of a few yards before attacking. They knew that there was probably one man on duty and could wreak havoc before the others could respond.

The 66th Infantry Division maintained a program of frequent ambush patrols for prisoners, combat patrols to neutralize German gun positions, and reconnaissance patrols to detect gun positions or changes in the German lines. Many of the Germans in the pockets were veterans of other campaigns and adhered to a no-surrender policy dictated by the Fuehrer. Rarely did they surrender voluntarily without provocation. Often when caught in an ambush, they would attempt to escape, sometimes initiating an intense firefight.

The frontline soldiers learned to live as animals and burrowed into the ground and hedgerows with a small pick axe–shovel combination tool. Any article of reflection was removed. The troops tried to maintain cover at all times, especially during daylight hours. Patrols followed hedgerows and ditches and never crossed an open field. Small-arms fire was used only when essential as it would disclose positions. No vehicles approached the frontlines. Any noise or light at night was prohibited as it carried for a long distance and would expose positions. No one was allowed a camera or to keep a diary for fear of capture and the information that either might give the enemy.

Patrols were sent out after dark and early in the morning before daylight. Reconnaissance patrols were usually four to eight men with a radio. Contact with the enemy was avoided if possible. The patrol was led by a squad leader or platoon sergeant. Combat patrols numbered twenty to thirty men with approximately one-third carrying automatic weapons. Missions were usually to capture prisoners or to eliminate an observation post or gun position. Radio contact was maintained with the company command post but kept to a minimum. Night patrols were usually reconnaissance patrols to locate gun positions. Darkness was good cover. If a position was detected, it was fired upon with fire direction provided by the patrol.

Company commanders had a lot of leeway in managing their sector. Each company had its own way of fighting. Small offenses were carried out by a platoon or company with the objective of advancing the company's line to a more advantageous position. The Germans opposed these moves with heavy artillery and mortar bombardment. The German 88mm cannon had a flat trajectory and extremely accurate as was their mortar fire.

The infantry soldier of the 66th Infantry Division was high in his praise for its own artillery units. Many patrols, when pinned down, had been rescued by the accurate artillery directed upon the enemy confronting them and allowing them to escape. The smoke shells provided a curtain to allow the patrol occasionally caught in an ambush to withdraw.

The German counterpart had 240mm cannon amassed in the early days of the war to protect their U-boat pens. On the Quiberon Peninsula was a battery of 340mm cannon that could propel a 700-pound shell twenty-one miles. These were coastal guns turned toward the land approaches to these fortresses. At Lorient, artillery forward observers were able to view ships in the harbor. By maneuvering constantly for a better position, the American artillery sunk fourteen vessels. The major prize came when they finally knocked out the battery of 340mm cannon.

In January 1945, an average of 450 rounds were fired per day against strongpoints, gun emplacements, patrols, bridges, water-purification plants, submarines, garages, repair shops, and bakeries. Later, when enemy activity increased, 1,000 rounds per day were fired. Because there was a 140-mile front, artillery support could not be given simultaneously to all infantry units. Considerable artillery movement was required based on priorities.

Already having suffered numerous aerial bombardments beginning in 1940, the artillery barrages finished the process of turning Lorient into a mass of rubble. Water systems were destroyed. A tanker bringing water from Port Louis was sunk. Electric power lines were destroyed. Ammunition dumps were set on fire. All daylight movement in Lorient ceased. Only the submarine pens offered safe refuge.

During the first week of February, French agents inside the St. Nazaire pocket notified the Allies of a planned German attack across the Brest-Nantes

Canal. On February 8 French patrols found that the Germans had crossed the canal and were occupying the two towns of Le Thenot and Coisnauté. The French took back both towns with small losses.

In March the 262nd Infantry Regiment (66th) put all three battalions on line in the Fay-de-Bretagne Sector. The Germans had become more aggressive and began attacking American positions with automatic weapons. The American policy at the time was to hold fire so as not to give away a position but the policy changed when eight American GIs were captured. Thereafter, the Germans were fired on at first sight, which reduced the number of German patrols and Allied casualties.

On March 9 a gun of the 194th Field Artillery unit sunk a 300-foot coastal freighter, hitting it twenty-one times. On March 22 a howitzer of the 721st Field Artillery sunk a 400-foot ship. On March 31, 1945, the 66th Infantry Division was placed under the 15th Army, which took command of the coastal sector of France under the command of Gen. Leonard Gerow. Remnants of the 106th Infantry, which had been overrun during the onset of the Bulge, joined the 66th Infantry Division on April 15, 1945. In April the Germans became very aggressive against the French units in the Jouteau and Laita subsectors in Lorient. The French retaliated, which precipitated vicious firefights and these persisted until the Germans capitulated in May.

A German attack near St. Croix was repulsed April 15, 1945. Several strongly constructed enemy positions were taken April 19–29, 1945. The offensive action of the American and French troops escalated greatly that month. Numerous small attacks and combat patrols were launched to intimidate the Germans into surrender. The 262nd Infantry Regiment (66th) maintained all three battalions on the line in the Fay-de-Bretagne area and attacked the Germans after extensive reconnaissance. The mission was to destroy enemy positions, take prisoners, and kill Germans. Bitter fights ensued. Artillery and mortar fire were heavy from both sides. The 3rd Battalion of the 264th Infantry Regiment (66th) sustained violent attacks on April 11, 16, and 21. The German raids began with artillery bombardments and were followed by infantry assaults. These raids were repulsed but were costly for the Americans.

Typical of these attacks was one launched by Company E, 262nd Infantry Regiment (66th) in mid-April 1945. The objective was to neutralize some German gun positions that had bombarded the company sector for several days. Approximately one-half of the company was involved. As the advance began, a machine-gun section was sent out on the left flank and a rifle squad from the 3rd Platoon was sent out on the right flank with a plan to join with a squad from an FFI unit. Through some confusion of communication, the French soldiers did not show up so the American squad slowly and undercover moved up to their designated position to lay down covering fire on the hedgerow which was supposedly just in front of the German artillery. The main body advanced along two parallel hedgerows. When they were detected, the Germans began laying down a devastating fire from multiple machine guns. The flanking rifle squad and machine-gun section began firing on the German position in hopes of pinning them down well enough so they could not fire accurately. As soon as this small-arms fire began, the Germans began firing their mortars and artillery with deadly accuracy, necessitating the Americans' withdrawal. One American officer was killed and approximately twenty-five soldiers were wounded. This was consistent with the formidable defense that the Germans had established in the bases at Lorient and St. Nazaire. The attack was aborted when ammunition was almost depleted. At the critique of this attack, several noncoms voiced rather strong objections that this attack took place, knowing first-hand of the intensity and accuracy with which the Germans could launch and sustain a defense from their well-entrenched frontline.

On April 19 a daring raid was carried out by a mixed American and French combat patrol consisting of two officers, one American and one French, and eighty-eight men. The objective was a huge stone tower forty-five feet high and 2,500 feet from the Allied line. The tower was used as a German observation post. Two hundred and thirty pounds of explosives were carried in backpacks. A demolition group planted the explosives, protected by security groups strategically posted to intercept any German opposition. The two officers stayed at the tower as the patrol withdrew and used a nine-minute fuse to ignite the explosives. It was a complete success without any casualties.

After Hitler's death, the Germans at St. Nazaire and Lorient considered surrender. Gen. Werner Junck, commander of the St. Nazaire garrison, was not sure of his authority to do so. The Allies had recently flown 1,200 planes over St. Nazaire as a persuasive show of force. The Germans merely retaliated by firing their big guns at American and French positions.

The Allied forces began putting a lot of pressure on the contained German forces during the first week of May and this continued until the capitulation of the Germans in both Lorient and St. Nazaire.

GERMANS SURRENDER

By May 1 the German artillery activity had decreased although German patrols persisted. Around noon on May 7, 1945, the American troops were notified that all firing would cease at 1300. The troops remained in position and alert. That night, the Germans began a general withdrawal with many explosions to their rear, which was probably the destruction of ammunition and supplies. Finally, on May 8, 1945, the Germans capitulated. Capt. Hauptmann Mueller, an emissary for General Junck, met with Col. John Keating, an American, who offered him the unconditional surrender that Captain Mueller took back to General Junck. General Kramer ordered a cease-fire after the surrender document was signed.

On May 9, 1945, elements of the 66th Infantry Division broadcast the news of the surrender from the captured transmitters in Adm. Karl Donitz's former headquarters to inform the surrounding population that after five long-suffering years, they were free at last. Immediately there was rejoicing in the streets.

On May 10 Gen. Raymond Chomel made an official announcement to all of the French in the area from the Place Royal in Nantes. Gen. Wilhelm Fahrmbacher surrendered the Lorient garrison to General Kramer and to French general Borgnis Desbordes at Caudan at 4:00 P.M., May 10, 1945. A brief ceremony was held and the band played "The Star Spangled Banner" and the French national anthem. General Fahrmbacher was presented to General Kramer and saluted. He held the salute until General Kramer returned it and then he presented his pistol to General Kramer. When presented to General Desbordes, General Fahrmbacher did not salute and finally broke the silence by telling General Kramer that he was surrendering unconditionally all German troops under his command. When in prison later, he was persuaded to write a letter of apology for this discrimination directed to the French general.

The official surrender ceremony of the St. Nazaire garrison took place at Bouvron on May 11, 1945. While this ceremony was being conducted, the soldiers of the 66th Infantry Division were dispersed to take over all military installations including the submarine base. At the ceremony, the French were represented by the 8th Cuirassiers, the famous cavalry regiment dating back to King Louis IV. The French and American national anthems were played. Generals Kramer and Foster with General Chomel were there to accept the surrender from General Junck, who was accompanied by Kriegsmarine Adm. Hans Mirow, two captains of the General Staff, and a Luftwaffe representative. General Junck handed over his pistol to General Kramer and saluted him. Thereafter all delegations returned to their cars. General Kramer handed over the civilian powers to Prefect of the Loire Inferieure Vincent who returned to La Baule for a meeting of the St. Nazaire town council. François Blancho was reinstated as mayor. The war was officially over.

The French constructed beautiful monuments in fields at Caudan and Bouvron commemorating the surrender ceremonies in the fields where they took place and honoring the American and French units who fought there. Another large granite monument was placed by a road near Pont Scorf where the 4th Armored Division had been stopped while trying to penetrate the Lorient defenses. The monument honors the 4th and 6th Armored divisions, the 94th and 66th Infantry divisions, as well as several FFI units. After five long years, there was peace in Normandy and Brittany. The cost in American lives had been very high.

Epilogue

SIR BASIL H. LIDDELL-HART, a noted British military strategist and correspondent, published two books following a series of interviews with German generals, most of whom were in prison post–World War II. His volumes, *The German Generals Talk* and *On the Other Side of the Hill,* give us much insight into the opinions of the German commanders who were major participants in the Cotentin Peninsula and Brittany campaigns.

Field Marshall von Rundstedt was the German commander opposing the Allies during the first month of the invasion of France and had been in that position since 1942. He was very cooperative with Liddell-Hart during a series of interviews. Field Marshall von Kluge, who replaced von Rundstedt, was dead by suicide but his opinions and views were given to Liddell-Hart by General Blumentritt who served both von Rundstedt and von Kluge as chief of staff. Field Marshall Rommel, who commanded the German Army Group B, was also dead at the end of the war but his staff was very cooperative when interviewed.

By 1943 von Rundstedt had done little to strengthen the coastal defenses so Hitler sent Rommel to the west coast of France in November 1943 to build a formidable defensive wall. Von Rundstedt told Liddell-Hart,

> The defenses were absolutely overrated. The "Atlantic Wall" was an illusion conjured up by propaganda to deceive the German People as well as the Allies. It used to make me angry to read the stories about the impregnable defenses. It was nonsense to describe it as a "wall." Hitler, himself, never came to visit it and see what it really was.

Von Rundstedt told Liddell-Hart that his defenses of the French coast were grossly inadequate. He had sixty divisions strung out along a 3,000-mile front. Many of these divisions were depleted on the Russian front and sent to coastal France for a rest. Blumentritt commented, "The disposition would be more likely described as 'Coast protection' rather than 'defense.'"

According to von Rundstedt and Blumentritt, a great controversy existed regarding a defense against the invasion. Von Rundstedt felt that with such limited forces, it was not possible to prevent a landing; therefore, he would rely on a powerful counteroffensive to defeat the invasion after the Allies had committed but before they were well established.

On the other hand, Field Marshall Rommel believed their best chance was to stop the Allies on the beaches. Rommel found in Africa that the Allied air forces were so strong that they would have a very detrimental effect on tanks traveling from a reserve base to the site of the invasion. He believed that the first twenty-four hours would be decisive. However, neither his nor von Rundstedt's plans prevailed. Hitler allowed neither of them a free hand and maintained a tight control on the reserve units, which could not be moved without his permission.

Liddell-Hart asked von Rundstedt if he had any hopes of defeating the invasion. Von Rundstedt replied,

> Not after the first few days. The Allied Air Forces paralyzed all movement by day, and made it very difficult by night. They had smashed the bridges over the Loire as well as over the Seine, shutting off the whole area. These factors delayed the concentration of reserves there. They took three or four times longer to reach the front than we had reckoned. Besides the interference of your Air Forces, the fire of your battleships was a main factor in hampering our counter-stroke. This was a big surprise both in its range and effect.

Blumentritt added that officers who had interrogated him postwar did not seem to have realized the devastation effect of the naval bombardments.

Von Rundstedt and Blumentritt continued to elaborate on the difficulty that Hitler had caused by not letting them withdraw so that they could refit and reorganize the armored divisions and follow with a powerful counterattack against the Americans' flank in the Cotentin Peninsula. Hitler would not allow any withdrawal and told them, "You must stay where you are."

Von Rundstedt made their position, at that time, clear to Liddell-Hart when he said,

> The Field Marshall [Rommel] and I had come to realize more and more clearly, since the second week, that we could not drive the invading forces into the sea. But Hitler believed it was possible. As he would not modify his orders, the troops had to continue clinging on to the cracking line. There was no plan any longer. We were merely trying, without hope, to comply with Hitler's order that the line Caen-Avranches must be held at all costs.

Because of von Rundstedt's pessimism and his objection to not having a free hand, Hitler removed him. Another factor was a conversation between Keitel, Hitler's top aide, and von Rundstedt. After a gloomy report from von Rundstedt, Keitel asked him, "What shall we do?" Von Rundstedt replied, "End the war, what else can we do?"

Hitler appointed Field Marshall von Kluge to replace von Rundstedt as commander in chief in the west. At first von Kluge was optimistic. He thought that the seriousness of their situation had been exaggerated. After reaching the front and having conferences with General Hausser, commander of the 7th Army and General Eberbach, commander of the 5th Panzer Army as well as with other corps commanders, he became very pessimistic. Hitler noted the change in his tone. When Rommel was severely injured on July 19, Hitler instructed von Kluge to take over the Army Group B temporarily. The attempt on Hitler's life with the briefcase bomb occurred on July 20, 1944. Hitler became suspicious of many of his generals, including von Kluge, who had been mentioned in some of the documents concerning the conspiracy.

Von Kluge had told Blumentritt that he had refused to be involved. However, another incident made Hitler more suspicious of him. At the time that General Patton's Third Army was breaking out of Avranches, von Kluge was absent from his headquarters for twelve hours. Hitler suspected that he was trying to contact the Allies to negotiate a surrender. Von Kluge maintained emphatically that he was trapped in a bombardment while visiting the front and that his radio had been destroyed. In the days that followed, the German defenses suffered as von Kluge was badly distracted, thinking that he could be arrested at any moment.

The event had detrimental effects on the Germans' effort to counter the Allies. Von Kluge was not performing his duties well. Many other generals were similarly affected and remained in a state of anxiety for fear that in some way they could be associated with the events of July 20.

Field Marshall Walter Model arrived unexpectedly to relieve von Kluge. Blumentritt visited von Kluge to tell him goodbye and found him very depressed. He committed suicide the next day while returning to Germany. One month later, Rommel was forced to do the same. Rommel, on one occasion, told Blumentritt that the only thing to do was to do away with Hitler and approach the Allies for a peace. Rommel thought it would be far better for the German people to live under a British dominion than to continue such a hopeless struggle.

Gen. Otto Elfeldt told Liddell-Hart that after the breakthrough at Avranches, he was sent to von Kluge's headquarters to take over command of the 84th Corps from General von Choltitz. On his initial inspection of the forces under his command, he found them to be very weak. There was no continuous front. Some of his infantry divisions were reduced to 300 men and, likewise, the artillery was very depleted. He was able to strengthen his forces with several new units. A counterattack with tanks was launched but failed. Elfeldt told Liddell-Hart that the Americans had several opportunities to completely subdue his forces but did not pursue their advantage. He further stated that the Allied air forces were his most formidable enemy. Elfeldt and his troops were finally trapped at Falaise and had to surrender.

When Liddell-Hart asked the German generals Heinrici, Roricht, and Bechtolsheim how the German soldiers compared in the two wars, Roricht made an interesting comment, "Between 1916 and 1918 the soldiers' morale was gradually undermined by the infiltration of Socialistic ideas, and the suggestion that they were fighting the Emperor's war, whereas, this time they had kept such extraordinary confidence in Hitler that they remained confident of victory in face of all the facts." They all agreed that this was a dominant factor in giving them the will to continue fighting.

Asked to give an opinion on the Allied commanders, von Rundstedt said, "Montgomery and Patton were the two best I met. Field Marshall Montgomery was very systematic. That is all right if you have significant forces and significant time." Blumentritt agreed and added that Montgomery was the one general who never suffered a reverse. "He moved like this." Blumentritt took a series of very deliberate and short steps, putting his foot down heavily each time.

Blumentritt was asked about the different qualities of the British and American troops. He answered that the Americans attacked with zest and had a keen sense of mobile action, but when they came under heavy artillery fire, they usually fell back—even after making a significant penetration. By contrast, once the British got their teeth in, and had been in position for twenty-four hours, it was almost impossible to shift them. He added that their losses were heavy when they tried to counterattack the British. In closing, he said, "I had many opportunities to observe this interesting difference in the autumn of 1944, when the right half of my corps faced the British and the left half faced the Americans."

Bibliography

PRIMARY SOURCES

Archives

City archives, Hennebont, France.
City archives, Lorient, France.
Le Grand Blockhaus Musée, Batz-sur-Mer, France.
Musée de la Resistance Bretonne, Malestroit-Morbihan, France.
Musée Memorial Liberté Retrouvee, Quinéville, France.
National Archives, Washington, DC.
Official Record of the 13th Infantry Regiment, 13th Infantry Regiment Association, North Olmsted, OH.
Official Record of the 66th Division, War Department Records Branch, SGO, Historical Records Section, U.S. Army Military History Institute, Carlisle Barracks, PA.
Public Library, Charleston County, SC.
U.S. Army Military History Institute, Carlisle Barracks, PA.

Unpublished Memoirs and Interviews

Bertrand, J. "Maquis et Liberation, 1944." On file at Le Grand Blockhaus Musée, Batz-sur-Mer, France.
Bichan, Yves. "Memoirs of December 21 and 22, 1944, Batz-sur-Mer, France." On file at Le Grand Blockhaus Musée, Batz-sur-Mer, France.
Dumas-Delage, Pierre. Personal communication to the author, France, 2001.
Fahrmbacher, Wilhelm. "Preparation for the Defense of Lorient" (MSB-731). On file at the National Archives, Washington, DC.

Fleury, Robert. Personal communication to the author, France, 2001.

Francois, Lucien. Personal communication to the author, France, 2001.

Gaddis, Henry. Personal communication to the author, Columbia, SC, 2005.

Gardner, William. Personal communication to the author, Greenwood, SC, 2005.

Picaud, Pierre. "Memoires de Guerre." On file at Le Grand Blockhaus Musée, Batz-sur-Mer, France.

Tardivel, Francois K. Personal communication to author, France, 2001.

SECONDARY SOURCES

"An Ambush in Brittany." *Cavalry Journal of the United States Cavalry Association* (September–October 1945).

Badsey, Stephen. *Normandy 1944: Allied Landings and Breakout.* Westport, CT: Praeger, 2004.

Bertin, Francois. *Saint-Nazaire sous l'Occupation.* Rennes, France: Editions Ouest-France, 1999.

Bloyet, Dominique. *1939–1945 St. Nazaire la Poche.* Montreiul-Bellay, France: Editions CMD, 1998.

Blumenson, Martin. "The Decision to Take Brest." *Army* (March 1960): 45–51.

———. "'To the Last Stone': The Siege of St. Malo." *Army* (August 1970): 38–48.

———. *United States Army in World War II: The European Theater of Operations—Breakout and Pursuit.* Washington, DC: Office of the Chief of Military History, Department of the Army, 1961.

Bourget-Maurice, Louis, and Josyane Grand Colas. *Et la Tanniere Devint le Village Histoire de la Base Sous-Marine de Lorient-Keroman, 1940–1947.* Rennes, France: Editions du Quantieme, 1947.

Bradham, Randolph. *Hitler's U-Boat Fortresses.* Westport, CT: Praeger, 2003.

Bradley, Omar. *A Soldier's Story.* New York: Rand McNally, 1951.

Braeuer, Luc. *La Base Sous-Marine de Saint-Nazaire.* La Baule, France: Imprimerie de Champagne, 2001.

———. *La Poche de Saint Nazaire, Aout 1944–Mai 1945.* La Baule, France: Imprimerie de Champagne, 1999.

Breuer, William. *Hitler's Fortress Cherbourg: The Conquest of a Bastion.* Briarcliff, NY: Stein and Day, 1984.

Burtin, Phillipe. *France under the Germans: Collaboration and Compromise.* New York: New Press, 1967.

Byrnes, Lawrence G. *History of the 94th Infantry Division in World War II.* Nashville, TN: Battery Press, 1982.

Calvocoressi, Peter, Guy Wint, and John Pritchard. *The Penguin History of the Second World War.* Middlesex, United Kingdom: Penguin Books, 1999.

Churchill, Winston. *The Grand Alliance.* Vol. 3 of *The Second World War.* Boston: Houghton Mifflin, 1950.

———. *The Hinge of Fate.* Vol. 4 of *The Second World War.* Boston: Houghton Mifflin, 1950.

———. *Tragedy and Triumph.* Vol. 6 of *The Second World War.* Boston: Houghton Mifflin, 1953.

Coffee, Carol. *From Tragedy to Triumph: An Historical Memoir of the 66th Infantry Division in World War II*. Houston: Odyssey International, 1999.

Collins, J. Lawton. *Lightning Joe: An Autobiography*. Baton Rouge: Louisiana State University Press, 1979.

Combat Chronicle. *An Outline of U.S. Army Divisions Series: Order of Battle*. Washington, DC: U.S. Army Military Institute, Historical Division, Department of the Army.

Combat History of the 6th Armored Division in the European Theatre of Operations, 18 July 1944–8 May 1945. Yadkinville, NC: Ripple Publishing, 1948.

Dorian, James. *Storming St. Nazaire*. Annapolis, MD: Naval Institute Press, 1998.

Dupuy, Trevor N., Curt Johnson, and David Bangard. *The Harper Encyclopedia of Military Biography*. Edison, NJ: Castle Books, 1992.

Frankel, Nat, and Larry Smith. *Patton's Best: An Informal History of the 4th Armored Division*. New York: Hawthorn Books, 1946.

Ganz, Harding. "The Breton Ports." *Journal of Military History* 59 (January 1995): 77–95.

Gawne, Jonathan. *The Americans in Brittany, 1944: The Battle for Brest*. Paris: Histoire Collections, 2002.

Gilmore, Donald, ed. *U.S. Army Atlas of the European Theatre in World War II*. New York: Barnes and Noble, 2004.

Heinnebont, Morbihan. *Les Heures Tragiques de la Liberation*. Hennebont, France: Imprimerie Artisanal, 1985.

Hirshson, Stanley P. *General Patton: A Soldier's Life*. New York: HarperCollins, 2002.

Hoffman, George F. *The Super Sixth: History of the 6th Armored Division in World War II and Its Postwar Association*. Louisville, KY: 6th Armored Division Association, 1975.

Irwin, Will. *The Jedburghs: The Secret History of the Special Forces, France 1944*. New York: Public Affairs, 2005.

Koyen, Kenneth. *The Fourth Armored Division: From the Beach to Bavaria—the Story of the Fourth Armored Division in Combat*. N.p., 1946.

Leroux, Roger. *The Resistance Movement in Saint Marcel*. Rennes, France: Editions Ouest-France.

Liddell-Hart, B. H. *The German Generals Talk*. New York: HarperCollins, 1948.

———. *History of the Second World War*. New York: Putnam, 1971.

———. *The Other Side of the Hill*. Chatham, United Kingdom: Mackays of Chalham, 1945.

Luger, Michel. *Missions de Bombardements Americains sur St. Nazaire: "Flak City," 1942–1943*. Rennes, France: Editions Ouest-France, 1998.

Maheo, Patrick. *Saint-Marcel: Haut Lieu de la Resistance Bretonne*. Ploermel, France: Rue des Scribes Editions, 1997.

Mansoor, Peter R. *The GI Offensive in Europe: The Triumph of American Infantry Divisions, 1941–1945*. Lawrence: University Press of Kansas, 1999.

Mitchell, George C. *Mathew B. Ridgeway: Soldier, Statesman, Scholar, Citizen*. Mechanicsburg, PA: Stackpole Books, 2002.

"Nazi 340's Damaged." *Black Panther Bulletin of the 66th Infantry Division* (May 1945).

Nordyke, Phil. *The Combat History of the 82nd Airborne Division in World War II*. St. Paul, MN: Zenith Press, 2005.

O'Connor, Jerome M. "Into the Gray Wolves' Den." *Naval History* (June 2000).

Pallud, Jean Paul. *U-Boote: La Base Sous-Marine de Lorient*. Bayeux, France: Editions Heimdal, 1997.

Partridge, Colin. *Hitler's Atlantic Wall*. Guernsey, United Kingdom: DI Publications, 1976.

"Picture Tabloid of German Surrender at Lorient and St. Nazaire." *Black Panther Bulletin of the 66th Infantry Division* (May 1945).

Pitt, Barrie, and the editors of Time-Life Books. *The Battle of the Atlantic in World War II*. Alexandria, VA: Time-Life Books, 1977.

Price, Frank James. *Troy H. Middleton: A Biography*. Baton Rouge: Louisiana State University Press, 1974.

Queuille, Jean Paul. *1939–1945 Bretagne: Lorient dans la Guerre*. Mortreoill-Belay, France: Editions CMD, 1998.

Roberts, Ray. *Survivors of the Leopoldville Disaster*. Bridgman, MI: privately printed, 1997.

Rondel, Eric. *Lorient et Saint-Nazaire: Les Poches de l'Atlantique*. N.p.: Editions Club 35, 1944.

Roskill, S. W. *The War at Sea, 1939–1945*. Vols. 1 and 2. London: HMSO, 1954.

Sanders, Jacquin. *A Night Before Christmas*. New York: Putnam, 1963.

Schoenbrun, David. *Soldiers of the Night: The Story of the French Resistance*. New York: E. D. Dutton, 1980.

Showell, Jak P. Hallman. *U-Boats under the Swastika: An Introduction to German Submarines, 1935–1945*. London: Allan, 1973.

Slader, John. *The Fourth Service: Merchantmen at War, 1939–1945*. London: Robert Hale, 1993.

Standifer, Leon C. *Not in Vain: A Rifleman Remembers World War II*. Baton Rouge: Louisiana State University Press, 1992.

Taylor, Maxwell D. *Swords and Plowshares: A Memoir*. New York: W. W. Norton, 1972.

Wessman, Sintos. *The 66th Division in World War II*. Nashville, TN: Battery Press, 1940.

Wilson, J. B. *66th Infantry Division, Armies, Corps, Divisions, and Separate Brigades*. Washington, DC: Center of Military History United States Army, 1987.

Zaloga, Steven. *Operation Cobra 1944: Breakout from Normandy*. Westport, CT: Praeger, 2004.

Index

About the Author

RANDOLPH BRADHAM is a retired thoracic and cardiovascular surgeon. Formerly a staff-sergeant squad leader, he fought against the Germans in Brittany during the Second World War. He is the author of *Hitler's U-Boat Fortresses* (Praeger, 2003).